Hwang

Moo Do Chul Hahk
무 도 철 학

A New Translation by

Hyun Chul Hwang

ISBN: 978-145750-304-7

Soo Bahk Do
Moo Duk Kwan

Moo Do Chul Hahk

A New Translation
by H. C. Hwang

H. C. Hwang
President World Moo Duk Kwan

武　道

Dedication

This book is dedicated first and foremost to my father, Hwang Kee, and my mother, Cho Kyung Kap, who endured tremendous hardship to build the Moo Duk Kwan; my lovely wife, Ji Seh Hun and my daughters, Hwang Ji Min and Hwang Ji Sun, and Hwang Sun Hee whose love, support and sacrifice make my work possible; to all Moo Duk Kwan members who have supported and contributed to our mission; and, to all who genuinely seek to understand and practice Moo Do Values.

Contents

Honorable Hwang Kee

*Founder of Moo Duk Kwan and
Author of the Moo Do Chul Hahk*

Moo Do Creed

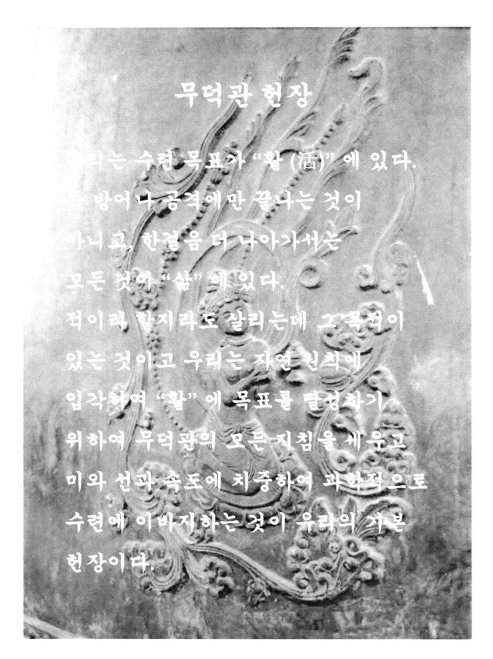

Moo Do Creed displayed on the Background Relief of the Emille Bell, One of Korea's Beloved Cultural Treasures (photo used with permission by Frank Bonsignore)

Moo Do Creed

The purpose of Moo Do is *Hwal* to cultivate ourselves

Moo Do does not end in offense or defense

It is one step further, the purpose is life itself

Even facing the enemy, our goal is to save them

The principles of Moo Do are the principles of Nature

Guided by Moo Do we may achieve the goal of *Hwal* in the principles
of Nature

To do so we must concentrate, stress the beauty, line, speed, and study
scientifically

To provide all this is our creed.

Detail of a nineteenth-century woodblock depicting a meeting between Confucius (left) and Lao Tzu (right) (Spiro, 1990, p. 25)

Acknowledgements

The first English translation of the *Moo Do Chul Hahk* was made possible because of the contributions of Saboms[1] Frank Bonsignore, Daymon Kenyon, Philip Bartolacci, Cash Cooper, Daniel Segarra, Charles Water, William Weber, Craig Hays, Joe Mele, Jim Harwood, Vincent Howard, Scott Magrann, Emily Hsu, Richard Wilcox, Daniel Bannard, Jeffrey Gross, Greg Bryan, Denise Mullin, Joseph Amico, Art Pryor, Lisa Donnelly, and Catharine Minichino. My gratitude is also extended to Master Noelia Lago, Kyo Sa Tonya Warren, Mr. Greg Ausfleg, and Mr. Tim Havican. I wish to thank these individuals in particular for their contributions, and especially Frank Bonsignore Sa Bom for his initiative, motivation, and guidance for this effort.

Special thanks and acknowledgement are extended to Mr. Charles Mueller for his initial translation. I would also like to recognize and extend appreciation to Master Daniel Segarra for initiating and organizing the first translation, engaging Mr. Mueller in this effort, and his dedication to editing and assisting with the translation of the first draft of this book. I also would like to thank Marylee Hendricks Sa Bom for her substantial contributions to proofing and editing of the final manuscript. Special appreciation is extended to Dr. Johnson Sa Bom for his contributions which include co-authoring the *Introduction and Historical Background* and editing and compiling the final manuscript for review and publication.

A very sincere appreciation is extended to Sa Boms Wha Yong Chung, Dr. Larry Seiberlich, Russell Hanke, and Victor Martinov for their guidance. My sincere appreciation is extended to Dr. Seiberlich Sa Bom for his deep interest, assistance and leadership that guided the initial writing of this book through its publication.

I also wish to express my sincere gratitude to Dr. Karen Mead, who made substantial contributions to the final editing of the translated text, with the guidance and assistance of Dae Kyu Jang Sa Bom rendering the content accessible and readable for a wide range of audiences.

H. C. Hwang

Preface

The *Moo Do Chul Hahk* was written by Hwang Kee and published in 1993. Hwang Kee was the founder of the Moo Duk Kwan, a traditional martial arts organization that rose to prominence in Korea during the 1960s and has continued to expand throughout the world. Hwang Kee experienced substantial challenges to the advancement of the Moo Duk Kwan due to political circumstances in the early 1960s that are explained in more detail in the *Introduction* to this book.

Hwang Kee was born in November 9, 1914 during the Japanese occupation of Korea (1910-1945). Hwang Kee was one of very few students entering and completing elementary and high school at the time. Despite the influences and control of the Japanese occupation during Hwang Kee's early childhood and young adult life, he developed an early, avid interest in the martial arts that ultimately became a lifelong commitment. He created the Moo Duk Kwan in November 9, 1945, three months after end of the Second World War (August 15, 1945) when Korea regained its independence. He introduced the techniques and philosophy of Moo Duk Kwan that continued to progress in spite of many challenges during the Korean War (1950-1953).

Some of his contributions and achievements include:

- Founded the Korean Soo Bahk Do Association Moo Duk Kwan.

- Authored and published *Hwa Soo Do Kyo Bohn*, the first modern Martial art book in Korea in 1949.

- Organized and hosted the first International Goodwill Martial Art Demonstration with China in 1955 demonstrating his lifelong commitment to improving human relations and achieving world peace through the practice of martial arts.

- Created and developed protocols and systems that embraced the value of history, tradition, philosophy, discipline, respect, and techniques of the art.

- Authored and published a number of texts demonstrating his value and the importance of infusing scholarship into the practice of martial arts.

- Positively impacted the lives of thousands of people through his visionary thoughts, presentations, communication, and personal contact.

- Presented and taught the value and benefits of Moo Do, an action philosophy based on the principles of Do that promote virtue, balance, and character, through his personal study and exemplifying it by the way he lived.

Moo Do (Martial Way) *Chul Hahk* (Philosophy) is based on the philosophy of Do (Tao). Hwang Kee's emphasis on the harmony between Western Philosophy and Eastern Philosophy is a key message of the *Moo Do Chul Hahk*. This book also introduces and expounds on key concepts including *shim gung* (spiritual effort), *neh gung* (internal effort), and *weh gung* (external effort) of human conditioning.

I believe this book may offer insights and opportunities for increased scholarship and academic study of the Martial arts. Furthermore, it is my sincere hope that this book will help readers understand the value of Moo Do Philosophy to developing their character, thereby leading to a greater understanding between Western and Eastern thought to promote and sustain harmony in the Universe.

Hyun Chul Hwang

Forward

This book is a translation of a unique Korean text authored by Hwang Kee, the Founder of the Moo Duk Kwan and who developed the traditional martial art, Soo Bahk Do. It is the only contemporary book that carefully describes an action-based martial arts philosophy that arises from, and is embedded in, a larger tradition of Eastern Philosophy.

The unique Martial Arts Philosophy presented herein, generated from the Eastern philosophical thought and traditions, and actually serves to respect and balance both Eastern and Western traditions, creating a natural harmony for the world to embrace.

If some lives exist for a purpose and if we are here for a reason, then surely the life of Hwang Kee is one of those that was destined to fulfill a mission. Hwang Kee's life may be characterized as pure in motive; endowed with spirituality, talent, vision, and dreams. He was certainly dedicated to the manifestation of individual growth as a means of achieving harmony among all people and world peace.

Hwang Kee, a highly esteemed and internationally recognized martial artist, describes in his book, the *Moo Do Chul Hahk*, the philosophy that he lived. The *Moo Do Chul Hahk* is a book of philosophy that presents the concept of the development of the "Authentic Person," and suggests that when acting selflessly, individuals who are dedicated to the concept of societal well-being can profoundly influence international well-being and contribute to world peace and harmony among all nations. This work reflects, in some measure, his exploration of our human condition and the most basic questions that confront us. He presents a blueprint or path to follow for bringing together in harmony a world philosophy through the understanding of Moo Do and the practice of his martial art, Soo Bahk Do.

The *Moo Do Chul Hahk* provides the reader with the general philosophical foundations supporting the martial arts philosophy, which is explained in detail including a presentation of the actual process of living the philosophical concepts – acting on the ideas as a practicum of life.

The book was written to:

1. Provide a general readership with a description of a unique philosophical construct

2. Establish the *Moo Do Chul Hahk* as a scholarly text describing a recognized and emergent philosophical tradition

3. Serve as a guide for those who wish to live the way of this "Philosophy:action"

4. Provide members of the Moo Duk Kwan a description of the philosophical structure that informs and guides their practice of the Art.

Although the text has been revised to be more easily understood by the Western reader, great care has been taken to ensure that the subject matter itself reflects the intent of the original Korean text. It provides for various interpretations based upon the reader's cultural contexts, worldviews, and personal life experiences.

The Senior Advisory Committee would like to express its deepest gratitude to Hwang Kee for his direct and personal guidance and instruction in their practice and understanding of Soo Bahk Do and his Moo Do Philosophy. The Senior Advisory Committee also thanks the many individuals involved in the translation and compilation of this book and for their dedication to bringing this important work to the public. We most respectfully thank this book's author and translator, Hyun Chul Hwang, for dedicating his life to the perpetuation and growth of the Moo Do Philosophy through Soo Bahk Do.

W. Y. Chung   Russell D. Hanke
Lawrence Seiberlich, Ph. D.   Victor Martinov

Introduction and
Historical Background

Hyun Chul Hwang
President World Moo Duk Kwan

John R. Johnson, Ph.D.
U. S. Soo Bahk Do Moo Duk Kwan Federation, Inc.

"Perfection results from the struggle." Chuang Tzu

Moo Do Chul Hahk

The *Moo Do Chul Hahk* presents a philosophical, theoretical, conceptual and practical framework for the study, understanding, and practice of the ancient Far Eastern philosophy referred to as *"Moo Do"* (literally translated as *"martial way"*). The *Moo Do Chul Hahk* was authored and published in 1993 in Seoul, Korea by Hwang Kee, the highly revered founder of a traditional Korean martial arts organization. The original text was written and published in Hangul (han'gŭl), the native Korean language. This book is the first English translation, and is authored and edited by Hwang Kee's son, Hyun Chul Hwang, the current President of the World Moo Duk Kwan. The World Moo Duk Kwan is the international organization and central administrative authority for the development, teaching and practice of Soo Bahk Do, a traditional Korean martial art.

This translation of the *Moo Do Chul Hahk* is intended for two audiences. The first is students, scholars, and researchers of Asian history, culture, philosophy, language, and traditions. The *Moo Do Chul Hahk* offers a unique insight and perspective into the mind, life and philosophy of a Korean scholar and martial artist who was responsible for organizing and founding one of the largest traditional Korean martial arts organizations in the world. The present text affords Western students and scholars of Asian studies access to a philosophy emerging from the application of principles drawn from Far Eastern philosophical and spiritual traditions understood and practiced by a modern day martial arts master and scholar.

While the original text of the *Moo Do Chul Hahk* was authored by a contemporary figure, the content of the text is founded on ancient philosophical constructs and principles of Taoism, Confucianism, Shamanism and Buddhism. Although the knowledge, understanding, or practice of a martial art and in particular, the martial art (Soo Bahk Do) developed and practiced by Hwang Kee, may be helpful to the reader, they are not essential for reading, studying, or understanding the *Moo Do Chul Hahk*. The intent of the author of this English translation is to provide an accurate and complete translation of the *Moo Do Chul Hahk* that is accessible to Western students and scholars, including non-martial arts practitioners.

This translation of the *Moo Do Chul Hahk* is also written as a guide for martial arts practitioners seeking to advance their practice and discipline with a deeper understanding of Moo Do Philosophy. For this audience, the text is a guide intended to help martial arts practitioners advance their practice to include a way of living, of understanding the self, the world, and the universe through the development of virtue and character.

The "martial way," referred to as *Moo Do* (武道) in Korean, *Wu Tao* in Chinese, and *Budo* in Japanese, is a key element of the practice and study of Soo Bahk Do and other traditional martial arts. While it has received substantial attention in the martial arts literature, it has received somewhat limited attention by the literature dealing with Far Eastern spiritual and cultural traditions and Asian Studies. Substantial evidence exists of the origins of the martial arts in the Far East. The practice of traditional martial arts is inseparable from the practice and understanding of Eastern philosophy and spirituality including Taoism, Confucianism, Shamanism, and Buddhism. Despite the ample historical evidence of the many martial arts in China, Korea, Japan, Thailand, the Philippines, and countries throughout the Pacific, few Asian and Pacific studies programs pay meaningful attention to the significance of traditional martial arts in Asian culture, traditions, and history.

In addition, there is limited research and scholarly inquiry and few professional publications addressing the historical and philosophical elements of traditional martial arts. Frequently, articles addressing the origins and development of a martial art fail to adequately reference primary source materials. It is notable that while there are many publications and volumes that provide substantive information about the history, background, philosophy, and practice of traditional martial arts and their founders, little attention has been paid to the historical and social influences of traditional martial arts. More recently, there has been an effort to increase the emphasis of more scholarly investigations and discussion of traditional martial arts (e.g., Cleary, 2008; *Electronic Journals of Martial Arts and Sciences, Journal of Asian Martial Arts;* Kim, 2000) that include journals and books devoted to the study of the history, culture, philosophy, and practice of traditional and ancient martial arts

Unfortunately, the lack of attention to the understanding of Moo Do Philosophy in the study and scholarship of Far Eastern culture and philosophy has led to a contemporizing and misunderstanding of the historical, military, social, educational, and philosophical value of traditional martial arts training. The popular media and film industries have often misrepresented the martial arts and promoted stereotypes and myths that lead serious students and scholars of Far Eastern and Asian culture to summarily dismiss the cultural and philosophical contributions of traditional martial arts. Yet, writings that many martial arts practitioners study and use in their training are also required reading in prestigious military academies and leadership development programs throughout the world.

Martial arts and combative sports literature are replete with publications and books that describe the physical and mental practice and application of martial arts techniques and philosophy. A substantially fewer number of publications include autobiographical or personal narratives of the lives of the founders of martial arts. However, serious students of the martial arts and Asian studies scholars understand that behind the physical prowess, skill, and ability of a true martial arts master and practitioner lies a deeper and more powerful understanding of the self, society, nature, and the universe that emerges from the practice of a traditional and ancient discipline and philosophy. In addition, practitioners of traditional martial arts training have employed the discipline of their training as a vehicle for achieving direct personal experience that is fundamental to acquiring the knowledge and wisdom afforded by the practice of traditional martial values.

At the core of all traditional martial arts training are an understanding and profound respect for and among those who would preserve and protect ancient values that have withstood the test of time, including history, tradition, discipline/respect, philosophy, and technique. The philosophical understanding and knowledge of traditional martial arts is the foundation of the mutual respect shown among martial artists within various styles who practice very different art forms. This respect is an acknowledgement of the struggles and challenges that martial arts practitioners endured in the practice of their respective discipline. The struggles and challenges faced and endured by all traditional martial arts practitioners who follow the "Way" (Do/Tao) are understood and seen as a common thread among practitioners. Their respect emerges from a mutual understanding that differences in physical skills, abilities, performance, technique, or practice are not the true measure of an authentic martial artist.

They generally hold one another's level of discipline, term of commitment, and level of training in higher regard than their level of physical skill. While physical skill is important it is but a small part of the struggles and challenges a martial arts practitioner has faced. Traditional martial arts practitioners understand that physical skills are constrained by many factors including one's current health, natural abilities, physical or mental limitations, and age. The real value and purpose of martial arts training is understood to be living a life of virtue following the path of "*Moo Do*"(Martial Way). For this reason, traditional martial art training is accessible to all regardless of ability or physical condition. Practitioners who train despite physical and mental challenges may be required to engage in more intensive discipline and effort to achieve levels of proficiency than those without such challenges may find much easier to attain. These challenges, limitations, and struggles may actually serve to deepen and accelerate a practitioner's discipline and understanding of core elements of traditional martial arts training and philosophy. This discipline and understanding may surpass the understanding of someone with superior natural physical skills and proficiency or who has access to expensive resources that might advance or enhance their performance. The important point is that the value of the challenge and the struggle is a recurring theme of most if not all traditional martial arts training.

More importantly, this high regard for the effort, discipline, and commitment to lifelong training and practice is based on an understanding and practice of the values and principles of a martial arts philosophy. Traditional martial art training that retains a martial philosophy at its core provides a number of benefits that are not available to practitioners of other systems. First, traditional martial arts are accessible to individuals regardless of ability or age since the physical skills acquired through training, though important, are viewed as a path of the martial philosophy rather than the ultimate goal. Second, physical proficiency and mastery are of secondary importance to the application of one's training to all aspects of one's life. While the importance of physical skill is not to be diminished or underestimated, it is understood that persons of varying physical abilities may achieve high levels of proficiency and mastery of a traditional martial art. Third, lifelong training and discipline are considered more important than competition or publicity. Finally, one's personal character, integrity, virtue and discipline are the ultimate measures of one's mastery of a traditional martial art that follows a martial philosophy. It is this final point that explains the very high regard and esteem in which Hwang Kee is held by the entire martial arts community.

The *Moo Do Chul Hahk*, literally translated as "Martial Way Philosophy," is a contemporary work that extends, expands and contributes to the attention paid to the study and understanding of Moo Do Philosophy that emerged from the life experiences of the author, Hwang Kee. Hwang Kee is one of the most revered and respected contemporary martial arts founders and practitioners of the 20th century. The *Moo Do Chul Hahk* is both a philosophical treatise and an autobiographical study and exposition of Hwang Kee's life that describes the principles and practice of Moo Do as a way of living. It is a comprehensive and scholarly work steeped in modern history. Hwang Kee's life journey began at the end of the First World War. His life was directly affected by the events of two major world conflicts, World War II and the Korean War. He personally experienced the impact of major political events in his home country, the Republic of South Korea, such as the coup by General Chung Hee Park in May 1961 that led to government efforts to dissolve and disband his Moo Duk Kwan. Hwang Kee's life spanned many international conflicts and events and he witnessed the impact of global events including the Viet Nam War, the appearance of AIDS as a pandemic disease during the 1980s; the rise and fall of apartheid in South Africa; major disasters such as the Chernobyl incident; the rise of ethnic cleansing in numerous ethnic conflicts; massive starvation on the African subcontinent, and the attacks on the World Trade Center on September 11, 2001. Despite the numerous struggles that Hwang Kee himself experienced and witnessed, his dedication and pursuit of Moo Do as a discipline, philosophy and way of life never wavered and his highest goal was to promote harmony and peace within and among all people.

An understanding of the *Moo Do Chul Hahk* as a scholarly and introspective study of Moo Do as a philosophy requires some understanding of the author and the historical context and events that shaped his life. The life of the author and the pre/post World War II and Korean War are intimately related. Serious students of the works of Far Eastern philosophy, Asian studies and others understand the tremendous influence of socio-political conditions of the historical periods on the lives of those who lived during these times. Philosophers who lived during these times reflected on their lives in several dimensions to address serious questions related to the nature of time, the origins of the universe and nature; the constructs of self and the community; the mechanics of the mind; the applications of cosmology; and practical approaches to addressing contemporary social and political problems.

The *Moo Do Chul Hahk* is a philosophical treatise set in an historical context that frames the author's understanding and development of a multi-dimensional philosophical perspective of the individual, society, nature, and the universe that emerged from deep personal reflection and personal history. It is a personal narrative that explains cosmologic elements addressing the relationship between the individual, nature and the universe. The *Moo Do Chul Hahk* also describes the responsibilities of individuals to one another and their communities based on the principles and spiritual values of Taoism and on a study of Confucian and Buddhist teachings.

According to Hwang Kee, "Scholarship starts with study and ends with theory. Moo Do starts with action and ends in theory" (Hwang, 1999, p. viii). Consistent with this belief, an understanding of Moo Do Philosophy as presented by Hwang Kee in the *Moo Do Chul Hahk* requires a basic knowledge and understanding of the author's life and the historical events during his life. This will give the reader insights into how his Moo Do Philosophy developed as a function of his direct experience (action) that led to his philosophy (theory).

Historical Context

To understand the historical context and times in which Hwang Kee lived it is important to understand the historical impact of the Chosŏn period on Korean culture, society and life.

Korea is a peninsula that is about 600 miles in length and some 85,000 square miles about the size of Utah. In width it ranges from 90 miles at its most narrow east-west points to 200 miles at its widest. It averages about 150 miles in width and resembles the outline of the state of Florida. The Taebaek mountain range runs up the east coast while the west coast is flat, muddy, and has many estuaries and indentations. The inland is characterized by hills, broad valleys, lowlands, and rice paddies (Goldstein & Maihafer, 2000; Fehrenbach, 2008). Fehrenbach (2008) notes that while the people of the Hermit Kingdom wish to be left in peace, "It is hopeless, for Korea is a buffer state (p. 10)." He also sadly notes that "So, Korea has suffered, without profit to herself. So she is suffering still. The crimes against her have been continuous, for Korea is a breeding ground for war (p. 11)."

The Chosŏn Dynasty, frequently referred to as the Yi Dynasty, was established in the late 1300's by General Yi Sŏng-gye. It was Korea's longest ruling dynasty lasting until 1910 (Cumings, 2005). During this period Korea's social structure was highly stratified and dominated by Confucian and Neo-Confucian orthodoxy. Society was organized according to a patrilinear familial lineage (Chi, 2001; Cumings, 2005; Library of Congress, 2007). This social structure included at the top, a ruling and upper class that included the king and *yangban*. The *yangban* comprised two groups, the literati (*munban*) and the military/martial class (*mooban*). The defining characteristics of the *yangban* were their scholarly knowledge and pursuits with a particularly strong emphasis placed on their knowledge and understanding of Confucian classics and Neo-Confucian thought. The *yangban* enjoyed a number of social and political advantages and privileges. Confucian scholars were considered the custodians of Confucian mores, rituals and ceremonies (Lee, 2007). The next level in the social hierarchy included a small middle class of government employees known as *chungmin*. The majority of the population including peasants, laborers and fishermen were known as *sangmin*. The lowest class (*cheonmin*) were slaves or considered low-born such as butchers, leather tanners, and beggars (*pakechŏng*).

According to Cummings (2005), the *Ta-Hsüeh*, or *Great Learning* was considered the classic text that established the foundation and rules that governed Korean society. Filial piety was considered the highest virtue. Society was structured by three relationships: ruler – subject; father – son; and husband – wife. Throughout the Chosŏn Dynasty all official records, formal education, and written discourse were expressed in classical Chinese as were the examinations required for achieving status and position in the social hierarchy. Education was considered so important that Korea was noted to have a "national devotion to education" (Cumings, 2005, p. 60). It was a central requirement for advancement in Korean society. The fifteenth century marked the pinnacle of the Chosŏn Dynasty and saw the emergence of han'gŭl under the reign of Sejong, known as Korea's sage king. Korea flourished as an agrarian society led by a structured bureaucracy that controlled entry to civil service, civil service itself, and taxation of landowners and farmers. Though Neo-Confucian thought was promoted, common people practiced Buddhism, folk religions, shamanism, geomancy and fortune-telling.

According to Cummings (2005), purges of the literati, and the Japanese and Manchu invasions during the 18th century marked the decline of the Chosŏn Dynasty. Numerous attempts to engage Korea politically and economically and open trade along with missionary work by Japan, the U.S., Great Britain, and France were met with staunch resistance. Korea attempted to remain secluded, isolating itself from Western and Asian influences. In short, Korea retained its heavily agrarian social structure through the late 19th century to the extent that there were no large commercial cities. The commercial class had very limited impact on Korea's economic status; merchants were considered to be of lower class than peasant farmers.

Japan's efforts to annex Korea began in 1876 with the Treaty of Ganghwa during the Chosŏn Dynasty. Ten years later after the Sino-Japanese War, Japan, used gunboat diplomacy to force Korean leaders to sign the Protectorate (Eulsa) Treaty in 1905 establishing Korea as a protectorate of Japan and authorizing the military occupation of Korea. The Japan-Korea Annexation Treaty was signed August 22, 1910 effectively ceding Korea's national sovereignty to Japanese rule and subjugation.

Japan's 35 year occupation of Korea had an enormous impact on Korean life and culture including:
- The removal of substantial raw materials and resources-to support Japan's colonial and military ventures
- The recruitment of hundreds of thousands of Koreans as soldiers and laborers
- The institution of the "comfort system" (*chongsindae*) involving the sexual enslavement of an estimated 100,000 to 200,000 Korean women
- Prohibitions on the teaching and use of the Korean language
- The imposition of the Shinto religion on the populace
- The mandatory requirement to use Japanese names
- Prohibitions on the expression of Korean culture and language and, the control of the Korean press
- The destruction of Korean textbooks
- The prohibition of teaching Korean history in schools and universities
- The brutal repression of peaceful independence demonstrations and,
- The plundering of thousands of cultural artifacts (Cummings,

2005; de Haan, 2002; Doll, 2002; Kim, 1977; Kristoff, 1998; Min, 2003; Schnabel, 1971; Yi, 2002).

In addition, Japan eliminated the Chosŏn leadership, destroyed the Korean Palace; reorganized the taxation system and evicted tenant farmers; exported rice crops to Japan causing widespread famine; instituted a repressive regime of governing that included killing those who refused to pay taxes; forced many Koreans into slavery in road works and mines; and, organized the first sweat shops in Korea. Although, systems of transportation and communication were built across the country modernizing the Korean infrastructure these resources were developed solely to serve Japanese economic and political aims and afforded little if any benefit to the Korean people (Cumings, 2005; Haggard, Kang & Moon, 1997; Kim, 1977). The study of the impact of the occupation and efforts to mitigate and reconcile that impact through diplomatic means and cultural activities continues through today (Dyke, 2006; Kirk, 2006; Kristoff, 1998; Sternhold, 1991, Min, 2003, Yi, 2002).

Japan's occupation of Korea ended with the signing of the Japanese Instrument of Surrender, September 2, 1945 at the end of World War II. The surrender included provisions of the Potsdam Declaration that stripped Japan of pre-war territorial annexations including Korea and Taiwan. Rhee Syngman was chosen to head the Korean government in 1945. He ruled as the dictatorial President of the Republic of South Korea until 1961 when he was forced to resign following a coup by Major General Park Chong Hee (Cummings, 2005; Schnaeble, 1992).

The status of Korea after World War II involved a complicated mixture of political factors that involved the U.S., Soviet Union, Japan, and China. Recommendations to divide Korea into Northern and Southern regions at the 38th parallel were accepted by President Truman and members of the U.N. Security Council (Fehrenbach, 2008; Halberstam, 2007). The United States and the Soviet Union agreed to a joint administration of Korea for four years, after which it was agreed that Korea would be self-governed. However, these arrangements were opposed by the Korean people, who responded with substantial protests and rebellion in the North and South. In 1949 the U.S. and Soviet Union withdrew from Korea, leaving South Korea under the rule of President Rhee Syngman and North Korea led by General Secretary Kim Il-Sung.

During the years before the Korean War, much suspicion, chaos and conflict among the population in South Korea developed involving the influence of North Korea. Fehrenbach (2008) reported that thousands of Communists and Communist sympathizers had infiltrated South Korea and specifically, Seoul. In addition, there are numerous accounts of Koreans falsely accused of being Communists who were imprisoned, tortured, and executed (Kim, 2002; Lim, 2006; Pak Wan-so as cited in de Haan, 2002).

The North Korean Peoples Army (NKPA) prepared for the invasion of South Korea months in advance of the initial attack on June 25, 1950. When North Korea attacked, it rapidly advanced west and south. On June 27, 1950, the United Nations Security Council passed a resolution calling for the cessation of hostilities and the withdrawal of North Korea back to the 38th parallel and agreed to aid South Korea. Several days later the NKPA captured and occupied Seoul and the Republic of Korea (ROK) army was destroyed. Three days later, President Harry Truman ordered U.S. troops into Korea. General Douglas MacArthur, Commander of the Far East Command (FECOM), was also placed in command of the United Nations forces.

The NKPA continued to advance and push south while the U.N. forces fought delaying actions across South Korea. The advance of the NKPA was halted when the U.S. landed forces at Inch'on and U.S. forces broke out of the Pusan Perimeter. U.S. and U.N. forces advanced from Inch'on and Pusan and eventually recaptured Seoul. By late November of 1950, U.S. and U.N. forces had captured P'yongyang and advanced to the Yalu River on the North Korea-China border. However, on November 1, 1950, the Chinese forces engaged and pushed U.S. and U.N. forces back south across the 38th parallel, captured Seoul on January 4, 1951, and continued to advance as far south as the 37th parallel. On January 25, 1951, the U.N. began to advance north, recapturing Seoul in March 1951 (Fehrenbach, 2008; Halberstam, 2007).

President Truman relieved General MacArthur of command for insubordination on April 11, 1951 based on communications issued by MacArthur in public opposition to the President's foreign policy. General Matthew Ridgeway was appointed as Commander of FECOM. U.S. and U.N. forces were finally able to recapture Seoul in March 1951 and advanced north to the 38th parallel in June 1951. Despite continued intense battles, little territorial gain was made by either side and a stalemate lasted through May 1953. Military hostilities finally ended with the U.N.'s acceptance of a Korean armistice and cease-fire July 27, 1953, holding military forces stationary around the 38th parallel, known as the Demilitarized Zone (DMZ) (Fehrenbach, 2008; Halberstam, 2007).

The Korean War left Korea a country of refugees, who had been constantly on the move, fleeing populated areas to escape the advance of the North Koreans and Chinese. Heavily populated areas were destroyed and Korea's economy and infrastructure were devastated. Hundreds of thousands of men, women, and children were dead or injured. Many were permanently separated from family and home by the DMZ, leaving hundreds of thousands of orphaned and homeless children, widows; and unemployed (Kim, 1998).

The end of the Korean War did not end internal political conflict within Korea. A military coup led to the control of the Korean government by Major General Park Chong Hee on May 16, 1961. This was attributed to the corruption of Korean President Rhee Syngman, subsequent failures of leadership by a parliamentary government under President Yoon Po-son and Prime Minister Chang Myon, numerous student demonstrations, and an inability by the government to establish law and order. These political events had significant implications for Hwang Kee and his efforts to promote and develop Soo Bahk Do Moo Duk Kwan as a traditional Korean martial art.

Brief Biography of Hwang Kee[2]

Hwang Kee's grandfather was born in March of 1841. He was a large man and a hard working farmer. Hwang Kee's father, Hwang Yong Hwan was born on June 13, 1862 and educated in the Chinese

Classics and History. He attended the Law Academy. Hwang Yong Hwan was awarded the prestigious Hong Pae (Red Scroll) around 1880 in recognition of the highest scholarly achievement after successfully completing the *Dae Kua Gup Jae* examination under the last king of the Chosŏn Dynasty, Ko Jong. This entitled him to wear a flower insignia on his clothing. His title was Hoon Mun Gwan (Extensive Literary Scholar). Hwang Kee's father was well known for his writing in the areas of history, culture, and in particular, philosophy and poetic literature. He later held the position of a Government Secretary. Hwang Kee's parents lived during the final years of the Chosŏn Dynasty (1392-1910) and were very likely members of the *yangban*, described in the preceding section. It is remarkable that Hwang Kee's father achieved this status since Hwang Kee's paternal grandfather was a farmer and advancement to positions of higher social status was extremely difficult and very expensive.

The Japanese occupation of Korea in 1910 resulted in a substantial decline in the development of Korean culture, arts, traditions, language and philosophy and a halt to any substantial scholarship in these areas. The Japanese began eliminating and killing Korean government officials and anyone connected to the Royal Family. Hwang Yong Hwan and his family returned to his home town of Changdan-Ni in Kyong Gi Province located immediately south of the DMZ between the Republic of South Korea and the People's Republic of North Korea.

This directly affected the status and ability of Hwang Kee's father to continue his scholarly pursuits and interests. In addition, the suppression of Korean culture under the Japanese culture resulted in a loss of any wealth accumulated by scholars during this time.

Hwang Kee was born November 9, 1914 in Jangdan, Kyong Gi Province. Hwang Kee was the youngest of three children with a brother about 20 years older and an older sister. Hwang Kee's family lived in very difficult and poor circumstances because his father was unable to pursue his livelihood. Hwang Kee's mother passed away when he was about five years of age leaving him to be raised by his father and other family members. Undoubtedly, his father's academic and scholarly interests and the high value placed on education in

Korean society influenced Hwang Kee's own value of education and scholarship which resulted in his writing many publications. His ability to fuse his knowledge of history, science, and philosophy into his study and practice of the martial arts is evident in his publications.

Early in Hwang Kee's childhood, at about age seven, he observed a man defending himself against multiple opponents using a method referred to as *Tae Kyun* and later watched as the same man practiced various techniques with a partner. Although Hwang Kee asked the man to teach him this martial system he was refused due to his age. Hwang Kee continued to observe and practice the man's movements. This fueled his lifelong interest and devotion to the study and practice of traditional Korean martial arts, the founding of a martial arts organization (Moo Duk Kwan), and the development of the traditional Korean martial art, Soo Bahk Do (traditional Korean martial art) that had been lost due to the occupation by Japan. Ultimately, his efforts led to a rebirth in the interest and study of Soo Bahk Do.

Hwang Kee entered elementary school at age 11 and graduated from high school in March 1935 at the age of 21 during a time when few students entered or completed high school. During his time as a student Hwang Kee, joined the high school track team and participated in other athletic activities. In addition, he became known for his high level of proficiency with the abacus to the extent that he competed and won a championship in this area. Hwang Kee also developed a strong interest in astronomy and was known for being an unusually talented and gifted child in a number of areas.

At age 15 Hwang Kee met his wife, Cho Kyung Kap. Mrs. Hwang was born May 13, 1914 and they were married April 12, 1928 in an arranged marriage typical of the time and the culture. Hwang Kee's wife was the only survivor of eleven children, ten of whom died either during childbirth or shortly thereafter.

According to personal conversations between the wife of the author of this text, Ji Seh Hun, and her mother-in-law (Hwang Kee's wife), Mrs. Hwang's parents sought the advice of a fortune-teller about their daughter's future. This was a common practice during this period and one that continues today on matters of marriage. Her parents were concerned about their young daughter's future and the possibility of losing her. The fortune-teller advised Hwang Kee's wife's parents that her marriage around age 15 would improve the future of the family and of the young girl and would avert bad fortune that might cause them to lose their daughter.

Photos of Hwang Kee from his high school yearbook including his school portrait, as a member of the school abacus team (standing second from the right), and track team holding the trophy).

Mrs. Hwang had another experience with a fortune-teller who worked on the main street of their home town. He told Mrs. Hwang that unless she paid respect to the god of the trees misfortune would befall her children. Only by deeply bowing in the center of the main street of the city could this misfortune be prevented. Mrs. Hwang complied with the advice of the fortune-teller. This experience had a deep impact on the author, who was approximately 14 years old at the time. Hwang Kee and his wife had five children, two boys and three girls. Mrs. Hwang passed away peacefully on October 14, 1997.

In 1935, after graduating from high school, Hwang Kee traveled to Manchuria where he worked for the railroad company. A year later in 1936 he met and trained under Master Yang Kuk Jin, a Chinese martial arts master in various martial arts training methods including *seh bop* (method of postures), *bo bop* (method of steps), and *ryun bop* (method of conditioning). He was also trained in *dham toi sip e ro* and *tae keuk kwon*, disciplines of form (patterns of defensive and offensive movements) and combat applications. Hwang Kee returned to Seoul, Korea, in 1937 and traveled to Manchuria in 1941 for a short term of additional training under Master Yang. It was the last time Hwang Kee would see Master Yang due to the outbreak of the Chinese Civil War. This armed struggle between the Kuomintang (Nationalists) and the Communist Party of China in 1946 ultimately left China under the rule of the Communist Party of China and Mao Zedong.

From the time Hwang Kee was born through August 1945, marking the end of World War II, the systematic study of martial arts was severely restricted by the Japanese during their occupation of Korea. Access to the martial arts by the general public at this time in Korea was limited to Gum Do (Kendo) and Yu Do (Judo). Ssrieum, a form of wrestling indigenous to Korea, was promoted by national leaders, though it was likely discouraged during the occupation period (Dong-kwon, 1963). Although training in other systems or arts was prohibited, Hwang Kee was able to obtain information about Okinawan karate from the library of the Cho Sun Railway where he worked in 1939. His study and practice of Okinawan karate[3] methods expanded his practice and skill as a martial artist and later the emergence of the martial art he taught. Thus, a substantial portion of the Hwang Kee's skill as a martial artist emerged and matured primarily through personal observation, study and practice. Drawing on his experience and skill in various Chinese and Okinawan martial arts systems he founded a martial arts organization that he named the Moo Duk Kwan (literally martial virtue school/institute) on his birthday, November 9, 1945. This occurred only three months after the end of World War II with the announcement of Japan's surrender on August 15, 1945. Hwang Kee was 31 years old.

Originally, he named the martial art he developed *Hwa Soo Do* (way of the flower hand) in honor of and reference to the *hwarang*, a military corps revered in Korean history for its dedication and highly acclaimed combative skill. The *hwarang* were also well trained in the literary and fine arts, music, and a code of honor and ethics (Hwang, 1995; Pieters, 1994; Young, 1993). Hwa Soo Do included many of the

methods Hwang Kee had mastered while training under Master Yang. However, due to the level of control over Korean life by the Japanese during their occupation of Korea, Hwang Kee faced numerous challenges and struggles achieving public recognition and acceptance of Hwa Soo Do as a bonafide martial art. Many of the methods influenced by Hwang Kee's training under Master Yang were not well accepted or understood.

Hwa Soo Do and Tang Soo Do Texts published by Hwang Kee

In addition, students were often looking for applications involving the faster striking movements common in Okinawan karate.

Hwang Kee eventually decided to incorporate elements of Okinawan karate into Hwa Soo Do to increase the visibility and acceptability of the Art. In addition, though he originally called the Art *Hwa Soo Do* he began referring to the art as *Tang Soo Do* since this name was more familiar to the general public. It should be noted that the names *Hwa Soo Do*, *Tang Soo Do* and *Soo Bahk Do* have all been used to refer to the same traditional martial art taught by Hwang Kee. Soo Bahk Do was the name he used when he incorporated his organization in 1960 and has been the name he has used since to refer to the martial art he taught. This name speaks to Korea's history and specifically, to a rebirth of the practice and study of Soo Bahk Ki. To adopt the traditional name of the martial art preferred by Hwang Kee, the U.S. Tang Soo Do Moo Duk Kwan Federation, Inc. changed its name to the U.S. Soo Bahk Do Moo Duk Kwan Federation, Inc. August 3, 1996. Other member organizations affiliated with Hwang Kee and the Korean Soo Bahk Do Association Moo Duk Kwan soon followed suit. The use of the name *Tang Soo Do* marked a period of growth of the Moo Duk Kwan organization of which Hwang Kee was named lifetime president. The first modern Korean martial arts text, *Hwa Soo Do Kyo Bohn*, was authored and self-published by Hwang Kee May 30, 1949.

During the years before the war and throughout the war there was a severe shortage of food. The mortality rate among newborns was particularly high (Tauber, 1946). Hwang Kee's first son, the author and translator of this text was born in 1947. Hwang Kee and his wife had another child two years later who died shortly after birth of malnutrition resulting from wartime conditions. Hwang Kee continued to work for the Ministry of Transportation during the war and attempted to continue teaching Tang Soo Do. However, for the most part he suspended teaching for 17 months until the war ended and he had relocated to Pusan (also spelled *Busan*). Hwang Kee and his wife experienced the loss of a number of family members, relatives, friends and martial arts students during the war.

Prior to the Korean War, in 1948, Korea was in political turmoil. As indicated above, there was much conflict in South Korea about the influence of North Korea and China and particularly of persons who were thought to have pro-Communist leanings. Many Communists and Communist sympathizers had infiltrated South Korea. The military and government officials made strong efforts to suppress opposition to Rhee's Syngman leadership and political activities thought to be supportive of North Korea. Before the war, Hwang Kee was one of many who were falsely accused of being a Communist sympathizer, detained, arrested, imprisoned and tortured. Although he alludes to these experiences in his "Preface" to the *Moo Do Chul Hahk* few details have been available.

According to his personal notes, Hwang Kee was subjected to this suspicion in 1948 and was arrested and tortured in an unsuccessful attempt to force him to confess that he was a left-wing Communist sympathizer. After several days of torture and imprisonment he was finally released. His personal notes indicate that one of his Moo Duk Kwan members reported that flyers had been discovered lying on the training hall floor where he taught that supported Communist activities and North Korean political policy. It later became clear to him that his arrest may have been precipitated by the discovery of these flyers in an attempt by a competitor to discredit him and disrupt the growing success and visibility of his martial arts organization.

In July 1950, one month after the Korean War began, Hwang Kee's family relocated from their home in Yong San, a village immediately north of Seoul, to Seok Got Ri a village located in the town of Jang Dan Myun, which was where he was born. At this time, H. C. Hwang, the author was about four years old. He had an infant brother about one year old and his sister who was about ten. The family relocated to be with family and relatives during these uncertain and difficult times. According to Hwang Kee's personal notes, the family walked from Yong San to Jang Dan Myun since there was no transportation available.

Although Hwang Kee had to stop teaching Soo Bahk Do, he continued to work for the Korean Ministry of Transportation remaining in Seoul after the North Korean advance and occupation of Seoul. Hwang Kee's biographical notes indicate that North Koreans began to investigate the loyalty of employees of the Ministry of Transportation. Persons found to be loyal to the South Korean government were routinely arrested and executed. Employees of the Ministry of Transportation including Hwang Kee were required to write a biography describing their history and employment, and answer questions about their political beliefs and loyalties. Recognizing the extreme danger he was in after turning in his biography, he fled to live with a relative of his father's in Seoul. Communist Party officials and the North Korean military began searching for him and when he was found he was placed under arrest. Hwang Kee's personal notes indicate that the chief investigator was an older man and refused to make eye contact with him appearing to be somewhat sympathetic to Hwang Kee's situation during his interrogation. The chief investigator eventually released him against the wishes of Communist Party officials who were present during the interrogation. After his release, Hwang Kee was followed by several party officials who attempted to re-arrest him based on their suspicions that he was anti-Communist and loyal to South Korea.

In his personal notes, Hwang Kee reported that this encounter did not end well for the party officials who experienced firsthand the effects of Hwang Kee's martial skills. After subduing the officials, Hwang Kee jumped over a fence and fled to a distant cousin's home located in Tchang Sin Dong. She took him in for a short time and found spaces under the roofs of homes where he could stay that were invisible to anyone on the ground from any direction. Upon the arrival of General MacArthur's forces into Seoul at the end of September 1950, Hwang Kee returned to Seoul to be reunited with his family.

Hwang Kee returned to work for the Ministry of Transportation. South Korean officials resumed investigations to identify North Korean and Communist sympathizers. The Director of the Ministry of Transportation began investigating employees. Again, Hwang Kee found himself the target of suspicions of being a Communist sympathizer. He was again arrested and tortured in another unsuccessful attempt to make him confess, until an official of the Ministry of Transportation (identified in personal notes as Mr. Kim) who knew him, found the biography the North Koreans had forced Hwang Kee to write. With this evidence, he was released and continued to work for the Ministry of Transportation.

In late October 1950 the direct involvement of the Communist Chinese Forces (CCF) in the war became apparent and by November 1, 1950 the CCF had engaged U.N. troops. The CCF advanced south and captured Seoul, which was turned into a ghost town as everyone fled in advance of the Chinese. Hyun Chul Hwang, was four years old and remembers it as a very dark and cold winter. In late December or early January as the Chinese advanced to Seoul, he, his father, mother and sister fled from Seoul south to Daegu (also spelled *Tae Gu*) located about 146 miles southeast of Seoul. At times they were able to use the railroad but more often they walked to Daegu. The family lived as refugees, sleeping in shacks, garages and storage areas behind people's homes. Very little food was available and famine was widespread. Drury and Clavin (2009) reported that the Korean winter of 1950 was the coldest winter recorded in thirty years. Numerous sources report subzero temperatures ranging from 10 to 40 degrees below zero (ANZAC Day Commemoration Committee, 1998; Drury & Clavin, 2009; Weider History Group, 2008; Westover, 1990). Fehrenbach (2008) reported "The cold, through the bitter days of December, would destroy as many American fighting men as enemy bullets (p. 239)."

In June 1951, Hwang Kee was once again subjected to arrest by Daegu police on the suspicion of sympathizing with the North Korean Communist regime. He was initially taken in for questioning and upon initial questioning was accused of being a criminal. When the police attempted to handcuff him, resisting the initial attempts, he was ultimately overcome by a number of police, handcuffed, and severely beaten. This incident turned into a long and torturous period during which he was repeatedly hung upside down and beaten and subjected to electric shock. Hwang Kee was also subjected to a water torture that involved placing a rag or towel over his face and mouth and pouring water over the towel. Water was also directly poured into his nose and mouth. These practices were reported by prisoners of war held by the North Koreans (Saffire, 2008). This torture was intended to force him to confess to the crime of being a Communist sympathizer despite the treatment he had received from the North Koreans. Hwang Kee refused to confess to being a Communist sympathizer or to crimes he had not committed. After one particularly brutal session, he was escorted by a guard armed with a carbine carrying a blanket that was typically used to wrap dead bodies to be transported to an unknown location. Hwang Kee was convinced he was about to be summarily executed and the blanket was to be used for transporting his body. The guard escorting him remembered that he had forgotten something and took him back to the office where the guards again subjected Hwang Kee to additional torture to see if he would confess to being a Communist sympathizer. Thinking of his family and convinced that he would be shot if he did not confess, he signed a confession giving the guards what they wanted. According to personal notes, the guards returned him to his cell and celebrated his signed confession as a victory.

During this period, Hwang Kee's family and friends were working diligently to free him. A distant family member, Hwang Jin Young, the first son of Hwang Kee's older brother, Hwang Kee's nephew, was notified of Hwang Kee's situation. Hwang Jin Young was a prosecutor which was a very powerful government position that carried a high level of authority. Hwang Jin Young traveled from Pusan to Daegu to visit and defend Hwang Kee. Upon seeing him, Hwang Jin Young demanded his release. He also commanded the police to apologize and rewrite their report and repudiate the confession signed by Hwang Kee.

Following his release, Hwang Kee and his family relocated to Pusan in October 1951. Pusan was where the government of the Republic of South Korea was operating during this time. Upon moving to Pusan he began teaching Soo Bahk (Hwa Soo) Do at the Cho Ryang Station. At this time, the author, Hwang Kee's son, Hyun Chul Hwang entered elementary school. Several months later Hwang Kee began teaching Soo Bahk (Tang Soo) Do for the Police Academy in Pusan and in April 1952, he began teaching Soo Bahk (Tang Soo) Do for the Ministry of Defense, also in Pusan.

After the end of the war in September 1953 he and his family again relocated to Seoul to teach Soo Bahk (Tang Soo) Do in a building that had no windows or floor. In May 1955, he leased a government building in front of the Seoul Central Railway Station that became renowned as the Joong Ang Do Jang (Central Do Jang/training hall). He organized and chaired the first International Goodwill Demonstration between Korea and China in 1955 and established a number of Soo Bahk (Tang Soo) Do training centers for the Korean military and police and eventually the U. S. Military. The late 1950s through the mid-1960s was a period of expansion and growth for Hwang Kee's martial arts community to the point that he retired from the Ministry of Transportation in October 1956, to focus his fulltime attention on the development of Moo Duk Kwan. In June 1960, Hwang Kee incorporated and registered his organization with the Korean government under the name *Dae Han Soo Bahk Do Hoe* (Korean Soo Bahk Do Association) as the traditional Korean martial art. The association was formed as a not-for-profit organization chartered to study, promote, and practice Soo Bahk Do to enhance personal well-being under the Moo Duk Kwan philosophy. The name of the association also signaled Hwang Kee's efforts to promote and institutionalize a traditional Korean martial art based on his research and study of evidence of the practice of ancient Korean martial arts referred to as *Soo Bahk Ki*. This eventually led to a transformation of the name of the martial art from *Tang Soo Do* to *Soo Bahk Do*.

Struggles and Challenges

Efforts to unify all Korean martial arts into one body with standardized training, teaching and testing methods were initiated in the early 1950s. These efforts were often led by founders of martial arts organizations who were high ranking members of the Korean military and had the support of leaders at the highest levels of the Korean government. The emergence of Tae Kwon Do and the decision by Hwang Kee to maintain the integrity and uniqueness of the Moo Duk Kwan has been the subject of a number of articles and debate (Burdick, 1997; Capener, 1995; Hancock, 1994; Hong, n.d.; Shaw, 2004). In June 1960, Hwang Kee's organization, the Korean Soo Bahk Do Association, Moo Duk Kwan was formally recognized by the Korean government. Less than a year later, Korea again found itself in political turmoil with a military coup led by Major General Park Chong Hee who later became President of the Republic of South Korea and held that office until 1979. Park's Chong Hee ascendency to the presidency led to significant impediments to Hwang Kee's efforts to advance Moo Duk Kwan. Hwang Kee's Moo Duk Kwan was one of the largest martial arts organizations in Korea after the Korean War and through the 1960s. However, the assumption of power by Park Chong Hee led to efforts by the Korean government to dissolve the Korean Soo Bahk Do Association, Moo Duk Kwan and impede Hwang Kee's activities. This included complete censure of the *Moo Yei Si Bo*, the newspaper he regularly published about Soo Bahk Do; terminating his position as an instructor for the Republic of Korea Air Force Academy and the National Police Academy; prohibiting instruction of Soo Bahk (Tang Soo) Do in middle and high schools throughout Korea; and, controlling the activities of the Moo Duk Kwan from 1961-1965. The pressures to unify under Tae Kwon

Do continued, during which time many of Hwang Kee's senior students and instructors yielded to the political pressures to leave the Moo Duk Kwan and join with Tae Kwon Do.

Additional problems emerged with the refusal by many employers to acknowledge the validity of Moo Duk Kwan certification for employment purposes, although it was recognized by the government; impediments to acquiring passports and visas by Moo Duk Kwan instructors to travel to foreign countries for the purpose of teaching Soo Bahk (Tang Soo) Do; prohibitions from attending international events; attempts to destroy the organization's record of rank and seniority; and finally, a countermand order revoking the Korean government's registration and recognition of the Korean Soo Bahk Do Association, Moo Duk Kwan. Though Hwang Kee initiated successful litigation that saved the association, the Korean Ministry of Education appealed this decision to the Korean Supreme Court. Hwang Kee's efforts led to the Korean Supreme Court's decision to deny the appeal of the Korean Ministry of Education preserving the existence of the Korean Soo Bahk Do Association Moo Duk Kwan. However, pressure to dissolve the Moo Duk Kwan and unify with Tae Kwon Do continued through 1979.

Despite these challenges Hwang Kee continued his efforts to develop and teach Soo Bahk Do which resulted in the establishment of branches of the Moo Duk Kwan throughout the U. S., Europe, Central and South America, Asia, and Australia. In addition, he wrote and published numerous publications including *Soo Bahk Do Dae Kahm*, a 700-page text describing core elements of Soo Bahk Do history, culture, tradition, philosophy, and techniques.

Hwang Kee's efforts to continue to develop Soo Bahk Do as a traditional Korean martial art continued to the end of his life. While Hwang Kee's maintained his primary residence in Seoul, Korea and the Korean Soo Bahk Do Association continued to be the central administrative organization for the Moo Duk Kwan, the focus of his efforts to strengthen the Moo Duk Kwan organization expanded worldwide. This focus resulted in the establishment of national federations dedicated to the teaching and practice of Soo Bahk Do in the U.S and throughout Mexico, Europe, Central and South America,

Asia, Australia and the Pacific. In 1998, the author, Hyun Chul Hwang organized the World Moo Duk Kwan. Members of this organization include federations and organizations from various countries around the world that are dedicated to the practice and study of Soo Bahk Do. The World Moo Duk Kwan directed by Hyung Chul Hwang is the current administrative body responsible for overseeing the study and practice of Soo Bahk Do.

In 1974, Hwang Kee toured the U. S. to promote Soo Bahk (Tang Soo) Do and his influence led to the founding of the U. S. Soo Bahk (Tang Soo) Do Moo Duk Kwan Federation, Inc. Hwang Kee was awarded *Black Belt Magazine's* 1989 Man of the Year award. He celebrated the 50th Anniversary of the founding of the Moo Duk Kwan September 23, 1995 in Seoul, Korea at the Seoul Education and Culture Center. This event was sponsored by the Korean Soo Bahk Do Association, Moo Duk Kwan and the Korean Ministry of Culture and Sports. He was also very active in conducting many instructional seminars throughout the world and continued to study and write about Soo Bahk Do.

Hwang Kee passed away peacefully July 14, 2002 at his home in Seoul, Korea. Subsequent to his death and according to his wishes the leadership and presidency of the Moo Duk Kwan organization was passed on to his son, Hyun Chul Hwang, the author of this book.

Hwang Kee's Contributions to the Development of a Martial Art and Philosophy

As interest in Tang Soo Do grew and the number of practitioners increased over time, Hwang Kee introduced unique contributions to the art. From the very beginning, Hwa Soo Do (Tang Soo Do) emerged as a martial art based on fundamental human values that required learning and practicing traditional and cultural disciplines that influenced human conduct and behavior. These values were initially taken from the principles that guided the training of the *hwarang* and were expanded by Hwang Kee to include tenets that formulated a philosophy, a code of ethics, and formal rules governing practitioner conduct before, during and after martial arts training. Demonstration of these values was adopted as a mandatory training requirement for practitioners of Soo Bahk (Tang Soo) Do. Hwang Kee also adopted goals and activities focused on promoting respect, courtesy, friendship, brotherhood, cooperation and goodwill nationally and internationally. Specific expectations and rules that governed how practitioners were to conduct themselves in the locations of martial arts training were taught and made explicit in training publications by Hwang Kee. The *Moo Do Chul Hahk* provides a comprehensive explanation and understanding of Moo Do as a philosophy.

Another key and unique contribution by Hwang Kee was his effort to advance the performance and execution of physical movement through the study and application of scientific principles. Hwang Kee was the first to include a detailed description of the application and understanding of scientific principles, specifically Newtonian physics (classical mechanics) and basic biomechanics (kinesiology), to the execution of each of the basic physical movements involved in the practice of Soo Bahk Do. Hwang Kee was the first to both theorize and apply a method of hip and waist movement with the execution of each physical movement that significantly increased the kinetic energy and force that may be generated in comparison to previous methods of executing these movements.

These are only a few of Hwang Kee's contributions. A brief summary of many of Hwang Kee's achievements and activities throughout his life are listed in the Appendix at the end of this book.

Efforts to Promote International Goodwill and Harmony

Hwang Kee organized a number of national and international goodwill events and introduced Tang Soo Do to the Korean and U. S. military. Many of these goodwill events included martial arts practitioners invited from China and Japan in an effort on Hwang Kee's part to promote world peace and harmony. In January 1961, a Moo Duk Kwan team, under the name of the Korean Soo Bahk Do Association, was invited by the All Japan Karate Federation for the Goodwill Martial Arts Championship. This was the first time in history that any Korean martial arts team competed in a foreign country. It was also the first time that the Moo Duk Kwan was internationally recognized. In May 1961 a Goodwill International Contest and Demonstration sponsored by the Korean Soo Bahk Do Association Moo Duk Kwan under the leadership of Hwang Kee and Ji Do Kwan (another respected Korean martial arts organization) was conducted in Seoul, Korea. China, Japan and Korea were invited participants. Hwang Kee was also instrumental in promoting international relationships among Asian countries leading to his appointment as the first president of the Asian Moo Do Federation in May 1961. Korea, China and Japan were key partners in the organization of this Federation.

Introduction to the **Moo Yei Do Bo Tong Ji**

According to Hwang Kee, 1957 was the most significant year of his martial arts career. During this year, Hwang Kee's constant practice and study of the martial arts led to his introduction to the original text of the *Moo Yei Do Bo Tong Ji* in the library of the Seoul National University. It is reported to have been compiled and published in 1790. The *Moo Yei Do Bo Tong Ji* is a book of martial methods comprising four volumes. It is the result of a comprehensive study of a number of ancient manuscripts that included illustrations and descriptions of fighting and military techniques and strategies (Kim, 1986; Kim, 2000). This text documents a martial method indigenous to Korea referred to as *Soo Bahk Ki* (or *Soo Bahk Heui*). According to Kim (1986), King Chŏngjo ordered Yi Tŏk-mu, Pak Che ga and Paek Tong-su to identify and survey ancient texts addressing military and fighting methods and strategies, research and field-test their effectiveness, and compile a manual describing them. The compilers and authors of the *Moo Yei Do Bo Tong Ji* drew on a number of ancient texts including a military manual entitled *Jixiao xinshu* by General Qi Ji-guang, the *Muyejebo*, the *Muyeshinbo*, the *Wujing qishu* and a number of Korean military manuals written during the Chosŏn Dynasty. This text is considered to be the only Korean book thought to be in existence from that period describing ancient martial methods and is of immense cultural value (see Kim, 2000 for a comprehensive English translation of the *Moo Yei Do Bo Tong Ji*).

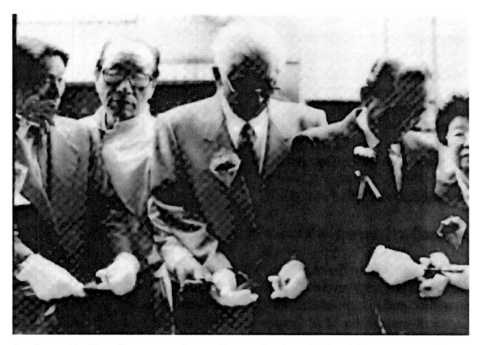

Professor Na Hyun Seong standing at Hwang Kee's right shoulder assisting with a ribbon cutting at the opening of the new headquarters for the Korean Soo Bahk Do Association in Seoul, Korea, March 1989.

Hwang Kee was introduced to the *Moo Yei Do Bo Tong Ji* by Professor Na Hyun Seong of Seoul National University. It appears that Professor Na and Hwang Kee had a prior association and friendship. Professor Na has been referred to as the Father of Modern Korean Sports and was a professor in the area of physical and health education at Seoul National University. Professor Na, aware of the immense value of the *Moo Yei Do Bo Tong Ji*, permitted Hwang Kee to study and photograph each page. These photographs served as his personal copy of the text.

Hwang Kee, recognizing the immense cultural and historical value of this work, realized that the book was clear historical evidence of the existence of martial arts techniques practiced over 1500 years ago in Korea—techniques that had gone largely unnoticed by the general public and martial arts community. Hwang Kee translated and published portions of the section of the *Moo Yei Do Bo Tong Ji* dealing with *kwon bup* in his martial arts newspaper, the *Moo Yei Si Bo*, in1960. These were the first contemporary translations and expositions of the *Moo Yei Do Bo Tong Ji*.

Appearance of the Moo Yei Do Bo Tong Ji in the Moo Yei Si Bo.

Unfortunately, little attention was paid to his efforts to document and disseminate scholarly information about the *Moo Yei Do Bo Tong Ji* in the *Moo Yei Si Bo* 48 years ago. Ironically, there is now much attention and interest paid to identifying, acquiring, and preserving ancient and traditional Korean cultural treasures including the *Moo Yei Do Bo Tong Ji*. Copies of photos of every page of the *Moo Yei Do Bo Tong Ji* were published in the Korean version of *Soo Bahk Do Dae Kahm* authored by Hwang Kee in April 1970 and later in an English version entitled *Tang Soo Do/Soo Bahk Do* in February 1978. While other translations of the *Moo Yei Do Bo Tong Ji* have been published subsequent to Hwang Kee's work (Kim, 2000; Della Pia, 1994, 1995), only Hwang Kee has incorporated content from his translation of the portion of the text dealing with *kwon bup* into the actual techniques, practice and application by a traditional Korean martial art (Soo Bahk Do).

The *Moo Yei Do Bo Tong Ji* so significantly influenced Hwang Kee's development of Tang Soo Do as a martial art that Tang Soo Do was eventually renamed Soo Bahk Do. The first demonstration of content translated from the *Moo Yei Do Bo Tong Ji* was presented by Hwang Kee on November 21, 1982 at the International Tang Soo Do Championship conducted in Atlantic City, New Jersey.

Demonstration of Hwa Sun Hyung by Hwang Kee in 1982, Atlantic City, NJ

The study and translation of the *Moo Yei Do Bo Tong Ji* by Hwang Kee has resulted in a fundamental evolution of Soo Bahk Do as a traditional martial art that includes techniques and methods practiced centuries ago in Korea known as Soo Bahk Ki. His study and translation of the section devoted to *kwon bup* (fist fighting method) revealed ancient ways and means of traditional martial arts training and practice that substantially expanded and advanced the practices and methods of training that standardized the practice of Soo Bahk Do. Hwang Kee was the first to infuse many of the training methods, strategies, and techniques learned from the *Moo Yei Do Bo Tong Ji*.

The integration of kwon bup movements and patterns taken from the *Moo Yei Do Bo Tong Ji* into the training requirements and practice of Soo Bahk Do is a major scholarly and cultural contribution by

Hwang Kee to the understanding, study, and preservation of a Korean cultural treasure and Korean culture and heritage. It is also important to note, that Hwang Kee, with the assistance and advice of Professor Na was the first to recognize, study, translate and disseminate information about the *Moo Yei Dobo Tong Ji* with particular emphasis on its potential benefits for martial arts practitioners.

In summary, Hwang Kee's work and translation of the *Moo Yei Dobo Tong Ji* cannot be overstated. Hwang Kee's recognition of the value of the *Moo Yei Do Bo Tong Ji;* his subsequent efforts to publish, disseminate and translate the text; and his efforts to incorporate the information directly into the training and curriculum of a traditional martial art that is practiced throughout the world must be understood and acknowledged in three ways.

First, Hwang Kee was the first to publicly disseminate and discuss the value and benefits of the *Moo Yei Do Bo Tong Ji*. This is clear since most, if not all, of the extant research and literature that discusses and describes the *Moo Yei Do Bo Tong Ji* is dated subsequent to the publication of Hwang Kee's work. As such, his efforts may be viewed as significant scholarly and cultural contributions to promoting the study and understanding of this ancient Korean text.

Second, through his direct efforts he has made a significant contribution to the knowledge, understanding, study and preservation of an ancient Korean cultural artifact, namely, the *Moo Yei Do Bo Tong Ji*, by incorporating key elements of the text into the training requirements for Soo Bahk Do practitioners. As a result, Soo Bahk Do has emerged not only as a martial art, but also as an important mechanism for the preservation, study and practice of a highly valued Korean cultural artifact. Soo Bahk Do elevates the academic study of the *Moo Yei Do Bo Tong Ji* to direct experience so that the serious student may derive benefits to personal health and well-being. Thus, as a *traditional martial art*, Soo Bahk Do embodies ancient Korean cultural and historical traditions and practices and significantly elevates the social, historical, and educational impact and contribution of the art for its practitioners and Korea as a country. This is one of the most significant and notable of the scholarly and cultural contributions made by Hwang Kee.

Third, the infusion of content from the *Moo Yei Do Bo Tong Ji* into the current practice of Soo Bahk Do and through his publications promotes the worldwide study, understanding and appreciation of Korean culture and history. This cannot help but increase the study and appreciation of Korean culture and history.

Hwang Kee's Publications and Scholarship

In addition to Hwang Kee's study, translation, publication and dissemination of key portions of the *Moo Yei Do Bo Tong Ji*, a considerable amount of time was dedicated to researching, writing, publishing and disseminating information about the traditional Korean martial art, Soo Bahk Do. He wrote and published a number of books including *Hwa Soo Do Kyo Bohn* in 1949, *Tang Soo Do Kyo Bohn* (Tang Soo Do Origin Instruction textbook) in 1958, the *Moo Yei Si Bo* (Martial Art Newspaper) and *Tang Soo Do Bo Sin Bop*. A partial list of publications authored by Hwang Kee in addition to the *Moo Do Chul Hahk* is provided on following pages. He is best known for his authorship and publication of *Soo Bahk Do Dae Kahm* the most extensive martial arts text describing the history, philosophy, values, traditions, and technique of the traditional martial art, Soo Bahk Do.

Hwang Kee's scholarship also includes his own translation of the original text of the *Tao Te Ching* by Lao Tzu and the *Book of Changes* (*Chou I*). His study of these works significantly influenced his thinking and writing of the *Moo Do Chul Hahk* which contains numerous references to these and other writings by Confucius and other Eastern philosophers and scholars. These translations are included in his original publication of the Korean version of the *Moo Do Chul Hahk*.

Selected Publications Authored by Hwang Kee

Title	Description	Language	Publication Date
Hwa Soo Do Kyo Bohn	First detailed description of the martial art taught by Hwang Kee	Korean	May 1949
Tang Soo Do Kyo Bohn	Updated description of the martial art taught by Hwang Kee	Korean	July 1958
Soo Bahk Do Dae Kham	Detailed description of the history, philosophy, culture, and technique of Tang Soo Do (Soo Bahk Do)	Korean	1970
Soo Bahk Do Dae Kham, Volume II	Introducing Yuk Ro hyung from *Moo Yei Do Bo Tong Ji*	Korean	June 1992
Soo Bahk Do	Translation of Kwon Bup from the *Moo Yei Do Bo Tong Ji*	Korean	March 1992
Tang Soo Do (Soo Bahk Do)	Translation of portion of *Soo Bahk Do Dae Kham* including all hyung through passai	English	1978
Soo Bahk Do (Tang Soo Do), Volume II	Latter segments of Korean version of *Soo Bahk Do Dae Kham*	English	1992
Moo Do Chul Hahk	Moo Do Philosophy as translated and described in this text	Korean	1993
Moo Duk Kwan	History of the Moo Duk Kwan and early development of Soo Bahk Do	Korean	June 1993

Title	Description	Language	Publication Date
Tang Soo Do (Soo Bahk Do) Moo Duk Kwan Instructional Guides	Guides for each rank level of Soo Bahk Do training	English	1993
The History of Moo Duk Kwan	A history of the emergence and development of Soo Bahk Do Moo Duk Kwan	English	1995

The Moo Do Chul Hahk: An Overview

Hwang Kee entitled his book, *Moo Do Chul Hahk* (*Moo Do Philosophy*),

> *...since this work, written on the basis of experience, seeks to bring together a synthesis of human philosophy, the philosophy of balance, and Moo Do Philosophy while looking at life through Moo Do* (*p. 150*).

Moo Do, literally translated martial way, is the essence and spirit of the martial art Soo Bahk Do Moo Duk Kwan and according to Hwang Kee the guiding philosophy of his martial art. More specifically, the term *moo* (武) comprises two Chinese characters, *ji* (止) translated as *to stop or prevent* and *gwa* (戈) translated as *knife* representing *war* or *conflict*. Therefore, the more accurate translation of the term *moo* is *to stop or prevent conflict or war*. Hwang Kee expanded the meaning of *moo* to mean stopping and preventing both internal and external conflict and promoting harmony within and without. The term *Do*[4] is exactly equivalent to the Chinese term *Tao* (道) often translated to mean way, nature or path. The terms *chul* and *hahk* combined are translated as philosophy.

Moo Do has been described by Hwang Kee, as an *action philosophy*. Dedicating his entire life to the pursuit, study and practice of Moo Do through the development, practice and teaching of Soo Bahk Do, the *Moo Do Chul Hahk* is the culmination of a philosophical theory that emerged from years of accumulated actions that characterize Hwang Kee's personal life. In short, it is a *theory* that has emerged from a lifetime of *action*.

The *Moo Do Chul Hahk* begins with a preface by Hwang Kee and is organized into eight sections. Each section addresses a range of topical areas organized into chapters. Some of the chapters are further subdivided into subtopics labeled "passages." Figures and tables are interspersed throughout the text. A summary of each section is followed by a discussion of some of the writing and stylistic conventions employed by Hwang Kee in the writing of the *Moo Do*

Chul Hahk. This summary introduces the reader to the content and message of the *Moo Do Chul Hahk.* It will be necessary to read and study the translation of the *Moo Do Chul Hahk* that follows this introduction to acquire more specific information and detail about content summarized below.

Preface. This section provides the reader some insight into Hwang Kee's state of mind as he wrote the book. It immediately introduces the reader to the conversational style and personal narrative of the author and explains the key elements of Moo Do Philosophy. He describes the purpose and intent of the book, indicating that it was his wish to develop authentic Moo Do practitioners. It is important to emphasize that while Hwang Kee devoted his entire life to the study and practice of Soo Bahk Do, he clearly wrote this book for both practitioners and non-practitioners of the martial arts. In addition, he does not limit the practice of Moo Do exclusively to practitioners of Soo Bahk Do, acknowledging that an authentic Moo Do practitioner may be a student of other martial arts systems.

Section I: The Importance of Philosophy. This section is composed of eight chapters that set the stage for the reader's study and understanding of Moo Do Philosophy. The first chapter addresses the perennial questions of the philosopher including the "why," meaning, and purpose of life; the self; the world in which we live; nature; and, the universe. The constructs of space and time are briefly discussed followed by a commentary on the transitory nature of man's life and activities. Chapter 4 initiates the reader into a discussion of Hwang Kee's philosophy with a historical perspective of the origins and emergence of philosophy itself. This is followed by an introduction to the *Book of Changes (Chou I)* and several principles from this work relevant to an understanding of Moo Do Philosophy. Hwang Kee's understanding of the importance of presenting a philosophy in the context of a world view and of historical events is evident in Chapter 6 as he describes key historical events and discusses the contributions of key individuals who have influenced philosophical thinking over time including Lao Tzu, Confucius, Jesus Christ, and Buddha. Considerable emphasis was placed on a description of the contributions of Lao Tzu and Confucius to the understanding and interpretation of Do (Tao). Section I ends with a comparison of

Eastern and Western philosophical orientations and a basic introduction to the fundamental elements of Moo Do Philosophy.

Section II: Realm of the Infinite Unlimited. Section II presents a conceptual framework for an Eastern philosophical orientation to the understanding of the origin and substance of nature. This perspective may be characterized as an Eastern ontological analysis of nature, life, the universe and the self. Hwang Kee begins with a brief discussion of "complete nothingness" which is considered mysterious and beyond comprehension. The next chapter deals with the "non-being ultimate" which has been likened to heaven or divinity. This construction deals with the paradox of the formless source and is described as the *Do* (*Tao*). Hwang Kee uses several analogies to liken the Do to a bellows, the atmosphere, water and man. He also introduces and discusses a conceptualization of the nature of Do as neutral. In this context, the question of which comes first, the chicken or the egg is addressed. He also presents the temporal order of *um* (*yin*) and *yang* noting that um precedes yang in the natural order of things. The significance of the neutrality of the Do is addressed in subsequent sections and chapters. Hwang Kee addresses the concepts of time and space in Chapter 4 of this section describing the equivalence between um and space and between yang and time and describes fate as the inexorable and inviolable cause-effect relationship between processes of the world and of the individual in accordance with the functions of time and space. Chapter 5 provides a cosmologic orientation that relates the origins and evolution of the universe, planets and nature to the concepts of um and yang. In addition, the author describes the relationship between um/yang and Do and the emergence of form and entities. Chapter 6 offers a personal insight into Hwang Kee's direct experience with enlightenment. He reflects on this experience and his observations about the extent to which humans cultivate the Do within themselves. The importance of understanding the neutrality of the Do appears once again in this chapter and he presents his own theory of Do. The final chapter of this section addresses Hwang Kee's perspective about God and heaven within a historical context. This chapter also recounts a childhood event involving a shamanistic ritual.

Section III: The Logic of Virtue. This section provides substantial evidence of Hwang Kee's deep reverence for virtue and its importance for all people particularly Moo Do practitioners. It should be of particular interest to members of the Moo Duk Kwan since Hwang Kee provides a comprehensive explanation of the concept of *duk* in this chapter. He begins a brief etymologic derivation of the Chinese terms *deok* (also spelled *deuk*) and a description of how the emergence of virtue involves *ki*[5], the energy associated with breath. In addition, the concepts of *mu* (formless/invisible) and *yu* (form/visible) are introduced. Hwang Kee integrates a Taoist and Confucian perspective of virtue and elaborates on how man is able to master his environment by possessing three types of intelligence including use of fire, the ability to write, and the development of superior weapons. Chapters 3 and 4 describe innate and acquired nature. Innate nature involves characteristics that cannot be altered and exist before the acquisition of learning and behavior. Acquired nature refers to characteristics and behaviors that are learned and can be altered. Chapter 3 includes a number of unique descriptors of human nature including *shim* (mind/heart), *jung* (centrality), *che* (body), *danjun* (point inside the body below the navel), *bonbang* (original defense), *kaesung* (individual/earthly nature), *cheonsung* (heavenly nature), *myeong* (luminosity) and *ji* or *jigak* (knowledge). Hwang Kee also describes in considerable detail the function of instinct and desire and introduces the innate ability for protection and defense. He also describes elements of human nature that are acquired including intelligence, balance and Moo Do that give humans mastery. Chapter 5, 6 and 7 move directly into Hwang Kee's observations and beliefs regarding the development and application of virtue in one's personal life. Chapter 5 presents the argument that we are born free of good or evil and that good and evil are ultimately developed as a function of how we live. He exhorts the reader to strive to develop and promote virtue and goodness in accordance with Do and the natural principles of one's conscience. He notes that excess and particularly excessive desire, is the source of evil and submits a rationale that striving to be "ordinary" rather than "extraordinary" is in accord with nature and the philosophy of balance. He ends this section with a discussion of 11 characteristics of a healthy society and a practical way of understanding heaven and hell with respect to the character and consequences of one's actions.

Section IV: The Philosophy of Balance. Hwang Kee presents his philosophy of balance in this section. He defines balance in terms of um, yang and neutrality which are basic elements of Do (Tao). Hwang Kee argues that in order to truly understand the philosophy of balance one must engage in authentic spiritual development (*suyang*). Hwang Kee describes the role of neutrality in achieving balance and harmony.

Section V: Moo Do Philosophy. This section introduces and describes in depth Hwang Kee's philosophy of Moo Do. It begins with a deeply personal reflection on Hwang Kee's life and the statement: "So here I am, setting down my view of life based on what I have learned of its ideology and what I know directly based on my own experiences. This is Moo Do Philosophy (p. 172)." This is a key statement since it points to the origins of Hwang Kee's philosophy, his own life experience. He introduces the Korean term *moodoin*, someone who engages in the authentic study and practice of Moo Do. Hwang Kee emphasizes that the true meaning of Moo Do is to train one's character and to strive to serve and help others through personal sacrifice. To this end, Hwang Kee introduces and explains the meaning of Moo Do, its purpose and key elements and explains that the aim of the book is to "... promote awareness of true Moo Do and promote the development of students with a truly humane character" (p. 173).

The second chapter of this section introduces the *Song of the Sip Sam Seh* (Song of the 13 Influences) concluding that it is an essential element of Moo Do Philosophy. The *Song of the Sip Sam Seh* appears in a number of ancient Chinese texts and the original source may not be known. Hwang Kee provides a translation and explanation of the song.

He explains that the *Song of the Sip Sam Seh* contains the complete basic teachings of Moo Do. Chapter 2 of this section stresses the importance of *munhak* (literature) to the understanding and practice of Moo Do, once again illustrating his emphasis on the importance of scholarship as a key element of martial arts practice. This chapter revisits the concepts of innate and acquired knowledge. He stresses the importance of a balance and harmony between *mun* (knowledge) and *moo* (martial skills) noting that neither should be considered more important than the other. This chapter also describes the meaning of

Moo and Do. The history of the development of Moo Do is discussed followed by the importance of the relationship of nature, balance, and life with Moo Do. Chapter 2 ends with a discussion of Hwang Kee's theory of change.

Chapters 3 and 4 discuss the related concepts of energy and ki. Chapter 3 provides an explanation of the relationship between energy and the concepts of um (a.k.a. yin) and yang. He characterizes um in terms of stillness and calm and yang as movement. He takes special care to emphasize that um and yang are not opposing entities but entities that have a "...positive tendency to harmonize (p. 190)." He describes the harmonization of um and yang in terms of the laws of Nature noting that their harmonization results in heat and light. He concludes that Do is the source of energy that harmonizes um and yang and defines it as intrinsic ki.

Chapter 4 provides the reader a detailed description of ki and its relationship with um, yang and Do. Hwang Kee begins by analyzing the Chinese character representing ki and the relationship between ki and basic Newtonian laws of motion (such as $F = MA$). He notes the prevalence of the character for ki in a number of Chinese and Korean words that deal with various types of energy. He presents Lao Tzu's concept of ki in terms of Do concluding that the Do, "... being neutral in nature can also be called central ki or empty ki..." (p. 194). Hwang Kee also delineates innate ki associated with birth ki and acquired yang ki which are associated with the elements required to sustain life. Together he refers to them as primal ki. He notes the importance of understanding the various aspects of ki in order to maintain, preserve, sustain and pass on life. He emphasizes and explains in detail the concepts of innate birth ki and acquired yang ki, their concentration in the *danjun* and ki circulation. This chapter ends with an emphasis on applying the principles of Do, the laws of balance, and ki as the core elements for promoting health and life.

The final chapter of Section VI addresses the practice of Moo Do based on the principles of Do. The relationship between stillness and movement, a theme that appears in a number of ancient spiritual texts, is addressed in the practice of the martial arts as Hwang Kee explains the importance of stimulus and reaction and the need for discrimination in action. He identifies and describes factors that a practitioner of Moo Do (*moodoin*) should attend to in their development with specific emphasis on Right Mind, Right Composure and Right Posture. This section ends with a description of seven essential elements of health for preserving human life mentioning that *un-gi* (ki movement) and *gigong*[6] (ki circulating through the body) are means of balancing and regulating body functions in terms of the seven essential elements.

Section VI: Practice of Moo Do Mind Training. Section VI comprises two chapters. Hwang Kee comments that the previous sections of the book dealt with theory and ideology and that Section VI focuses on the actual practice or essence of Moo Do. This section begins with an introduction to Soo Bahk Do, a traditional Korean martial art. The technical elements of this art are explained in detail in previous publications authored by Hwang Kee (e.g., Hwang, 1970). This section focuses specifically on the mental training required of a *moodoin* and describes the essence, significance and goal of mental training. Hwang Kee stated, "The purpose of mind training is to establish and regulate the mind on the basis of training so as to stimulate spiritual development and thereby promote spiritual health" (p. 207). Hwang Kee provides a basic taxonomy of the elements of mental training followed by a description of methods of mental training and discipline. He delineates two basic rules for training and developing the spirit including *sullibeop* (Accordance with Principle Method) to develop *shim gung* (mind training) and *yungnibup* (Opposition of Principle Method) to address conflict situations in opposition to nature and balance. Five levels and five methods of mind training including methods of healing are described.

Chapter 2 of this section includes a description of *Sun Do*, a method for cultivating the Do that Hwang Kee notes has much in common with the Moo Do Philosophy. A brief description of this practice is accompanied by an overview of the practices and principles of *Sun Do*.

Section VII: Education for Character Development. Of all the sections of the text, this is the largest, comprising 14 chapters. The last chapters of this section include the guiding principles for the practice of Soo Bahk Do including the 10 Articles of Faith and the Elements and Points of Emphasis for Mental and Physical Training. Hwang Kee also clearly emphasizes spiritual development and, specifically, the cultivation of Do over the development of technical skill in the practice of Moo Do and Soo Bahk Do. He takes issue with the attitudes of individuals who value martial arts training based only on their belief of its effectiveness for winning a fight and notes that "Anyone studying Soo Bahk Do should emphasize its spiritual aspects over its technical aspects" (p. 254). In short, Hwang Kee unequivocally asserts that the true value of Moo Do Philosophy, Soo Bahk Do and martial arts training is the development of virtue and character.

Section VII begins by comparing and contrasting Eastern and Western ways of "knowing" and "reasoning," arguing that true knowledge is comprehension of the Do that naturally results in virtue and goodness. Chapter 2 is a discussion of virtue and the consistent demonstration of virtue in one's life expanding on his exposition of the "Logic of Virtue" in Section III. The notion of "inwardly wise" and "outwardly regal" is introduced. Hwang Kee asserts, "The greatness of a legacy is determined by the extent to which it represents a sacrifice of one's self for the good of others" (p. 231). He describes the Three Essentials, the Three Esoterica, the Three Moderates and the Three Practices that help to develop a virtuous life and comments on the importance of reflection, judgment and discrimination directed by *dodeok* (virtue), ethics, and a mind of goodness.

Chapters 3 through 6 address Hwang Kee's perspectives on the relationship between mind and God; Do and man; and, the relationship between generator and generation. Chapters 7 through 9 discuss the construct and phenomenon of intuition expanding on Hwang Kee's discussion of Eastern and Western ways of knowing and reasoning. Intuition is characterized as a way of knowing. Form and image are differentiated to show that intuition involves attention to image rather than form. Hwang Kee concludes that because Do is beyond the senses and unimaginable it cannot be knowable or intuited.

Chapters 10 through 12 expand on the notion of the virtuous man distinguishing the Confucian and Taoist notions of virtue. Five types of people are designated by varying levels of virtue and character. Hwang Kee argues that discarding knowledge, eliminating emotions, reducing desires, and transcending birth and death lead to one's natural state. Hwang Kee also notes that to grasp fixed entities, the faculty of knowing is required, while intuition is required to perceive phenomena that are fluid and becoming.

Chapter 13 clarifies moo as a means of promoting vitality which extends physical, mental and spiritual health and welfare. Do is characterized as the source of the physical body, activity and technique.

The final chapter of Section VII is devoted to a discussion of principles and guidelines for the practice of Moo Do Philosophy and Soo Bahk Do. Hwang Kee states that the goal of training is vitality and includes both defense and the extension and preservation of life. This chapter lists and explains the 10 Articles of Faith of Martial Virtue, key elements and points of emphasis for mental and physical training. Hwang Kee emphasizes that the cultivation of Do is superior to the development of technique and physical skill. He identifies 13 areas that Moo Do and martial arts practitioners should pay particular attention to in their training and practice.

Section VIII: Personal Reflections. This section discusses the application of the principles of Moo Do Philosophy to the problems of contemporary society based on the observations and experiences of the author. This section includes 15 short chapters that present Hwang Kee's views on political philosophy, leadership, social organization, economic systems, military doctrine and his philosophy of life. He begins by orienting the reader to Lao Tzu's Taoist perspectives on political leadership and governance. Hwang Kee presents his own observations and political philosophy in the second chapter which are revisited and expanded upon in subsequent chapters. The second chapter takes issues with political systems that ignore the needs of common people and engage in various forms of corruption, and class systems that promote an underclass. Consistent with the previous chapters Hwang Kee again emphasizes the need for cultivating virtue and putting into practice a lifestyle based on Do. He specifically notes the need for people of the world to focus on spiritual training to develop their own individual natures and become truly humane

Chapters 3 and 4 summarize Lao Tzu's philosophy of economics and the effects of desire, possession. and domination, and presents his own personal economic perspectives. Chapter 3 presents scenarios of the economic and social effects of acting in harmony or conflict with Taoist principles. Hwang Kee offers his personal philosophy of economics. He identifies 12 conditions he believes are necessary for achieving economic stability in the world and stresses the need for controlling the desire for material possessions, wealth and domination to support a viable and just economic system.

Hwang Kee, noting that he is not a military expert or soldier, argues for adherence to the Moo Do and specifically, understanding the Do. He identifies five great principles of national defense and describes U. S. conduct during the Cold War as an example of the application of these principles. He also clearly differentiates the goals of the Moo Do practitioner and the military.

Chapters 6 through 8 present Hwang Kee's views on the ideal society predicated on adherence to a philosophy of Do and balance (Moo Do Philosophy). He begins with a comparison of America and Asia and reflects on his visit to Philadelphia where he viewed the Liberty Bell (now located at the Liberty Bell Center, Independence National Historical Park) and original documents of the founding of America. He concludes that the American system of government appears to be consistent with the principles of Do. He elaborates on the influence of Confucian philosophy on political leadership and governance in East Asia concluding that it may have overemphasized theory and form at the expense of actual application. Chapters 7 and 8 elaborate on the ideal society based on Taoist and Confucian schools of thought. He draws from the work of Lao Tzu and Chuang Tzu. He noted that the ideal society from a Taoist perspective is based on the principles of non-action; discarding or detachment from knowledge and desire; living simply, and the philosophy of *muwi*, non-aggression and non-desire. In contrast, the Confucian perspective views are described in terms of governance of the nation and pacification of all under heaven. The former is based on familial, social and national ideals while the latter is based on extending one's values from one's individual self to society at large.

Chapters 9 through 12 are very short and deal with the temporary nature of life while emphasizing the need for living in accordance with the laws and principles of balance and Nature. Chapter 9, "Doctrine of Return," reminds us of how short life is. Hwang Kee acknowledges the natural process of life and death as a cycle of change from non-existence (*mu*) to existence (*yu*). Hwang Kee describes this as a fundamental principle of nature. Chapter 10 deals with the weakness and frailties common to humanity. He describes the ego and the necessity for a natural and sacred life by living in accordance with the principles of balance and Nature by avoiding human insensitivities. Chapter 11 discusses the importance of hope and the paradox that often leads to confusing hope with desire. Hwang Kee notes that hope is a spiritual quality while desire that becomes excessive can be enslaving. Finally, he admonishes us to be a master of the external by mastering one's instincts to avoid becoming a slave to our instincts and knowledge.

In Chapter 13, Hwang Kee takes strong issue with the statement, "Life is War" and argues that such a perspective is wholly inconsistent with Moo Do Philosophy. He directly states that the practice of Moo Do Philosophy and specifically, Soo Bahk Do, is a movement to "...bring the entire world together as siblings within the same family. The ultimate goal is to eliminate war, violence and envy, get rid of hatred, and cooperate in a spirit of harmony so that all of mankind can enjoy happiness, peace, health and freedom" (pp. 285-286). Hwang Kee categorically rejects war as a valid or moral instrument for achieving political or social ends (p. 285). He notes how technological advances for the purpose of engaging in warfare often result in the decline of civilizations and that civilizations advance with sincere efforts of the people, leaders, and scholars.

Chapter 14 extends Hwang Kee's views on war by describing some of its costs to society and human civilization. He argues that human peace and happiness are only possible when tendencies for war and violence are suppressed through mastery over the desire for superiority.

The final chapter of this section begins with a list of the acquired qualities and principles of Do, balance and Nature. The author elaborates on each of the qualities and principles and presents his views on what is necessary to achieve true happiness. He promotes the practice of Moo Do and specifically, training in the art of Soo Bahk Do as means of calming the mind, eliminating desire, and training the body. He further describes the requirements for achieving happiness.

In the context of happiness, Hwang Kee also discusses his views on and the importance of the concept of heaven and hell. He comments on the value of a belief in heaven and hell to urge people to live good lives and presents a case for his belief that heaven and hell exist on earth. He ultimately concludes that while perfecting the self in a natural, balanced and good way, we must also live for the sake of others. To accomplish this he describes the three essentials of Right Mind, Right Posture and Right Composure.

This chapter also compares the relative characteristics and value of academic study (*mun*) and martial arts (*mu*) and notes the need for a balanced application and practice of both. Hwang Kee explains that *mu* is active and moving while *mun* is characterized by calm and stillness and that Moo Do is the balanced practice of both. To achieve the ultimate goal of happiness, Hwang Kee identifies eight requirements. He ends this chapter by noting that when people think only of their own benefit and live only for themselves they cause great harm. He leaves the reader with four questions that one should be able to answer to determine the value of their lives.

Section IX: Trends in Modern Philosophy. This section provides some insight into Hwang Kee's perspectives on modern philosophy with particular attention paid to Immanuel Kant. Hwang Kee describes his perspectives and appreciation for contemporary Western philosophers. He contends that mathematic logic and phenomenology are methodologies that do not represent substantive theories. Hwang Kee also comments on the work of Henri Bergson, William James and Ernst Mach.

Section X: The Philosophy of the Infinitely Large and Infinitely

Small. The final section of the *Moo Do Chul Hahk* is a short exposition of the relationship between the macrocosm and microcosm. He ultimately concludes that the energy, nature and philosophy of the infinitely large and infinitely small are the same. He ends this section with an interest in seeing additional investigation of the relationship between philosophy and science.

Writing Style and Conventions

This is the first published edition of an English translation of the Korean version of the *Moo Do Chul Hahk* which was originally written and published in han'gŭl in 1993. It is the culmination of a number of draft translations of the Korean version. The organization of this book retains the organization of the original Korean text with two exceptions. The original Korean version authored by Hwang Kee includes his translation and interpretation of the *Book of Changes* (*Chou I*) and the *Tao Te Ching* by Lao Tzu. Given the large number of scholarly translations of both of these texts, the author of this book chose not to include Hwang Kee's translation of these texts in order to focus the reader on the sections addressing Moo Do Philosophy[7]. The translations of the sections of the *Moo Do Chul Hahk* addressing Moo Do Philosophy are included in their entirety. The author of this text refers readers to two widely read and accepted translations of the *Chou I* entitled the *I Ching or Book of Changes* edited and translated by Wilhelm and Baynes (1967); the translations of Lao Tzu's *Tao Te Ching* and Chuang-tsu's *Inner Chapters* by Gia-fu Feng and Jane English (1974), and the *Analects of Confucius* translated by Chichung Huang (1997). Another reference that may be particularly useful for readers who may be new to the topic is *A Source Book in Chinese Philosophy* by Wing-Tsit Chan (1969) which also includes the writings of Mencius and Neo-Confucian philosophers. The translations of the *Chou I* and *Tao Te Ching* by Hwang Kee may be made available in the future.

The original translation of the *Moo Do Chul Hahk* was subjected to a number of reviews and revisions culminating in the present translation by the author of this text. This text includes updated figures drawn from reliable sources. The translator and author of this book made every effort to preserve the integrity, accuracy and meaning of the original text of Hwang Kee's *Moo Do Chul Hahk*, while offering a translation that is readable and accessible to a wide audience.

The reader will observe early on that Hwang Kee wrote the *Moo Do Chul Hahk* in first person clearly establishing that the book reflects his own uniquely personal perspective and narrative. In addition, some portions of the text appear to be presented as a chronological narrative, that is, as a series of essays on topics that are published in the order in which they were written. For example, there are chapters in which Hwang Kee addresses a topic such as "war" that he discusses again in a later chapter. To improve the organization and flow of the content, the translator combined sections that discuss the same topics. A few chapters of the original text were combined and others were organized into different sections to improve the organization and readability. A "Table of Concordance" between this text and the original *Moo Do Chul Hahk* may be found at the end of this book. This table identifies the sections of this text that correspond with the translation of each section and chapter of the *Moo Do Chul Hahk* for readers who may wish to refer to the original version of the *Moo Do Chul Hahk* printed in Korean.

Another issue with translating a text of this nature is that many Korean and Chinese characters and concepts cannot be literally translated into English. As such, some of the original text involves interpretation by the author of this book. Several Chinese characters are included to provide the reader familiar with these characters with the exact terms used by Hwang Kee in the original text. Korean terms are italicized to identify it as a Romanized spelling. A glossary includes both the han'gŭl and Chinese characters used in the *Moo Do Chul Hahk* for all Korean and Chinese terms included in this text with the exception of proper names. The glossary also includes the English spelling and a translation of the terms. This provides the reader direct access to the actual characters for Korean and Chinese readers familiar with the language to derive their own understanding of the meaning.

The most widely accepted method of Romanizing Korean into English is the McCune-Reischaur system (Tistory, n. d.). The Korean government recently adopted a simpler method for Romanizing

Korean. The Wade-Giles system is frequently used to Romanize the spelling of Chinese into English. For the purpose of this text, the pronunciation and spelling of a Korean term is secondary to understanding the meaning intended by Hwang Kee. In general, the McCune-Reischauer system has been used for the English spelling of Korean terms. Exceptions are terms that frequently appear in the literature addressing Korean and Chinese martial arts whose spelling may differ from the McCune-Reischaur system. The typical spelling found in this literature has been used. Readers may refer to the glossary for Korean and Chinese terms that are included in the text.

While Hwang Kee was clearly a scholar in his own right, the conventions that are typically applied in the writing and publishing of scholarly work were not conventions that he was familiar with nor are they uniformly adopted in the publication of scholarly works in the Far East. The author of this English translation has attempted to compile and cite all of the sources and references employed and cited by Hwang Kee in his writing of the *Moo Do Chul Hahk*. Footnotes are also included to provide additional information and explanation where necessary. References have been compiled and citations inserted where appropriate to provide supporting evidence of information included in the "Introduction." Future editions of this book may be forthcoming and include updated citations, footnotes, references and commentary as more information becomes available regarding Hwang Kee's life, philosophy and primary sources.

The spellings of the names of ancient Chinese philosophers that frequently appear in the literature have been used throughout the text. The Korean tradition of presenting a name is typically to present a surname followed by the given name. This tradition has been maintained in this book for Korean names while presenting the given name followed by the surname for Western names. Exceptions are some persons of Korean nationality, such as the author of this text, Hyun Chul Hwang, who may be more commonly known by the Western presentation of their names.

It will become apparent to readers that Hwang Kee's writings and thoughts emerged from a deep personal reflection on his life and were affected by world and national events. The reader will ultimately see his contributions, practice, study and development of Soo Bahk Do leading to the description of his Moo Do Philosophy in the writing of the *Moo Do Chul Hahk* as inevitable. He was an astute observer and student of history, sociology and human behavior. His philosophy is a reflection of his experiences and his reflections on the relationship between the self, life, society, nature, the universe and Do validated by his study and translation of ancient philosophical texts. He often presented his philosophy in the context of his observations showing how many of the struggles and follies of humanity may be avoided or rectified by practicing a Moo Do Philosophy.

As a scholar, Hwang Kee recognized the need to review and study the historical foundations of Taoist, Confucian and Buddhist philosophy to understand the foundation of Moo Do Philosophy. He consistently presented this information before presenting his own perspectives and understanding of Moo Do Philosophy. This is an important stylistic component and reflective of Hwang Kee's respect for engaging in scholarly inquiry in the conduct and practice of Moo Do Philosophy. This is also consistent with Hwang Kee's earlier writings and publications where he presented information based on his study of Korean history, culture, traditions and philosophy and on the information available to him at the time.

Recurring Themes

Recognizing that Hwang Kee's Moo Do Philosophy emerged from a life of action will lead to the realization that the *Moo Do Chul Hahk* is the result of deep personal introspection and reflection. His writing began in the early 1960s and the *Moo Do Chul Hahk* was finally published in 1993 spanning 30 years of his life. A number of consistent themes emerge from his work. The first is his emphasis on awareness and comprehension of the Do. The second is his focus on understanding, developing, and personally living a life of virtue, balance and character. However, knowing and understanding these are insufficient. Hwang Kee clearly emphasized that direct application of the principles of Do, balance, and virtue is essential. Understanding theory is not enough. One must live and practice Moo Do Philosophy to be an authentic human being. The last section of the book is a compilation of essays reflecting his thinking about the application of

Moo Do Philosophy to the problems of contemporary society and world events.

Notes to the Reader

It is important to understand that the *Moo Do Chul Hahk* spans the life of one man through very turbulent and conflicting times. Thus, the information presented in this book and this translation reflects Hwang Kee's understanding of Soo Bahk Do and his personal Moo Do Philosophy based on his own personal life experience and the information that was available to him and others at the time of the writing and publication of the book. This also applies to the many other publications authored by Hwang Kee. As new information becomes available revisions and corrections may be needed. In addition, readers are advised to consider the period during which many of Hwang Kee's books were written (pre/post WWII and pre/post Korean War). Korea was subject to the Japanese occupation before and during World War II during which many Korean cultural artifacts were taken and the expression and study of Korean culture were suppressed. Korea sustained much destruction during the Korean War that also affected the study and understanding of Korean culture. Efforts to preserve Korean cultural, historical and archeological treasures are relatively recent through a number of Korean and international cultural organizations (UNESCO World Heritage Centre; International Council on Monuments and Sites, Korea; Korean Cultural Heritage Administration) that have led to more accurate and complete information and evidence that was not available to Hwang Kee at the time he published many of his earlier books. Despite any new information that may come to light, the contributions of Hwang Kee to the study and preservation of Korean culture, traditions, history, and philosophy through his study and practice of the traditional Korean martial art, Soo Bahk Do, are undeniable.

Readers are also advised to make the distinction between philosophy and dogma in their reading and understanding of the *Moo Do Chul Hahk*. Hwang Kee's description and understanding of Moo Do Philosophy emerged from a reflection on his life which was clearly influenced by a number of significant socio-political and historical events. It was not and is not a philosophy that demands or expects authoritarian or rigid compliance. It requires self-examination in the context of an understanding of the principles that govern the conditions under which we live with a value for human life, society, virtue and character. It would not have been Hwang Kee's wish, nor is it the wish of the translator and author of the current text, for any reader or martial arts practitioner to thoughtlessly and blindly adopt any belief, principle, or value without full consideration and sincere respect for one's own and others' beliefs, experience, culture, traditions, and circumstances. In addition, there is always room for additional research and study of both the theory and application of many of the ideas and conclusions presented in the *Moo Do Chul Hahk*.

About the Author and Translator

Hyun Chul Hwang was born in 1947 the second of five children. Consistent with the wishes of his father, he was appointed as his father's successor for the Korean Soo Bahk Do Association Moo Duk Kwan in July 2002. The Board of Directors of the U.S. Soo Bahk Do Moo Duk Kwan Federation, Inc. unanimously appointed him as its lifetime president in 2005. He has served in a number of key positions nationally and internationally. Hyun Chul Hwang began his martial arts training May 5, 1954 at the age of 7. He earned his first dan (equivalent to a 1st degree black belt) at the age of 9. At that time he was the youngest dan[8] holder in Korea. Hwang earned a degree in Oriental Philosophy from Korea University in 1969.

Hyun Chul Hwang is a charter (founding) member of the U.S. Soo Bahk Do Moo Duk Kwan Federation, Inc. organized and incorporated in 1976. When the Federation was founded he was appointed by Hwang Kee as Chairman of the Technical Advisory Committee responsible for the technical quality of

Soo Bahk Do practitioners as well as preserving the history, tradition and philosophy of Soo Bahk Do in the U. S. He was appointed to serve as his father's designee and representative of the Korean Soo Bahk Do Association Moo Duk Kwan abroad.

In 2004, Hyun Chul Hwang was awarded *Black Belt Magazine's* Man of the Year award, the most prestigious award offered to an individual who has made significant contributions to the martial arts community in the U. S. and internationally. Currently, H.C. Hwang resides in the U. S. with his wife and three children.

Hyun Chul Hwang has invested his life since his early childhood in supporting his father's efforts to support and advance the traditional Korean martial art, Soo Bahk Do. The table on the following page provides a brief summary of the achievements and contributions he has made to this end. It is notable that while his father, is clearly acknowledged as the founder of the Moo Duk Kwan, Hyun Chul Hwang has dedicated his life to supporting his father's efforts since his early childhood.

The focus of his current activities and vision are on promoting five values among Soo Bahk Do practitioners: history, tradition, discipline/respect, philosophy and technique. This book is a major contribution to this effort. Hyun Chul Hwang is the co-author of a number of instructional texts for Soo Bahk Do practitioners and a major contributor to books authored by his father. He has also written a number of articles published in the newsletter for the U. S. Soo Bahk Do Moo Duk Kwan Federation, Inc. and in international Federation newsletters. Future works include compiling and translating an autobiography of his father, Hwang Kee. A listing of books that he has co-authored and has made substantial contributions to include:

- *Tang Soo Do (Soo Bahk Do) Moo Duk Kwan Instructional Guides*
- *Tang Soo Do (Soo Bahk Do)*
- *Soo Bahk Do (Tang Soo Do), Volume I,*
- *Soo Bahk Do Dae Kham, Volume II*
- *Soo Bahk Do*
- *Moo Duk Kwan*

- *Moo Do Chul Hahk*
- *The History of Moo Duk Kwan*

Brief Listing of the Achievements and Contributions of the Author and Translator, Hyun Chul Hwang, to the Traditional Korean Martial Art, Soo Bahk Do.

Date	Achievement/Contribution
May 5, 1954	began training in Soo Bahk Do
October 27, 1957	Promoted to Cho Dan (1st Dan) in Moo Duk Kwan
March 1959	graduated Yong San Elementary School
March 1962	graduated Sun Rin Middle School
March 1965	graduated Yang Jong High School
November 15, 1965	promoted to Sa Dan (4th Dan) in Moo Duk Kwan
September 1969	graduated Korea University (Major in Oriental Philosophy)
May 24, 1970	promoted to O Dan (5th Dan) and Sa Bom in Moo Duk Kwan
1970-1973	served as the chief Sa Bom at the Central Headquarters Dojang.
1973-1974	served as the chief Moo Duk Kwan Sa Bom in Athens, Greece
June 30, 1975 - July 2002	served as the chairman of Technical Advisory Committee of the U.S. Soo Bahk Do Moo Duk Kwan Federation
1989 - July 2002	served as the Vice President for the World Moo Duk Kwan
1998	Organized the World Moo Duk Kwan comprising federations and organizations of countries from around the world dedicated to Soo Bahk Do
August 31, 1999	promoted to Gu Dan (9th Dan) in the Moo Duk Kwan

Date	Achievement/Contribution
July 2002 - present	appointed as President of the World Moo Duk Kwan
2004,	*Black Belt Magazine* Hall of Fame, Man of Year Award
July 20, 2005	appointed as lifetime President of U.S. Soo Bahk Do Moo Duk Kwan Federation by Board of Directors

Summary

This "Introduction" provides a historical context for emergence of Hwang Kee's Moo Do Philosophy. It also provides an overview of the content of the book, the organization and character of the book, and some of the unique writing conventions and style of Hwang Kee. However, the single most important point that the reader should understand is that Hwang Kee's Moo Do Philosophy emerged from his own personal life involving intense challenges, conflict and struggles. These struggles were influenced by the occupation of Korea by Japan; the liberation of Korea subsequent to World War II; the division and occupation of Korea by the U. S. and the Soviet Union; and, the involvement of the three superpowers, the U.S., Soviet Union, and China, in Korea's internal politics and the Korean War. These historical events directly affected Hwang Kee's life and family. Efforts to suppress, dissolve, and merge the Moo Duk Kwan with Tae Kwon Do added to Hwang Kee's lifelong struggle.

Despite these challenges Hwang Kee had a vision. This vision resulted in the emergence of a network of international organizations dedicated to the study and practice of the Korean martial art, Soo Bahk Do, that integrate values, tradition, history, philosophy, culture, and technique. He singularly understood the value of the *Moo Yei Do Bo Tong Ji* and incorporated it into the practice of Soo Bahk Do making a major contribution to the preservation and study of an ancient Korean cultural jewel throughout the world. He refused to sacrifice his beliefs and values for political expediency or financial gain and his accomplishments came at an incredible personal cost and sacrifice.

Hwang Kee's Moo Do Philosophy cannot be fully understood until one understands that this is a man whose philosophy was fired, tested, and endured in the crucible of incredible personal struggle, war, imprisonment, political conflict, hatred, and personal loss. Yet he never lost sight of his vision and mission, a vision and mission that he saw others carry on and in the end he died at peace. Hwang Kee's life and philosophy are his legacy. Understanding his leadership and contributions to humanity requires a study of both his life and his philosophy and will lead one to ultimately conclude that Hwang Kee lived the Moo Do Philosophy he presents in the *Moo Do Chul Hahk*.

It is the hope of the author and translator of this text that this translation of the *Moo Do Chul Hahk* provides the reader a means of understanding and living the Moo Do Philosophy. In a world of overwhelming complexity, despair, conflict, extremism, and malevolence the *Moo Do Chul Hahk* offers a message of simplicity, hope, harmony, balance and virtue. One thing is certain, the *Moo Do Chul Hahk* and the impact of Hwang Kee on the lives of hundreds of thousands throughout the world clearly demonstrates that Hwang Kee's life exemplifies the quote taken from Chuang Tzu and stated under the title to this introduction; "Perfection results from the struggle." Ultimately, the serious reader will come to understand after studying and reading the *Moo Do Chul Hahk* that Hwang Kee's philosophy was his life and his message. Finally, Hwang Kee would have advised the reader that to truly understand Moo Do Philosophy, study alone is insufficient. The authentic *moodoin* is one who actualizes and practices Moo Do values in their daily life.

Hwang Kee

Moo Do Chul Hahk
무 도 철 학

A New Translation by

Hyun Chul Hwang

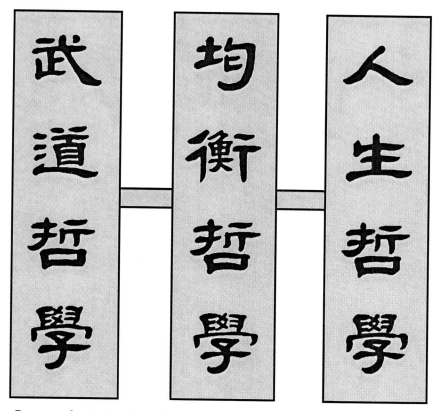

Banner depicting the relationship and connection between Moo Do, balance and life in Hwang Kee's philosophy.

Translation

Left Column: Moo Do Philosophy

Middle Column: Philosophy of Balance

Right Column: Philosophy of Life

PREFACE

Hwang Kee

The Korea into which I was born was a turbulent place, enduring political chaos and annexation by Japan. From the moment of my birth in 1914, the rough course of my life has been full of tribulations and trials. I have experienced much suffering, threats, blackmail, hunger, and disease. Through others' slander and intrigues, I have, on a number of occasions, had the harsh experience of being held in police detention centers. And I have had several close brushes with death.

Yet within these difficult circumstances, I have never let go of my sense of self-dignity, hope, and righteousness. When I look back, I do not have the least regret. And my conviction that we must walk the correct and humane path remains unchanged. I feel that it is solely this conviction that has sustained me on life's journey. I have, therefore, worked to live naturally and in an ordinary manner, as a man of nature. If there is something that makes my life's journey different from others, it is simply the fact that I have spent my life as a martial arts practitioner. This practice has involved many harsh trials, but at the same time, it has allowed me to see different natural environments and sights from around the world and has allowed me to have direct and personal human contact with people from various social classes and walks of life.

During this time, I have received warm welcomes and hospitality from people all over the globe. Based on such contacts with all of existence, be it narrow or wide, high or low, shallow or deep, I have formed a philosophy that synthesizes the *Do (Tao)*, man, and martial arts. The Korean word for Tao is Do (pronounced "doe"), and martial arts is *Moo Do*. My philosophy, which I refer to as "Moo Do Philosophy" is the subject of this book. Key elements of my approach are as follows:

1. Moo Do philosophy is based on the Do, the fundamental principles of Nature.

2. Moo Do Philosophy is a philosophy of balance based on the Do.

3. The fundamental essence and structure of Moo Do philosophy serves as the ideological basis of Moo Do practice.

4. In presenting Moo Do Philosophy, which is based on the philosophy of the Do, I have made practical efforts to establish a synthesis between Eastern and Western philosophy.

5. Using the knowledge I have developed in this area, I have set forth the essential character of the Do—which has previously been expounded only in a vague conceptual manner. I have explicated the principle of neutrality, explaining the importance of this principle in a logical and practical manner.

6. The central points of Eastern philosophy, the middle way, balance, and Moo Do, share common characteristics. The concept of the middle way is difficult for people to understand and, therefore, to practice. For this reason, I explain it through the philosophy of balance, using the simile of a scale.

7. While the term *ki* is frequently used and its importance often acknowledged, there have not been, as far as I can tell, any concrete explanations of its essence. In this work, I elucidate the nature of ki's basic essence.

8. Wherever possible, I have avoided difficult philosophical expressions and terms, and have instead tried to use terms and phrases more readily understood, with an emphasis on ideas that relate to our lives.

9. In the world today, numerous figures and religions have set forth doctrines regarding heaven, paradise, and hell, but I have set forth a doctrine of paradise and hell existing on

earth.

10. The thing we must keep in mind is that the *mo che*[9] (literally translated as "mother-body"; may be interpreted as the natural mother or the nurturing and sustaining source or origin) of the philosophies of life, Moo Do, and balance is Nature, the philosophy of the Do. The fundamental essence of this is centered on man. Thus, in respect to their essential content, these philosophies are one and the same.

My basic intentions in publishing this book on Moo Do Philosophy are to develop awareness in the present generation of Moo Do practitioners and to facilitate their development as authentic practitioners. Moving beyond this, I feel that Soo Bahk Do (Moo Do) is something that transcends national boundaries and religious and racial differences, and can help bring the people of the world together in a spirit of brotherhood. In this way, it can promote the true happiness, health, tranquility, freedom, and equality of mankind and help us create a world without violence, weapons, war, famine, disease, or fear. With such faith and ideals, I record the contents of this book.

I

THE IMPORTANCE

OF PHILOSOPHY

Chapter 1

Personal Reflections

Before I was born, my father had a birth-dream of the Three Great Stars (*Sam t'ae sung*). Perhaps this is why I love nature and stars, and have always felt a sense of intimacy and interest in the stars. I remember one night in the space behind our house, looking up absent-mindedly at the Milky Way and countless other clear stars twinkling in the tranquil, clear, blue night-sky of autumn.

When, where, and how did these beautiful stars appear? How high and far away were they? I secretly had a desire to go to them. Haven't these numerous stars been twinkling in the same way for millions, or actually, billions of years, for a period of time that we human beings cannot even imagine? If this lovely, mysterious light from these stars continues unchanged for billions of years, why is it that we human beings are so inconstant? From the standpoint of Great Nature (*Tayjayun*), our earth looks like a minor accident, while human life and its changes seem like nothing at all. Our most ancient ancestor must have seen the beautiful light from these stars, as do all the people living on the earth today. And in the future, our descendants will look up at these same stars.

Looking down at us, the stars must know all the events and hardships of mankind's history. Within the impermanent, futile life of man, why are there so many vicissitudes? Are these due to man's struggle for survival, his attempt to satisfy his instinctual desires, or just his fate? When I look up at the stars, these thoughts occur to me, but everyone is different: some view the stars from an astronomical perspective, others write poetry, while others are indifferent. But there is one common thought that occurs to everyone. This is the feeling that the stars are mysterious, that they contain some riddle. Perhaps this is man's original nature, unadorned nature, which is the symbol of the Do (Tao).

When I abruptly return to my basic feelings and take a cold, hard look at things, it suddenly occurs to me that I am both imperfect and fragile, no better that a lily blooming next to a mountain path. It's true. For that lily is nature as it is, without exaggeration or arrogance, pure, innocent, free and peaceful. And when in full bloom, it gives all the people in the world assistance and an edifying message, bringing joy and sharing its sentiment. In a natural fashion, it grows and disappears.

On the other hand, what was I born into this world to do? What have I done? In this unnatural environment, in this world without freedom that is fettered by instinct and formalities, what have I done for others? What is it that I've been trying to do? From time to time, I've had a desire to live beyond the ordinary, and have made an effort to live for others. I have tried just about everything, but it seems as if I've done nothing and have lived an ordinary and solitary life.

Looking back through mankind's history, there have been many great men and heroes. Through the power of emperors, both fortresses and the Great Wall were built. Rome rose and fell. Greek culture was created, and also fell. Throughout history, great sages have appeared. Yet they, too, have long since left this world. Awesome and absolute powers, once prosperous and glorious, have risen and fallen, becoming nothing more than a spring dream. Wielding power at will, the ancient kings left behind coercion, suffering, and remnants of material culture stained by blood and sweat, while the sages left behind immaterial culture.

Humans may recognize these physical and cultural remnants that are said to be so magnificent. However, they are of no concern to the other animals on this earth or to other things, and the numerous stars have absolutely no interest in them. Moreover, when viewed from the perspective of the Do, culture is absolutely nothing, yet human beings fight over it, criticize one another, are jealous, hate, betray one another, hatch schemes, deceive their conscience, become angry, sad, excited, and even kill.

With these thoughts in my head, I walked along the country path strewn with fallen leaves, toward the big gate of our house. In the solitude and quiet of night, the crunch of leaves underfoot sounded unusually loud, breaking the silence and stimulating my mind. For some reason, fallen leaves always give me a lonely feeling. And they remind us of autumn—the season of fruition.

I am referring to the fruition of the hope, vitality, exuberance, difficulties and efforts of all plant life. Just as with past hopes, difficulties, and effort, fallen leaves are the preparation for the future; not just withered leaves, they are full of significance as the expectation and groundwork for tomorrow.

Suddenly a thought occurred to me. The plants of this world are in a rush to prepare their fruit to greet the autumn and fallen leaves. As a human being living in this world, what fruit do I plan, what fruit do I intend to bear? Among the vast numbers of humans, only a few have realized a beautiful fruition. With what mission was I born into this world? All felt so vain and unknowable. As they say, "With empty hands I come into the world, and with empty hands I leave."

Chapter 2

Space and Time

Most people in the world today are not interested in philosophy or in such abstract concepts as space and time. If someone talks about the true essence of time, they are treated as an eccentric. When most people think of time, they think of it as one o'clock or two o'clock, or as how summer naturally follows spring, and after summer, fall, and after fall, winter. Or they think of how, when daytime ends, night comes, and when night ends, day comes again, or how January is followed by February, or this year followed by the next.

Of course, time and space are granted fairly to all, and people are free to use time however they wish. Thoughtful people stress the importance of time, saying that it is more precious than gold. Since time, once gone, never returns, they stress the importance of utilizing time effectively.

It is said that the green spring is short and life is no more than a "spring dream." This is a warning about time and life's transience. Yet people tend to have little interest in time, or in the atmosphere, sunlight, water, or parents. In the next section I will discuss the importance of space and time to Asian philosophy, for these things are valuable and have an absolute, inseparable relationship with man. Yet people take these things for granted because they are so ordinary, free, and grand that they pass unnoticed and receive no gratitude.

When we go to a playground and get spun around, we are all directly aware that we are spinning as we get dizzy. Yet no one senses the earth, where we live, rapidly spinning around. To the contrary, we understand and sense the sun rising in the east and heading towards the west. Even so, this earth is rapidly spinning.

Chapter 3

Man's Transience

Humans are like ants busily running around a round bamboo sieve that has been hung in the air. The ant, apparently unaware that it just keeps running around the same circle, races around in order to survive. People watching this ant might each have different thoughts, but most would find this ant's behavior unfortunate, pitiful or foolish, and feeling a bit perturbed, would think that this ant is truly an ignorant, idiotic and undeveloped animal. With a sigh or with disdain, they would look at this pitiful, foolish ant, thinking even if the ant runs around all day long, it will never get past the point where it started.

But if we look on ourselves not as the large but as the small, if we look at ourselves from the perspective of the Do, the stars or Great Nature, human behavior is not a bit different from the ant busily running around a sieve. We must realize that we are the same. Human beings have a positive, sensitive, and sharp interest in, and take action on, that which they can see with their eyes, but take lightly or are even unconcerned about that which they cannot see. They must realize that that which is not visible is actually more important to human beings than that which can be seen. Only after this realization can they enjoy the principles and happiness of an authentic life.

Chapter 4

The Source of Philosophy

The essence of philosophy existed from the beginning of Nature, the frontier of the Non-being Ultimate (*mugeukkyung*). In the beginning, the myriad images, forms, and things lacked intelligence and were thus unable to understand this, and the *Mugeukkyung* remained unmanifested. The myriad things (*manmul*) include inanimate objects, animals, and human beings. Even in the beginning, their actual lives accorded with the principles of Nature, so even though they were unaware of it, they led a life in accordance with philosophy.

With the development of human knowledge, man became inquisitive about the things of this world. He created ideologies to explain them. From twenty- or thirty-thousand years ago, these developed into systems of thought regarding Heaven and spirits. These systems underwent further development so that, from around five or six thousand years ago, the essence of philosophy began to manifest. During the Chou Dynasty in China (1027-256 B.C.E.), a purely philosophical document was written, known as the *Chou I* (*I Ching* in Chinese, *Chu Yeok* in Korean).

From this time, interest in philosophy increased significantly. Toward the end of the Chou Dynasty, as Chinese society slipped into chaos, a large number of scholars sought to discover the principles of natural and social order that might help to restore peace in their world. The greatest of these was Lao Tzu (*No Ja* in Korean), known in his own time (570-490? B.C.E.) and through the present as the great philosopher of the Tao.

After Lao Tzu, numerous philosophers and their texts appeared in Asia, and philosophical thought spread throughout the world. In the West, a large number of thinkers appeared, including the great philosopher Socrates (470-399? B.C.E.). Socrates established the basis for Western philosophy. I believe that with the further development of human knowledge, civilization, and science, there will come a day when all of mankind is one family with a more evolved philosophy that respects the essence of both East and West. Such a philosophy must help man live naturally and practically according to the principles of Nature and contribute, in a logical and practical manner, to a happy, healthy, peaceful, and free lifestyle for all of mankind. With such faith and ideals, I have elaborated the Moo Do philosophy.

Chapter 5

The Goal of Philosophy

Philosophy sets out to make all men aware of the truth of Nature's principles and to evoke interest and thought regarding these principles. By promoting a natural lifestyle for all mankind, it promotes the inclination towards developing humane people who are virtuous, for it is such people who are able to manifest happiness, health, tranquility, freedom, and equality.

Busy eating and living in this complicated world, many people tend to ignore philosophy, thinking that there is neither the time nor the need to reflect on space, the past, or the future. They think, "Why should one waste one's valuable time and energy on such matters?" People take the invisible principles of Nature and the harmony and changes of um and yang (Chinese yin and yang) for granted. Instead, they value and pay close attention to those phenomena that they can see, in the spirit of Western philosophy. Practical problems of the moment are important, but I believe what is more important are those things that cannot be seen.

The reason for this belief is that all material things in this world have an end, while the principles of Nature have no end and are vast. Therefore, the person who endlessly searches for that with no end is much wiser in the principles of the Do than he who searches endlessly for that with an end. In other words, the endless quest for that which is posited on the finite is a kind of greed, whereas the endless search for the infinite is not based on greed, but on hope.

I would like to present a practical example of this. Everyone in the world eats food each day in order to preserve his or her life. Food is something that we can all see. The fact is that the people of this world fight one another, and nations even go to war, in order to gain more food for their subsistence. And this precious food is indeed important for our survival.

Yet people ignore something of more practical and pressing

importance than precious food, namely, the atmosphere. Anyone can live two or three days without food, but would die within a single hour if he or she were unable to breathe the air. In spite of this, human beings have an excessive interest in food, which is visible, and are concerned about its quality, quantity, and preservation. When it comes to the atmosphere, not only are they disinterested, they do not hesitate to pollute and degrade it and regard it with disdain.

The atmosphere does not complain, ask people not to do so, or seek revenge. To the contrary, it remains indifferent, unperturbed, placid, and natural. If our unconcerned and scornful attitude towards the atmosphere continues and we recklessly pollute it, we are clearly committing an act of suicide that will lead society inevitably down the road towards destruction.

Since Nature is vast, great, and eternal, its reactions take a long time and are thus invisible. Even so, if one performs any action, one will, through the principle of cause and effect, definitely receive the corresponding results of that action. We human beings do not understand this great natural principle. Man has an indivisible relationship with Nature, just as our lives and fates are controlled by the Do. Philosophy is the field of learning that looks at the laws and principles that form the basis of mankind. For this reason, the most important thing in this world is philosophy.

Chapter 6

The Changes of Chou I

In Korea and China when philosophy is mentioned, we automatically think of Nature. When we think of philosophical literature, we think of the previously mentioned *Changes of Chou I*, the ancient text commonly referred to in English as the *Book of Changes*. The word "*I*" refers to alteration or transformation. The myriad things of the universe may differ in method, time, or form, but the "*I*" elucidates the principles and laws behind endlessly changing natural phenomena.

Who authored this important work? One account says that the Chinese Fu-hsi (Pokhui in Korean) received a revelation when he saw markings like a diagram on the back of the mythical dragon-horse emerging from the Yellow River. Looking at celestial patterns, terrain features, and the transformations of this world's infinite appearances, forms, and things, Fu-hsi created the Eight Trigrams, which he later developed into the 64 Hexagrams, the six-lined diagrams that serve as the basis for philosophical guidance and divination. The Chinese scholars Wang-pi and Ssu-ma Ch'ien also think that the Eight Trigrams were created by Fu-hsi, but that the 64 Hexagrams and other sections were created by King Wen.

Still another scholar, Ma-jung, credits Fu-hsi with the Eight Trigrams and the 64 Hexagrams, and King Wen with the "Judgment on the Hexagrams," but states that the "Judgment on the Lines" was created by the Duke of Chou and the *Ten Wings* by Confucius. These accounts have been passed down from ancient times, and there is no way to be certain which is correct. But whoever the authors, the importance of the *Chou I* cannot be overestimated.

Here I would like to explain the essence of the changes, and defer discussion of the Trigrams and Hexagrams to a later part of this book (Appendix I deals exclusively with the *Chou I*). Um and yang are a dualism, and everything in this world is comprised of um and yang. Heaven is yang while Earth is um; the sun is yang and the moon um;

the powerful are yang and the weak um; that which is high is yang and the low um. The principle of the *Chou I* is that all opposing objects and phenomena are distinguished as um or yang, and these things endlessly transform in accordance with the position, condition, and laws of these forces.

According to a principle of the *Chou I*, when that which is strong reaches an extreme, it once more goes into decline, while that which has declined gradually becomes stronger. In a similar fashion, if a person in a difficult situation struggles to overcome it, in accordance with the principle of um and yang, difficulties will pass and the situation will get better.

Chapter 7

World History, High Antiquity, and Philosophy

Passage 1: High Antiquity

Any explanation of philosophy must be accompanied by a discussion of history. However, I will restrict the discussion to brief notes on aspects of ancient history, especially those that have a deep connection with the philosophy of this book.

The term "high antiquity" refers to the period four to five millennia ago when humans began to shape civilizations out of less organized ways of life. The first civilizations developed in the great river valleys. In East Asia, civilizations developed in the Yangtze and Yellow River basins that today are in China; and the Indus and Ganges basins that today are in India and Pakistan. In the West, the early civilizations stretched from the valley of the Tigris and Euphrates Rivers to Africa's Nile River basin, a region that today includes Iraq, Syria, Lebanon, Israel, Jordan, Egypt, and Sudan. All of these areas were well suited for human habitation. They had good climates and fertile soil and were conducive to irrigation. As many people gathered together, agriculture began providing the people with spare time in which knowledge could be developed. As a result, the people formed cooperative groups seeking common benefit, and these eventually coalesced into states.

Passage 2: Western Antiquity

The key points of ancient history in the West are those most ancient cradles of civilization, Egypt, which was centered on the African Nile basin, and Mesopotamian culture centered on the Tigris and Euphrates.

Egypt was a state that developed five millennia ago and reached its zenith (though not necessarily in philosophical terms) around 1500 B.C.E. At this time, people were polytheists and worshipped the sun in particular. Believing that the soul was eternal, Egyptians had the custom of preserving the deceased as mummies. Egypt achieved numerous cultural developments, with those in the areas of architecture, sculpture, and art especially noteworthy. Giant structures such as the pyramids and the Sphinx particularly amaze us today. The Egyptians also developed hieroglyphs and made great progress in astronomy and mathematics. However, we can see no remarkable developments in philosophy.

Babylonia represented another of the world's cradles of civilization and one of the great nations of Western antiquity. Moreover, it is noteworthy since the monarchy it established in Mesopotamia, centered on the Tigris and Euphrates, was the most developed area two millennia prior to the present with great achievements in astronomy, architecture, and weaving as well as in the development and use of cuneiform writing.

The Hebrews, Phoenicians, Assyrians, and Persians were major peoples of Western antiquity, but their relationship with philosophy is not considered as significant to the West as that of the Greeks.

Greece developed somewhat later than the above-mentioned nations. In its geography of mountainous terrain, bays, and nearby islands, each of its regions formed separate independent states, but ideologically it was a unified culture in terms of language and religious customs. In response to its environmental circumstances, it had a developed sea trade and the numerous colonies developed as city-states. Among these, Sparta and Athens are most famous. Sparta prospered as an aristocratic

regime with a strict military education. In the sixth century B.C.E., it attained its greatest development, bringing almost all of southern Greece under its control. Athens, on the other hand, initially had an aristocratic form of government but switched to

Panathenaic amphora showing Pankration (Metropolitan Museum of Art, 2008)

democratic rule around the end of the sixth century B.C.E. As the power of Athens grew and developed, it brought most of central Greece under its dominion. In short, Athens, with its strong navy and focus on culture and technology, achieved cultural development and prosperity.

The great Athenian statesman Pericles (495-429 B.C.E.) appeared on the scene and presided over a golden age of cultural development often called the Age of Pericles. Holding the rule and rights of the people in high regard, he developed the navy and worked towards developments in the arts. In addition, he gathered together the various outlying regions and colonies for the great rites of Olympus where competitions were held in the cultural and military arts. These have developed into the Olympics we have today. Nowadays Athens is a city of ancient ruins, and the glory of the temple known as the Parthenon will never fade.

The fifth century also witnessed the birth of the philosopher Socrates (470-399 B.C.E.). The philosophy of Socrates, as it was passed down through Plato and his disciples, became the source of Western philosophy. He held an objective belief in concepts such as justice, virtue, and especially self-knowledge. For Socrates, virtue was knowledge, and he prized rational argument.

 Jesus Christ belongs to a later era, but since he is a holy and great person of history, I will briefly write of him here. Jesus was born in Judea. Observing how the people of the time lived lives of great suffering due to the corrupt and chaotic society of the time, he worked towards their salvation, espousing a doctrine centered on universal love and equality. He was warmly welcomed as someone who gave the people a sense of hope and respect. However, he was despised by the Judean rulers and eventually ended up vanishing on the cross. In other words, he sacrificed his own precious and holy life for the salvation of those in difficulty. Afterwards, his disciples, heirs to his sacred teachings, diligently engaged in spreading his word, spreading the message through the Roman Empire where they suffered persecution. The

number of believers gradually grew and eventually received official recognition by Emperor Constantine in 312 C.E. After this time, the religion gradually grew, spreading throughout Europe.

Passage 3: Eastern Antiquity

Brief mention must be made of ancient India, whose history began in the Indus River Valley around 2500 B.C.E. But here I will primarily discuss the important series of events related to the era of Shakyamuni, the historical Buddha.

Around 4000 years ago, one part of the Aryan tribe living in Central Asia moved south into the area that would become India. After establishing a state, they formed a society consisting of four castes according to Brahmanism: the priests, aristocracy, commoners, and slaves. Of these castes, the priests monopolized the right to perform Brahmanic

Śākyamuni Buddha. statue at the Seokguram Grotto on the slopes of Mount T'oham (Used with permission of the family of Joseph Amico)

ceremonies. The other three castes were forced to live under their harsh suppression. As a result, the people of these castes, discontented with their lot, lived lives of misery. In 485 B.C.E., Shakyamuni was born. Since he advocated a philosophy of compassion, many people welcomed him warmly.

Born in the highest social position as an Indian prince, Shakyamuni wielded power and wealth, yet he was not satisfied. He pondered the question of why the people of this world took the precious lives of others, why they were subject to starvation and suffering, and why they ended up groaning in agony upon their sickbeds. At last, he decided to renounce his glory, power, and wealth, and take leave of his luxurious palace. Undertaking ascetic practices and spiritual cultivation in the firm belief that the suffering of man must have a cause, he finally clarified this cause and awakened to the realization that it was necessary to give this teaching to others through a heart filled with compassion. He gave his entire life to the service of others, explaining how man could overcome his adverse circumstance through a compassionate heart and action.

China is one of the world's oldest nations and the one most important to the discussion of philosophy. Five-thousand years ago, the Han tribe settled in the Yellow River, area driving out the Miao tribe who had previously inhabited the area. After this, the Han tribe developed under the reign of an emperor, unifying numerous villages and establishing the "Central Kingdom" (China). At this time, China already had carts and boats. It had established a fixed system of music and had begun sericulture. Kings Yao and Shun ascended the throne. Due to their good government, the society enjoyed ongoing peace. As a result, later generations have called these kings "the sage rulers."

After this, Shun passed on the throne to his minister Yu in recognition of the latter's accomplishments in dealing with a flood of the Yellow River. Yu called his state Hsia, and this state prospered under his good governance. Up until this time, most of the Chinese enjoyed freedom and equality, but Yu passed on the throne to his son Ch'i and from the Hsia period his grandson came to power. Over four centuries later, the rule was finally passed down in this way to the tyrannical Chieh. The hereditary system of rule thus began during the

Hsia Dynasty. The Kingdom fell to T'ang of the Yin Kingdom. His descendants ruled the kingdom for over 600 years. In the end, the kingdom fell to the Chou Dynasty's King Wu around 1027 B.C.E., as a result of violent rule.

King Wu set up the Chou capital at Hujing. He organized his family and ministers into a hierarchy of five titles and ruled with good governance. After King Wu's death, King Cheng ascended the throne, but due to his young age he was advised by his uncle Prince Chou. The latter provided good leadership, setting up numerous governmental organs and establishing rules of ritual and music. These became the basis for Chinese tradition. For many decades the Chou Dynasty enjoyed peace but eventually fell into decline with ministers rising up in revolt internally and foreign incursions by the Manchurians and Xirong. The twelfth Chou ruler, King You, was murdered during a Xirong invasion, and his son King Ping thus decided to move the capital to the town of Luo in the east. After the move, the social atmosphere grew still more chaotic. The period of time after this, spanning roughly three centuries, is known as the Spring and Autumn Period (722-481 B.C.E.).

During the Spring and Autumn Period, the Chou royal house gradually became weak, ruling in name only. Regional feudal lords fought one another and the Yi and Rong invaded. The country fell into chaos and the population suffered immensely. As central rule weakened, the country was run by feudal lords instead of the king, and commanded by lesser feudal princes. These lesser princes are known as *paeja* (regional despots). Prince Huan of Ji, Prince Wen of Chin, Prince Chuang of Chu, Fu-chai of Wu, and Kou-tien of Yueh are known as the "Five Despots of the Spring and Autumn Period."

The Spring and Autumn Period extended for more than 240 years as over 50 states were annihilated and more than 30 kings massacred. During these turbulent times, Sun Wu (Sun Tzu) published the work *Sun Tzu: Military Methods*, popularly known as *The Art of War*. In this period of continuous warfare, kingdoms rose and crumbled, aristocrats fell, and innumerable goodhearted commoners unjustly died as others experienced harsh suffering. There must have also been countless men of intelligence who, unable to bring their noble intentions and study to fruition, vanished like the morning dew. Yet along with Sun-wu, the work of many important philosophers was preserved. Not only did the previously mentioned *Chou I* (Book of Changes) appear during these years, but both Lao Tzu (570-490) and Confucius (551-479) lived and worked during this period.

Photographic reproduction of Confucius as Scholar from the Qing Dynasty and a depiction of an original painting of Lao Tzu Riding an Ox in the Cleveland Museum of Art (2008) collection.

The two centuries following the Spring and Autumn Period are known as the Warring States Period (403-221 B.C.E.). At this time, most of the smaller feudal states of the Spring and Autumn Period fell, leaving the seven stronger states of Chin, Chu, Yan, Ji, Han, Wei, and Chao. These are called the "Seven Heroes of the Warring States." These seven "heroes" each took on the appellation of king, wielding power according to their own whims. The Chou royal house, on the other hand, was weak, ruling in name only, and was, in effect, no more than a regional principality based in Luo. During this period also, great thinkers were born. Chuang Tzu (370-301), like Lao Tzu before him, taught his followers to follow the Tao. Mencius (371-289) was the great proponent of the ideas of Confucius.

Among the "Seven Heroes," the state of Chin was the mightiest. The Chin King Zhao-hsiang destroyed the royal house of Chou and his son Cheng destroyed the other six nations to unify China. He called himself Chin King Shi Huangti, and he established his capital in Hanyang. During his violent rule, he set up a splendid palace and began to build the Great Wall. Losing the support of the people, his state of Chin fell after a mere 21 years.

It is the Chou Dynasty, with its 37 kings and 867 years, that is far more important. In seeking to restore the peace and order of the dynasty's early years, both Lao Tzu and Confucius elaborated their philosophies during the difficult Spring and Autumn Period.

Passage 4: Lao Tzu's Theory and Confucius's Philosophy of Tao

Lao Tzu was born in Ch'u-jen hamlet, in Li-hsiang, in the district of K'u, in the state of Ch'u. His family name was Li, his name Erh, his sobriquet was Pai-yang, and his pseudonym Tan. He left his hometown and went to the Chou Kingdom where he worked as the official in charge of the royal library. Aware that the Chou kingdom was losing virtue and gradually falling into decline, he left the kingdom and went to the Han-ku Gate. At the urging of a gatekeeper by the name of Yunhui, he composed a work about the Do and virtue in two volumes. The work contains 5,000 phrases. After this, he left for another place. Nobody knows about Lao Tzu's final period. From the beginning to the end, he was a mysterious figure. Various scholars have put forward a number of theories about him, but that stated above is considered the most reliable.

Confucius was born some twenty years after Lao Tzu in the state of Lu. He served as the overseer of a granary in Lu and later as minister to the state. Like Lao Tzu, he was concerned by the decline of morality in his times, and he left his ministry to wander from state to state. As an expert in matters of culture, ceremony, and rites, Confucius tried to educate state leaders on the ideals of a previous era in order to restore moral government and security in daily life. Lao Tzu is said to have prophesied that the state of Chin would reign supreme 129 years after the death of Confucius.

Both Lao Tzu and Confucius emphasized the Do and virtue. Confucius said that if one heard the Do in the morning, one could die in the evening. Yet these two figures have different starting points. Lao Tzu's thought is centered around the principles of Nature as the macrocosm, whereas the Do of Confucius considers nature as the microcosm or the natural principles of the human realm. For Confucius, the concept of Do can be said to be derived from the concept of virtue, which in turn is derived from the concept of Heaven, which comes from the concept of God.

Lao Tzu, using Nature as his starting point, treats the Do and virtue as a commonality, while Confucius takes them as principles for human life. Regarding this point, I basically regard the Do, virtue, Heaven, God, and spirits as being conceptually inclusive terms. However, in this world, the term Do has been chiefly used within the sphere of natural philosophy, virtue within the sphere of human philosophy, and Heaven, God, and spirits within the realm of religion or superstition. One other thing to be noted about Confucius is the sentiment expressed in the *Book of History*: "Heaven cannot be trusted. My Do is to extend the virtue of King Wu." In other words, Heaven is inconstant and so cannot be trusted. Only the virtue transmitted from the ancestors is reliable; hence, the Do of Confucius is to perpetually extend this.

It was Confucius who, having received the mandate of Heaven, developed this conception of the Do. To repeat what has been said, it is clear that the Do and virtue are performed by nature and man. Straightforwardness was the beginning of the thought of Confucius and authentic human-heartedness forms the core of Confucian ethical philosophy.

In contrast, Lao Tzu's response to the chaos of the Spring and Autumn Period was to turn people's attention from the phenomenal realm to the realm of substance, from the limited to the unlimited, from the visible to the formless, from the relative to the absolute; in other words, to the absolute realm of life, existence, and value. While people were baffled by present problems, Lao Tzu, setting his sights on the transcendent realm, found the Do as the ultimate source of transformation, existence, and being, and firmly established himself based on those principles.

When considering Lao Tzu as a lover of nature and an authentic promoter of freedom, some come to the hasty conclusion that he left himself to fate, letting the world go as it would. Lao Tzu was imprisoned many times and was ridiculed by some. Many considered him a wanderer who let things be. Some even saw him as a dissolute madman. But Lao Tzu was not this kind of person. Then and now, most people are caught up solely by the current situation and their material desires. As soon as someone pursues the Do, which runs opposite to these desires and being empty, invisible, limitless, and changeless, transcends the present situation and physical desires, the person's words are considered to be no more than senseless sleep-talking.

Lao Tzu did not advocate a vague return to nature where one would do nothing, spending each day as it came, wasting away one's time, living a meaningless existence in seclusion, claiming that such a life was the Do. Rather, the Do is a study that is endlessly deep, endlessly mysterious, and without limits. The truth of the Do is infinite and the *mo che* of all Nature. The fact of the matter is that when it came to principles of Nature and the world's practical problems, Lao Tzu sought a greater aim and more central truth, from the standpoint of calm and tranquility. He strove to spiritually develop himself as a human being. His thought was an expression of cool judgment and discrimination in the sense that he critically perceived things according to the principles of Nature. Lao Tzu believed that the more one strove to do something, the more one lost one's original identity. Through his sober critique and authentic observation of nature and man, he set forth an ideal of man as a free agent, one who does nothing yet leaves nothing undone.

Man's failure to attain an accurate and widespread awareness of the august and magnificent Do as the source of this world's myriad images, forms, and things can be attributed to human contrivance and other factors. While the Do lies at the center of our everyday lives, it is extremely magnificent and infinite and is therefore invisible to the eye of man. Yet as I mentioned earlier in this book, if such an invisible aspect of nature as the atmosphere were to disappear from this world for just 30 minutes, human beings, and all other life for that matter, would be completely destroyed.

In spite of this, almost nobody feels gratitude towards the atmosphere. While aware of our indebtedness to it, there are still those who pollute it. One wonders whether they are aware of the dire consequences that their deeds will inevitably incur. Or whether it has ever occurred to them that if the Do, conceived as the principles of Nature and the source of this world's myriad images, forms, and things, did not exist, all the things of this world would return to the void of non-existence. We are reminded of human beings constantly running around in circles, eating, etc., while not being aware of the rapid revolutions of the Earth.

It is true that human beings are attached to things that are directly or indirectly visible and disregard that which does not appear before their eyes. In our everyday lives visible objects are important, but those who understand that the invisible is also important and take interest in it are able to enjoy happier lives, while those who take no interest bring misfortune upon themselves. Historically, this phenomenon has been repeatedly observed and experienced, whether during chaotic eras like the Spring and Autumn Period, or peaceful eras like that of China's Yao and Shun, or the present day.

In Lao Tzu's philosophy of Do, there is no urgency to force his thought on others or transmit it to future generations. While this may have something to do with Lao Tzu's character and thought, the most important reason is that the philosophy of the principles of the Do, being infinite and eternal and forming the basis for Nature's myriad images, forms, and things, possesses an absolutely inseparable relationship with these things. Thus, Lao Tzu was confident that there would come a time when people would inevitably treasure the Do, take interest in it, and awaken to it.

To summarize, Confucian and Taoist thought mutually influenced each other, with the philosophy of the Do undergoing greater development. Those who developed this philosophy of the Do (Tao) were known as the Taoist school. During the chaos of the Spring and Autumn Period, scholars and other followers of Confucius, putting their faith in human reason and ability, sought to rectify the world through social virtues. Those of the Taoist school, on the other hand, believed that they could rationally solve the problems by promoting understanding of the principles of Nature rather than directly confronting the great powers of the chaotic world. The inability of the Confucian school to wield major influence during this period reinforced the Taoist belief that one should not irrationally step to the forefront.

Passage 5: The Further Development of Taoist Thought

During the long Spring and Autumn Period, various thinkers continued to develop the ideas of Lao Tzu. The Taoist learning of the Yang-chou faction, a successor to the thought of Lao Tan, agreed with his assertion that the most meaningful life for man was to regard himself and the myriad things all as nature in existence, and to fully examine the fundamental elements of human nature (*seongjeong*[10]) considered as the natural proclivities of the human heart in its natural state. This faction rejected interventionism, claiming that the world would be ordered of its own accord if only complete freedom were given to man. Furthermore, Sung-yen Yun-wen complained that whereas man originally had few desires, these few desires had been endlessly expanded. He put forth a theory of non-aggression (*bujaeng*), claiming that if war were to be eliminated, men had to be willing to embrace humiliation.

Ten-ping and Shen-tao said that if one did not discriminate among the myriad things, considered them all as equal, threw away knowledge, renounced the ego, ignored sages and wise men, and became like the mindless dirt or a block of stone, one could exhaustively penetrate the Do. Shen-tao, in a further development of his thought, advocated authority that accorded with natural law, which transcended the individual's knowledge, sentiment, or intentions.

And King Wei of the state of Chi provided a government-funded school for the average people and students of the Do, a move affording scholars of the Do a favorable environment for their studies. This school became the forum where philosopher-Taoists like Sung-yen Yun-men, Shen-tao, Ten-ping, Huan-yen, and Tie Tzu set forth their doctrines.

Chapter 8: Eastern and Western Philosophy

Passage 1 Eastern Philosophy

Drawing together that which we have discussed so far, if we talk only about the bare bones of Eastern philosophy, it is the philosophy of the Do, and of um and yang. It concerns itself with the visible and invisible realms and the production of being from non-being. It places importance on virtue, on the mean or middle way, and on living in harmony with Nature. Followers of Eastern philosophy are a bit negative and tend to overemphasize theory.

Passage 2: Western Philosophy

Western philosophy is ontological, meaning that it concerns itself with the nature of existence. It holds that the essence of things is fixed and can be understood through thought. Followers of Western philosophy place primary importance on the actual.

In an attempt to harmonize Western and Eastern philosophy, I advocate a philosophy *of* balance. In accordance with the principles and laws of Nature, Eastern and Western philosophy must be synthesized in a rational manner so as to establish an autonomous philosophical system that can bring benefit and happiness to the everyday lives of all mankind.

I believe that the source of all this world's learning and civilization is the Do. The logical source of the world's reasoning emerged from Eastern philosophy. Yet, in the case of modern science, the West is ahead of the East because of Western philosophical thought. Science, the logic pertaining to all fundamental principles, was created first within Eastern philosophy, and then Western philosophy, taking this as a basis, actualized it. To name just one example, in accordance with the principleof harmony between um and yang, we can understand the principles of electricity in the present. In this respect, the harmonization of Eastern and Western philosophy is already underway. My hopes and efforts are that this may continue to occur in the realm of philosophy.

Passage 3: *Moo Do Philosophy*

In order to confirm this harmony between East and West, I have advocated the Moo Do philosophy from the very beginning as a practical expression of the philosophy of balance—an essential element in the synthesis of Eastern and Western thought.

Moo Do philosophy serves as a rational, natural, and practical model of East-West philosophy, harmonizing the Eastern stress on the logical with the Western stress on the actual. The essence of Moo Do is its incorporation of both theory and practice. It agrees with the principle that literary (*mun*) and martial (*moo*) skills both must be developed. Theory or mun corresponds to the East, while practice or moo corresponds to the West.

In conclusion, the "Moo" in Moo Do corresponds to Western philosophy, while the "Do" corresponds to Eastern philosophy. The incorporation of both theory and practice in the authentic Moo Do results in the natural and rational harmonization of both the philosophies and cultures of the East and West. This book is, for the most part, written from this standpoint.

II

REALM OF THE

INFINITE UNLIMITED

Chapter 1

Forward

Up to this point, I have explained the importance of philosophy, its goals, its history, and my wish to bring East and West together. Now we turn to the philosophy itself.

Since philosophy is closely tied to an understanding of Nature, in this section, I present the realms of Nature. The first is the Realm of Complete Nothingness. This is a realm of the unknown, nothingness, which human beings cannot even imagine. Second is the Realm of the Non-being Ultimate (*Mugeukkyung*), which is the realm of the Do. This refers to our conceptual images of that which is imageless and formless. Third is the Realm of the Great Ultimate (*T'aegukkyung*), which is the realm with images but no forms, the world of Nature.

The fourth is the Universe of the Mysterious Realm—that referred to through concepts having images and form—nature as we understand the universe, solar system, and Earth. Fifth is the Realm of Reality, of the myriad things, appearances, and forms. This is our existential conceptualization and chiefly refers to the human and natural realms. Sixth is the Realm of the Future, and it refers to that which follows death.

Chapter 2

Realm of Complete Nothingness

The Realm of Complete Nothingness symbolizes the completely empty unknown realm of darkness. As a realm transcending the ability of modern men like ourselves, it cannot even be conceived of through imagination, premonition, or other means. As a result, it is an absolute nothingness devoid of space, time, um, neutrality, or yang. It is a philosophical riddle untouched by the realm of inspired conceptualization.

Chapter 3

Realm of the Non-being Ultimate

Passage 1: Forward

Realm of the Non-being Ultimate refers to the infinitely large realm that is the vital origin and source for the Universe and Nature's myriad appearances, forms, and things. I also call this the realm of the Do. Other scholars also call it Heaven or God, and some people call it the Divine Sovereign (*Shinju*).

Literally, *mu* may be translated as "no or not" and "without limit"; *guk* means "ultimate" or "extreme focal point." *Mugeukkyung* or the Non-being Ultimate is without image or form. The symbolic imageless and formless Do is the creator of the *mo che* for this world's myriad images, forms, and things. I call the transformation from non-being (*mu*) to being (*yu*) "mysterious transformation" (*hyunhwa*), and the development from one being to another "evolution."

The Do itself is neither um nor yang but is neutral. It produced the um characteristic, which is space, and the yang characteristic, which is time. The Do thus controls this world's fate and life, as well as phenomena and principle. Phenomena (*sa*) and principle (*ri*) are two major categories in neo-Confucian thought, and I use them frequently to refer to the difference between the visible and the unseen. Phenomena refer to that which is manifested in the world, that which is visible. Principle (*ri*, translated as *noumena* in Buddhist thought) refers to the principles and laws by which the visible things are manifested. Do is the *mo che* of the myriad images, forms, and things of Nature.

Lao Tzu said the following about the Do's designation:

> There is something obscure formed before Heaven and Earth. Quiet and calm, standing alone and unchanging, it operates everywhere yet is not in peril. It could be called the mother of [everything] under

> *Heaven. I do not know its name. If forced to write it
> down, [I may] call it "Do." If forced to give it a name,
> [I may] call it "great".*

This is from Chapter 25 of the *Tao Te Ching*, the text left by Lao
Tzu. In the above passage, Lao Tzu writes of the vast nature of Do
that can embrace anything and is infinitely large beyond the reach of
human words. Another approach to the Do is below.

Passage 2: The Do Likened to a Bellows

Lao Tzu said the following about Nature: "The Do of Heaven and
Earth are like the bellows of the world." (See Chapter 5 of the *Tao Te
Ching*). To explain it in more concrete terms, Nature is devoid of
desire, emotion, or love. It is aloof and completely fair. Nature is
apparently cold, unconcerned, and indifferent when it comes to this
world's myriad images, forms, and things. Its space is empty like the
bellows used in a blacksmith's shop, which are empty, yet ceaselessly
move, limitlessly producing wind. Likewise, Nature's *un-gi*—its
moving ki—like Do, is without limit.

The space of Nature is filled with infinitely minute images and ki
that is beyond even the imagination of man. As something unknown,
one cannot know whether it is material, emptiness, atmospheric
phenomena, moving liquid, or minute solid bodies. But it is a fact that
ki exists throughout space.

Passage 3: The Do Likened to the Atmosphere

If, for the sake of explanation, the Do is likened to this world's
phenomena, it resembles the atmosphere. The atmosphere is without
form and is invisible. Even so, it has an indispensable relationship
with man and all living beings.

The atmosphere, being impartial and devoid of selfishness, is a
vapor that exists everywhere at all times. It can be both calm and
moving. While it seems like the weakest thing, it is also the strongest.
It plays a vital role in maintaining and developing the precious life of
all things; yet it asks for absolutely no praise or compensation for this.

Passage 4: The Do Likened to Water

The Do also is likened to water. Water is vital for the maintenance of the life of this world's myriad things. It is at once the weakest thing in the world and the strongest. And liquid water can transform into both a solid and a gas.

As the most common form of matter in this world, it is precious; nevertheless, it is at times an object of disdain. Water is good at both joining together and dividing. If it joins together, it becomes the vast sea. And drops of water can drill through a boulder. If water is put into a triangular vessel, it becomes triangular; if put in a round vessel, it becomes round. And no matter how water is used, whether or not it is looked down upon, it is never thankful or angry. It does not rebel, complain or refuse to comply, but only acts in accordance with the dictates of nature.

If water is calm for a long time, it becomes foul. If it moves, it is fresh. Water flows from high to low places. Moreover, when flowing water hits obstacles, if it is weak, it either stops or goes somewhere else, but when its force is strong, it sweeps the obstacle away or goes over it. In this way, water is free and unrestrained. It is, therefore, one of the world's materials that best resembles the essence of the Do. The same can be said of the atmosphere.

Passage 5: The Do Likened to Man

As mentioned before, the Realm of the Non-being Ultimate is the mysteriously transformed realm educed from the Realm of Complete Nothingness. As such, it is an unknowable realm that man cannot fathom. Yet it is a mysterious realm that evokes spiritual intuition, the sense that there is something essential that can be known.

Within the process of the gradual mysterious transformation from the Realm of Complete Nothingness to the realm of light, there is a vague sense of ecstasy and arcane manifestation. This is neither darkness nor light; it is neither um nor yang. It is the Do, and the Do is neutral.

The Do in its neutrality is neither this nor that, but is merely recalled through man's ideation. It is, however, the original source of Nature's myriad images, forms, and things, the *mo che* that serves as the source. The Do is aloof, stern, eternal, limitless, and mysterious, a neutrality possessing transcendent force replete with myriad abilities. Human intellectual capacity has a difficult time explaining such an august Do.

Let me explain this using a simile from human life. We human beings begin our lives within the dark void of our mothers' wombs. When first conceived from the harmony of um and yang, we are initially the neutral Do. Gradually transforming into um (female) or yang (male), we are born nine months later as human beings. It is clear that this process of development is similar to that of the Do. The root source of man is the Do; he is the microcosm of the universe, along with any of the images, forms, and things of Nature.

Passage 6: Neutrality of the Do

I realized the following regarding the Do: the Do is imageless and formless; it is fair and devoid of selfishness; it is limitless, void, and eternal; it is neither um nor yang; its basic character is an unlimited, eternal neutrality. In other words, neutrality is a singular profound mystery. This is because the most primal of the myriad images, forms, and things of Nature is neutrality.

To bring up a practical example, an egg is neutral. If iron is hung below a hen's nest during the incubation period, the incubated chicks will all be male. In the case of humans, medical techniques can be used to create a male or female child. In other words, the ironclad rule of Nature is that it never prefigures the image or form of a thing beforehand. If this was not true and the fetus or egg was male or female upon its conception, it would be impossible to alter via artificial means. This world's myriad images, forms, and things are, in the very beginning, neither um nor yang but neutrality. This neutral Do through its potent mysterious force produces um and yang, the Great Ultimate, space and time.

People of this world pose the riddle: Which comes first, the chicken or the egg? Unable to reach a clear conclusion, their discussion ends in a puff of smoke. I, however, have three reasons to believe that the egg is first.

First, the egg is a living organism in a calm state while the chicken is in an active state. The basic principle of Nature is that um chronologically precedes yang in the order of things. Second, the very beginning of the myriad forms and things of this world is derived from the natural principle of neutrality. Third, after the forms and things of this world have completely developed into either um or yang, they no longer revert to their former state.

People might attack my position, saying, "Since it was actually the chicken that laid the egg, isn't the chicken first?" And indeed, it may appear so when looking directly at the present reality. I, however, do not speak only of the present, but rather speak philosophically according to the natural principles and laws. Then, where did the egg come from? As something created from the Do, it gradually evolved from microscopic life in prehistoric times. Thus, this problem is a mysterious enigma.

Something I would like to add at this point is that while the manipulation of the sex of a human fetus may, from a certain standpoint, seem to be convenient, from the standpoint of the principles of Nature or of human morality, it is a grave problem. Hence, the reason I mention such artificial manipulation is not to encourage the practice, but rather to illustrate the philosophical principle.

Chapter 4

The Realm of the Great Ultimate

We pass from the Realm of the Non-being Ultimate to that of the Great Ultimate (*T'aegukkyung*). As mentioned previously, the Realm of the Great Ultimate is that with image but no form. It appeared through mysterious transformation from the Non-being Ultimate, the Do. The Great Ultimate contains space and time--absolute and omnipotent power that can be cognized by man. Space is um whereas time is yang. It follows that the Do has produced um and yang. It seems to me that when viewed from the perspective of the philosophies of East and West, um and yang are Eastern philosophical expressions while space and time are Western philosophical expressions. The thing I would like to add at this point is that the Do, that is neutrality, by producing space (the um aspect) and time (the yang aspect), has necessarily elicited the principle of equilibrium.

Passage 1: Space

Space, as the symbol of that with an image, has no beginning or end, no color, no form. It is invisible and inaudible, intangible and impartial. It has no feelings, no sound, no words, and no opposition. It is absolute, and as truth, which is eternally non-moving, non-alternating and non-changing, it is infinitely fixed and calm. Space is um. Space is accompanied by the aspects of position, direction, and distance, and though empty, it solemnly exists. And Nature's myriad images, forms, and things all exist at a particular point in space.

Passage 2: Time

Time has no beginning or end, no color, no feelings, no breath, no shape. It is invisible and inaudible and impartial, neither fast nor slow. As an absolute, it is infinitely and eternally fair and equitable, is non-alternating and non-changing, never rests for a moment but is eternally flowing. It follows that time is truly motion. Time is accompanied by the past, present, and future. Time is yang.

Although space and time cannot be seen, they definitely exist. Though they seem to be impotent forces in this world, they are the strongest, wielding a power of the most infinite magnitude. This world's most robust energies and powers, severe cold or fireworks, heat or explosions, cannot exert even a slight influence to change space or time. Human beings can observe the flow of water and store it. The flow of the atmosphere is not readily visible but can be detected.

People are indifferent to the infinite, authentic calm of space and the changeless, eternal movement of time. Yet it can be hypothesized that if a great change or revolution were to alter space or time, it would mean the end of this world's phenomena and, indeed, the whole macrocosm. Thus, the things that control and govern the whole universe and, of course, the existence and life of all the myriad images, forms, and things of this world, are space and time. Space and time are the creator. It follows that space is the mother (um) of everything within the macrocosm and time corresponds to the father (yang).

Space and time have the transcendent, magnificent power to embrace the entire limitless universe, authentically love it, sacrifice for it in an infinitely fair, impartial manner, and protect, develop, and manage it. Space and time are indifferent to heat and cold. They are not perturbed nor do they harbor emotions, become ill, or break down. Whether amidst white brilliance or darkness, rain or snow, and even if the macrocosm breaks open and becomes extinct, space and time are indifferent, without change, flowing on nobly and infinitely, without rest. Even the greatest power of the universe cannot block their flow. For this reason, the basis for solving all the issues and problems regarding the myriad images, forms, and phenomena of the macrocosm is space and time.

People think that it is man who solves all the problems and crises that occur in the world, but this is man's vanity and delusion. To give just one example, when a mother conceives an embryo, nine months must pass before an infant is born. Violation of this principle definitely leads to complications. In the same way, this world's myriad images and things, beginning with man himself, only form within the mandate, duties, and mission of the basic principles of space and time. They only form while living in accordance with the order, procedures, and cause-effect relationships of space and time. This is also called fate.

Chapter 5

Universe of the Mysterious Realm

As mentioned previously, due to the mediation of the Do's neutrality within the Realm of the Great Ultimate, um and yang, space and time, harmoniously combine to bring forth the universe. This is the realm of mysterious existent entities that are visible and have form. The universe is a totality, without limit, vast and eternal. This Universe of the Mysterious Realm exists in accordance with the balancing principles, which necessarily appear from the Realm of the Great Ultimate, the source and the sustainer, the *mo che* (literally mother-body).

Passage 1: The Solar System

Our solar system is one constitutive element within the macrocosm of the mysterious universe. *Taeyanggye*, the Korean word for solar system, literally means Great Yang System just as *taeyan* means sun. The solar system eternally and impartially embraces and develops this world's myriad images, forms and things in accordance with the principles of Nature. The solar system also forms and exists in accordance with the balancing principles, which appear from the Great Ultimate.

Passage 2: The Earth

As touched on earlier, the Earth was brought forth from within the solar system. The Earth can also be seen as being equivalent to a single cell within the totality of the macrocosm. In accordance with the balancing principles of Nature, the Earth constantly rotates while revolving around the sun at a specific orbit and speed. The earth represents a mysterious totality that maintains an intrinsic, indivisible relationship with us humans, and all concrete entities on the Earth's surface.

The Earth is formed of gases, liquids, and solids. The gases are um, the liquids a neutrality, and the solids yang. The representative entities existing on the Earth are animals, plants, and minerals. Minerals are classified as um, plants as neutrality, and animals as yang. These three types of entities mutually aid and support one another so as to maintain life, in accordance with the laws of Nature; they therefore have an indivisible relationship. To explain this in more concrete terms, gases are the atmosphere, liquid is water, and solids are earth. Based on these three elements, animals, plants, and minerals take form and exist. These six things unite, harmonize, and transform, existing according to the laws and principles of Nature.

We human beings exist as one life-form among animals. We humans are unique spiritual entities; hence we are called the lord of all creation.

The solar system and Earth make up the phenomenal realm, possessing a direct relationship with humans: we exist and live within them. For this reason, the most pressing issue would seem to be how to live our lives in accordance with the reality and the conditions of our environment. We therefore cannot help but take interest in the philosophy of Nature and, of course, the philosophy of life. For the sake of discussion, I have collectively referred to the celestial spheres beyond the earth as Nature, and that which is below this sphere as the human realm. The Earth and the myriad things on Earth also develop and exist in accordance with the principles manifested within the Great Ultimate.

People in this world often use the word Tao or Do. If you ask such people what the Do is, they say they don't know, or that they use the term since others use it. Or they say that it is a philosophical term or symbol. Or that it is the source of all things.

The Do that I advocate is neutrality and this doctrine is something that I have never heard from anyone else or in any other book. My doctrine refers to the nature of yang, the nature of um, and the nature of neutrality. From the Do, from neutrality, the um-nature and yang-nature are produced; the Do is neutrality, um is space, and yang is time. The *mo che* of um and yang is the neutral Do.

At the same time, from neutrality, the heterogeneous um and yang forces transform; and through their unity, the myriad images, forms, and things are produced.

Passage 3: Process of Development Regarding the Ten Thousand Images and Things

Lao Tzu says the following regarding the Do as the source of Nature and the original laws and principles of its development. The Do, which is the source of Nature, gave birth to one primal Do. From the one Do, two were produced, um and yang. From two, three were produced, and from three, the ten thousand things. The ten thousand things formed, carrying um on their back, obtaining yang and harmoniously combining with empty ki. (see Chapter 42 of the *Tao Te Ching*).

Passage 4: The Ten Thousand Things are Produced Through the Harmony of Um and Yang

As humans, we search for a visible, phenomenal symbol from within the realm of no image or form to help us understand the mysteries of Nature. For this reason, when we say that the um and yang nature of things are the basic elements of Nature, it is helpful to think of space and time. Though they have no form, they have an image. Though they do not seem to be, they subtly exist in a way we can imagine.

If we observe phenomena from an unemotional standpoint, after deep and thorough deliberation, I honestly believe, that the mysterious basic starting point, the endless harmonization and change, and the eternal existence under the fundamental laws of Nature, is that um is in all cases the changeless um, and yang is in all cases the changeless yang. And um's characteristic nature is calm while yang's characteristic nature is movement. And calm knows nothing beyond calmness while movement knows only how to move.

I will provide a simile from the Universe of the Mysterious Realm: the moon always shows the same side to Earth, appearing not to spin or rotate but always fixed. It is therefore complete calmness, or um, and to the extent that nothing acts upon it, will forever be as it is.

Earth, unlike the moon, rotates and spins and is always moving, or yang, and unless something acts upon it will forever be complete movement.

It occurs to me that since um and yang are fundamentally heterogeneous aspects, if um forever remains steadfastly calm in accordance with its Heaven-ordained nature while yang remains steadfastly moving in accordance with its Heaven-ordained nature, change or reversal arising from um or yang cannot occur. Yet the Do, absolute and of manifold capacity, manifests its basic essence of neutrality, which is neither um nor yang, and acting as an intermediary, guides and stimulates um and yang, taking these diametrically opposite principles and synthesizing them to produce the macrocosm.

From this opposition and synthesis, this world's myriad images, forms, and things eternally derive and abide. Thus the cosmos consists of three basic aspects: um, yang, and neutrality. Um and yang, as innate heterogeneous aspects, are mutually negating and contradictory antithetical forces. Neutrality, being neither um nor yang, serves a mediating function, positively harmonizing um and yang, effecting a synthesis of the dual forces so as to produce a new phenomenon beyond the duality.

The cosmos is constantly changing and transforming in accord with the harmonization of um and yang, and the basic element of this harmonization is balance. For example, the planets of the solar system always move through specific spatial locations at particular times in a set speed and direction. Because they move regularly according to the principles of Nature, they are able to abide in absolute stability. This relative equilibrium is present in the entire universe. We human beings along with all of this world's myriad images, forms, and things are produced and exist in accordance with these principles of Nature.

I would like to introduce here my philosophy of balance, which I will discuss in more detail later. The Do, along with um and yang, is the mother-image of balance. Equilibrium consists of um, yang, and neutrality. Equilibrium has an inextricable connection with the maintenance of the life of this world's myriad images, forms, and things.

As described above, the cosmos (or macrocosm) was produced in accordance with the principles of um and yang. Um-space is the mother of Nature, while yang-time is the father. In dialectical terms, the cosmos-Nature is the offspring of um and yang, and is therefore the grandchild of the Do. And the cosmos is eternal and absolute, possessing image and form. The cosmos, thus brought into being, was initially neutrality, but as it matured with the passing of time, it transformed into the manifested cosmos consisting of um, yang and neutrality. However, when we human beings observe the cosmos, we are confronted by a number of riddles. This is Nature's marvel and mystery, and it is what calls forth philosophy.

Chapter 6

Realm of Reality

Passage 1: Enlightenment

As a martial arts practitioner, I have devoted my life to the art of Soo Bahk Do and have dedicated myself to exploring the wonders of *moo* and *do*, these two essential parts of Moo Do. Always seeking a better understanding, I searched for the true significance of these two concepts, looking for meaning in the realms of Great Nature and the nature of animals and plants.

Perhaps because of a lifetime of contemplation or perhaps a spark of revelation, at the age of 79, I found myself changing direction. Instead of looking for answers to the mysteries of moo do in the most infinite and far-reaching realms, I focused on a very simple place.

I considered from the theoretical and practical perspectives that a human like myself is a small part of a heavenly body—a microcosm of the great universe. It was as I contemplated the course of human formation in the greater solitude that my mind instantaneously perceived that the Do is neutral. During this blinding flash, I was filled with hope and jubilation; I felt joy and emptiness at the same time.

Not only is Do the source and the creator of all the myriad things, it is also the source of change and transformation of all things in the universe of our Great Nature. Therefore, Do is divine and yet it is also not; it is heaven and also not; it is empty and yet it is not empty. Once I thought that the Do was infinitely high and existed only in the unknown realm, yet eventually I realized that the Do also exists in my body and therefore in all bodies.

But among humans there is an absence of willingness to cultivate the Do in themselves, or to develop their inborn character. We give insufficient effort to become familiar with and control the instincts we are born with. Nor do we work hard enough to change and improve our external environment. The balance in our lives is destroyed, yet we allow our darker selves to shield us from the true color of the Do in our bodies. Among all humans, some are not aware, others are not willing to know or not willing to give the effort to study, but most cannot imagine enlightenment and thus remain far from it.

Therefore the focus of self-cultivation must be to remove all malice but even more difficult, to strip away all that is superficial, falsely ingratiating, or unctuous. Unctuous means oily or slick, like flattery that is self-serving. Of course these characteristics vary in different people and different cultures, but the principle is the same. If we can remove all hypocrisy and the falseness that comes from non-engagement with ourselves, then we can experience enlightenment in our hearts and feel the Do that is within our bodies, within ourselves.

Because this is such a core issue in our lives, it seems that this task should be common and simple, yet it is the most difficult task. If we humans wish to overcome our hypocrisy and superficiality, we must accept the importance of virtuous living within the essence of Do.

Passage 2: The Importance of Do as Neutral

It is not easy to understand my insistence that the Do is the very inception of Nature, the creator of all things, and at the same time is neutral. I believe that the beginning of all kinds of visible phenomena, shapes and things is neutral. Therefore, Do is neutral even as it is infinitely eternal, absolute, and mysterious. Yet the neutrality of Do cannot bring about transformation and evolution by itself.

The Do is neither um nor yang. It is imageless and formless, limitless, void and eternal. The omnipotence of Do in the Realm of Non-being Ultimate and in the Great Ultimate remains neutral and, at the same time, the source of heterogeneous meaning through the formation and transformation of relative opposites, um and yang. Um and yang share the characteristic traits that enable them to harmonize with each other or separate from each other.

Do is neutral but possesses the fundamental quietness (*jung*) that is um and the action (*tong*) with the character of yang. *Jung* stimulates the *tong*, and *tong* stimulates the *jung*. As we have seen and will continue to discuss in later chapters, tranquility always wants to retain its character as eternal *jung*, just as *tong* wants to retain its character as eternal action. The neutral Do has the character to unite *jung* and *tong* when needed and, through that union, creates the harmony of um and yang through the neutral energy.

This is the energy that generates life. Earlier I discussed this in the context of Great Nature and using the example of the egg. The identical principles hold true for humans as well. The beginning of fertilization is neutral, but cannot create the true essence of human life alone. With the change of time and atmosphere and through the principle of Do, the spine of the human develops as neutral, the brain develops as the essence of um, and the heart develops with the character of yang. Eventually, the human person is born with the complete body structure, and this appearance is consistent with the principles of Do and the very inception of Great Nature itself.

This unimaginable mystery of the Do in the presence of the human body has long been the subject of medical study as revealed in the famous 1613 treatise written by Huh Joon, *The Complete Medicine Book of Korea*.

Passage 3: My Theory of Do

What is this Do that seems so strange and so absolute? Already we have pages of discussion and yet it is impossible for anyone to give a complete answer to this question because of the eternal mystery and emptiness of the Do. Still, I think that by combining the attempt to explain Do with an account of the development of philosophy, it will deepen our understanding and help us to devise the method to cultivate ourselves.

We must begin with Lao Tzu. He is not the only man in history to have left a written record of the philosophy of Nature. But he was the first person to contribute so extensively to logically systematize the philosophy. For this reason, Lao Tzu and the Do ideology are inseparable from each other.

The simple word "Do" or "Tao" means way or road that anybody can freely travel in all directions. With this simple concept we also use the word Do to denote a philosophical way. We use the word do at many levels, for example Soo Bahk Do, Kendo, Soh Do (calligraphy), Hapkido, Cha Do (traffic lane), and so forth. So it is good to consider how Do is used as a philosophical way.

Since the time of Lao Tzu and even before, we used the word Do practitioner or Do person to refer to those who sought to practice better health, longer life, mental stability, and peaceful living by departing from this world to go to the mountain. The physical aspect of the deep mountains made it possible to have a better connection with Nature and to move beyond human selfishness. By furnishing their bodies and spirits with clean air and natural food, these Do practitioners not only improved the health of their bodies and minds, but developed excellent personal character as well. Laymen and others who were not able or willing to go to the mountain tended to cherish these ideals and respected these people close to Nature.

Thus there is a long history of people who have perceived the Do as inseparable from the desire to cultivate the mind and body and to build character. Most of the time we are not able to retire to a mountain to cultivate ourselves, but many people do set aside specific times and places to enjoy activities that cultivate their minds and bodies in their daily social lives. Those who do this regularly not only plan and achieve physical health and spiritual depth; they enjoy stability of mind and peacefulness, which helps them to have a quality life as a good human. To describe the intention of their desire to study Do, we also use the character Do.

What is Do? What is the creator of all things? We cannot answer these questions because of the mystery and eternal vastness of Great Nature. But the investigation of this puzzle is philosophy, and philosophy is the foundation of all literature. It is that humans can ask such questions and write their answers for others to study that has made man the lord of all creation. As such it is our responsibility to apply all effort to behave with the dignity that such a role implies.

Do is the *mo che* for and creator of Great Nature, and we think of it also as the rational way to discover the appropriate direction to be taken in order to live in harmony with Great Nature. It is as if Do exists and does not exist. Only humans are not able to perceive the Do because the principle of the Do is infinite and enormous. Most of the myriad ten thousand things exist comfortably within the Do, but humans must study to find the appropriate path. We know the earth rotates but cannot comprehend how fast it is spinning. In the same way, it is difficult to gain a sense of the reality of the Do. People who approach this understanding are called *chunin*, one who has attained Do, or sunin, a sage.

In this life, it is through Moo Do that we may begin to cultivate ourselves and find the appropriate directions to live in greater harmony with Nature. In this Realm of Reality that we share with the myriad things, appearances, and forms, Moo Do practice can help us to develop healthy bodies and more peaceful minds.

Chapter 7

Realm of the Future

Passage 1: The Concept of God

In order to understand thought regarding God, one must take a look at the circumstances surrounding its origin by considering the texts of antiquity and the simple inscriptions on excavated tortoise shells and animal bones, along with legends and oral tradition.

During remote antiquity, though the human intellect was undeveloped, people felt that all things in the world were controlled by some great force. The weak relied upon this force that they thought possessed great power. When it comes to survival, man is so frail, powerless, and weak in comparison to Nature. For this reason, when he is confronted with adverse circumstances such as threats to his survival, misfortune, disease, loneliness, pain, or sorrow, he wants to give unconditional obedience or subservience to a symbolic force or great power. Man wants to achieve his desires, happiness, and health through the grace, aid, and salvation of the force of Nature, which possesses absolute, manifold power. Hence, man turns to superstition, God, *Haneul* (Korean for Heaven), or *Hananeunim* (Korean for God).

During ancient times, religions were polytheistic. The forces of Nature were obvious to ancient peoples, and so, they believed in diverse spirits and created numerous altars where they prayed for good fortune. Such altars might include the *sungwangdang* (abundance king altar) and the *sanshillyeongdang* (mountain spirit altar). One of the more representative altars was the *chajukkari* placed in the back of the house. At this solemn spot, shamans conducted prayers and worshipped. When the people, whether common people or the ruler, intended to undertake something, they would first consult the altars or perform divination and then act accordingly. Gods had great authority and were believed to be higher than the ruler. Polytheism was widespread in ancient times, from China's Hsia Kingdom to the middle of the Yin Kingdom (ca. 2000 to 1350 B.C.E.). This view of gods resembles that of the ancient Greeks in the West.

I would like to share a personal experience from when I was eight or nine years old. In the back courtyard of our house, we set up a *chaju*, bundled rice straw representing a protective deity that measured about one meter wide and one and a half meters high. I remember covering it so that rain would not get on the rice straw. We created a crown and clothing for the chaju, which was reverently maintained. Whenever there was an event, I recall how a female shaman would hold a service or recite prayers. At this time, such events were called *chajukkari, teojuragi* or *teoju daegam*. Nowadays, these things are no longer seen. In light of the fact that this resembles the *chaju* deity tablets of the ancient Chinese kingdom of Yin and yet is not found in other countries, there appears to be an inextricable connection between Korea and the Yin of Chinese antiquity.

The ideas associated with this practice gradually changed from the middle Yin period and during the early Chou period. In the Chou Kingdom, persons of noble virtue, figures such as the sovereign, became deified. In Heaven, such a person was called the "High Emperor of the highest position, the Jade Emperor." It was believed that below this figure, many spirits existed through the order of the High Emperor (God). The Korean word *shin* can be used either for spirits or gods. It is also sometimes used for God, especially when used in the more abstract, academic sense. These beliefs about Heaven were mirrored on Earth. It was thought that there were sovereigns who become deified as a result of their illustrious virtue, with their ministers and the people organized below them. It was from this point on that we start to see an ideology of virtue. It is my belief that the terms *do* (Tao), *shin* (god/spirit), *cheon* (Heaven), *Hanuenim* (God), and *yeong* (spirit, spiritual force) are somewhat different depending on time, place, and person, but that the fundamental thought is the same.

Passage 2: The Concept of Heaven

People have thought of Heaven as referring to the infinite and vast cosmos, and have therefore conceived of the sun, moon, or all the stars as being the place where the High Emperor (God) resides. People have called this figure *Je* (Emperor), *Hwangje*, or *Hocheon*. In the ancient Kingdom of Yin, people often consulted spiritual mediums regarding the future. They held the belief that since it is difficult to determine the auspiciousness or inauspiciousness of a certain event through human means, one could rely on a superior person who possessed great capacity and perspicacity as a solution. Later in the Chou period, people began to have a more unified idea of a supreme God. God (*Sangje*) was also called *cheon* (*Heaven*).

The people of this era believed that the supreme God or "Heaven" possessed a will and emotions, and was able to judge good and bad and give man directions and commands regarding what was inauspicious or auspicious, and what would lead to misfortune or good fortune. This concept of God is similar to that of the Ancient Hebrews in the West. And Heaven, used in this sense, is a term of utmost reverence.

Toward the end of the next section, we will return to the notion of the Realm of the Future as that, which follows death, considering Heaven in its relation to virtue.

III

THE LOGIC OF VIRTUE

Chapter 1

Introduction

Sculpture displaying Virtue's control overEvil

Virtue is the basic element underlying thought and action as man lives his life in this world. Yet modern man finds this virtue to be abstract and of little interest. Ancient people, in contrast, placed great importance on virtue in their everyday lives and expended tremendous effort to put it into practice. If the mo che of Nature is understood as Do, the mo che of man is virtue. Thus, a man of virtue is said to be a "good man." When many such men of virtue appear in the world, the world becomes happy and tranquil; and when the opposite is the case, the world is clearly unordered and chaotic. For this reason, we must always strive to become persons of virtue, in the belief that virtue is man's essence. It is the expression of the philosophy of Heaven, the Do, and the expression of that which is "straight," meaning honesty.

Many sages of the past associated virtue with the concept of "obtaining." In English, the connection between "Virtue" and "obtaining" is not apparent, but the ancient Chinese words "deok" and "deuk" appear to be etymologically related. And Lao Tzu, for example, said that one "obtained" virtue via emptiness.

Lao Tzu believed that only when virtue was understood as emptiness could one achieve the Do in one's actions. He said that the space between Heaven and Earth was empty, but empty like a bellows so that when active it was not exhausted, but to the contrary it is increased. Lao Tzu's concept of emptiness is *mu* (*wu* in Chinese), the nothingness from which existence (yu) arises. Mu is invisible, but its beginning is associated with ki, the energy associated with breath. It is said, "*Mu* is called 'great emptiness,' *mu's* beginning is called ki. Emptiness is identical with ki." In this way we can see how Lao Tzu thought of emptiness as something active that could serve as a force.

It also becomes easier to understand how Lao Tzu believed that in human society, emptiness or ki is interchangeable with virtue. We are talking here of a human being who is capable of transforming ki to inspire others; a natural man who, in agreement with the order and principles of Nature, is able to harmonize his virtue, transcending artificial actions that could never be compatible with *mu*. The Do is the *mo che* and basic essence of the universe, which accords with the fundamental principles of Nature. The Do does not refer to man's understanding of scientific laws or to the "artificial" knowledge that is separate from Nature. For Lao Tzu, the goal was to manifest virtue based on Nature as it exists outside of man, to become a "man of Heaven" by acting in accord with mu and with Do rather than forcing action in accord with artificial knowledge.

For Confucius, however, the way of Heaven and the Do of Nature were not constant and were therefore, not something people should rely on. Only the virtue of the ancestral shrine was worthy of faith. The eternal preservation of this virtue was the Do of Confucius. The goal was seen as emphasizing the virtue within man so as to manifest it and become a sage. Man could become humane when he was able to transform virtue. He was able to inspire others with his human virtue so that those doing evil would be moved to do good. The Do of Confucius was to be straight (honest and upright); to be straight is benevolence, benevolence is intimacy and love, and intimacy and love is virtue.

This was how the Confucian concept of virtue originally meant an "obtaining." When the mandate of Heaven was received in a person's heart, this was called the straight heart (*jikshim*) or the rectified mind. The Chinese character for straight is the ancient character for virtue.

To the Western mind, this straight honesty produces unexpected forms of virtue. For example, even if one's father did a terrible misdeed, one could not tell others. It goes without saying that one could not accuse him of a crime. This is the "straight heart" that arises naturally from the heart of authenticity. It was also said, "If one repays one's enemies with virtue, with what is one to repay virtue? Virtue is to be repaid with virtue; one's enemies are to be repaid with the straight." This is because if enemies are repaid with virtue, this is deception in terms of one's true feelings, and in this respect, one's heart is not being straightforward. It is also said that when conducting a ritual for the spirits of the deceased, it is the moral value of the ritual rather than the existence or non-existence of these spirits that is important. For this reason, when a ruler or a wise man is respecting the spirits, it is his duty to draw close to the common people with the awareness of the moral significance of their lives. Benevolence and virtue are things that man freely controls, but the mandate of Heaven is not something controlled by the will of man.

Chapter 2

Man's Uniqueness

As man lives in this world, he always has an interest in the when, where, or why of everything. This sense of inquiry serves as philosophy's starting point. Yet we have already discussed how often people are interested only in the phenomenal aspect of things, the visible parts they can see. They stop before they ponder the cause or invisible parts of reality. Of course, there are a few rare people in this world who attempt to fully clarify this, and among those who strive towards this purpose are those whose efforts are rewarded. This ability to inquire into such matters is like a gem possessed by all men but polished by few.

Man takes his place as one of the Earth's animals. Yet man is the master of everything. What is it about man that makes him uniquely different from the other animals? Is it because he's bigger? No. Cows, horses, elephants, and whales are many times larger, yet they are not masters. Is man more powerful? Elephants and whales are many times stronger than man, yet they are not masters. Does man attain mastery due to inventions such as fire, guns, knives, planes, and bombs? Once again, the answer is no. Man becomes master because he possesses three particular types of intelligence not found in other animals or things in our world. Man's use of fire, his development of writing, or his use of superior weapons is possible because he possesses these elements that enable him to transform his environment. Before we can understand this intelligence, we must explore man's innate nature.

Chapter 3

Regarding Innate Nature

Passage 1: Introduction

When we begin to think of human nature, we must be careful not to confuse this use of the word "nature" with that of Great Nature. Human development and growth can generally be explained in terms of two stages, the innate and the acquired. The term *suncheon*, literally "before Heaven," refers to that which is innate or natural. *Hucheon*, literally, "after Heaven," refers to that which is acquired or artificial. In other words, the former is linked to the Do and is therefore eternally changeless. The latter is achieved through effort and discipline, which by their nature are also linked to Do since the source of effort and achievement is Do.

Man comes into this world with his mysterious and absolute life force, which is innate. The human body is the practical vessel for life, and this vessel comprises the three components of *shim* (mind/heart), *choong* (centrality), and *che* (body). *Shim*, *choong*, and *che* are essential, not accidental, and constitute innate nature, basic instinct and basic defenses. The innate nature corresponds to *shim* or to clarity, basic instinct corresponds to balance, and basic defense corresponds to *moo* or martial.

It goes without saying that the most important thing in this world is life. Life is solemn, mysterious and unknowable. When we die, it is the end of everything. In other words, it is absolute nothingness (*mu*). For this reason, it is both a special privilege and a duty for us to maintain our lives. The Do is the source of life. In order to maintain and extend our lives eternally, we give birth and rear children. With these thoughts in mind, murder of invaluable life is a most immoral, cruel, and hateful crime. If humans are to preserve and maintain life so as to attain happiness and peace, they must lead natural lives in agreement with the fundamental laws of the macrocosm and must authentically strive to rationally develop their innate nature. While doing so, they must harmonize their innate nature with their acquired nature in a rational and natural manner.

Passage 2: Regarding Shim, Choong and Che

Shim, as a term referring to man's innate heart/mind, corresponds physically to the brain, and also to the spirit (*shin*). *Choong* as a term meaning center or pivot corresponds physically to the spine, and also to the spiritual essence (*jeon*[11]). *Che*, signifying the body, corresponds to the physical body, and especially to the heart organ, which is the basis for the body. These three things are the core elements of human life. After all, even if other parts of our bodies are not present, life can be maintained, but when one of these three elements is missing, we clearly cannot survive.

The term "brain" is used in speaking of the physical body whereas the term *shim* (heart/mind) refers to one's innate nature which in philosophical terms is the spirit and corresponds to um. The vertebrae are a reference to the physical aspect whereas "center" or "pivot" or *choong* refers to innate nature which is in philosophical terms instinct and corresponds to neutrality. The heart is spoken of in physical terms while defense is spoken of in terms of the innate nature—in philosophical terms, this is described as heat and it therefore corresponds to yang. The brain, spinal cord, and heart are the "Three Great Essentials" that appear in this world to innately perform the function of life.

At this point, I would like to add a discussion of the danjun. We know that this refers to the point inside the body below the navel, but I have never come across, in books or conversation, a convincing explanation of the danjun. Literally, the term means "cinnabar field," and it is merely said to exist three *chon* below the navel. (In Korea, a *chon* is 3.0303 cm). Yet people go on and on about "danjun breathing," about gathering the ki into the danjun or how the *danjun* is the source of ki. I would like to explain the essence of the danjun in a concrete and systematic manner based on the fundamental principles of Nature.

The danjun is the focus of the harmonization of the Three Essentials of mind/*shim*, spine/*choong*, and heart/*moo*. When the

Three Essentials are in balance, one is able to maintain the physical body in the most complete manner so as to keep from getting ill. The stimulants for the Three Essentials are the atmosphere, sunlight, and food, and to realize greater effectiveness, they must be accompanied by training in *shim gung* (mind training), *neh gung* (inner training), and *weh gung* (outer training). In terms of reproduction, when um and yang positively harmonize through the male testes and reproductive organ, refined ki (sperm) is emitted and life is produced. This process requires Nature's laws of balance--motion and stillness, emptiness and fullness, restriction and change. When these are present, human life is preserved and advanced.

Passage 3: More on Innate Nature

There are other ways to think about innate nature. For example, the term "original nature" or *bonsung* is pleasing for its linguistic association with the term *bonneung*, which means instinct or "original ability." I also use the term "original defense" (*bonbang*) to preserve these associations. The term *bonbang* includes innate defenses, justifiable defense, and unconscious defensive actions. It is the source for the martial arts (*moo*) of today. Original or innate nature is also referred to as individuality (*kaesung*) or Heavenly endowed nature (*cheonsung*).

When man, via the providence of Nature, receives life from his parents and appears within the phenomenal realm, he appears with an innate or Heaven-endowed nature. This original nature, individual for each person, does not change through a person's life. Each of us must effectively develop, manifest, and cultivate one's own particular innate nature and adjust it according to place and situation in our daily life.

Lao Tzu called one's Heavenly endowed nature "luminosity" (myeong) to distinguish it from acquired intelligence, which he called "knowledge" (*ji* or *jigak*). He wrote that one's capacity to fully comprehend the Do was linked to luminosity rather than artificial knowledge.

Passage 4: Instinct

Instinct refers to man's innate desires. Just as every human being is endowed with the Three Essentials that maintain life, everyone is also born with innate possession of instincts that serve to protect the Three Essentials. These are absolutely vital to human life but can also be a cause of misfortune in some circumstances. Instinct comprises three types of desires. First is sexual desire, referring to the desire for sex acts and the preservation of life. Second is material desire, which is chiefly made up of the desire for food. I would add a third, the desire for superiority.

Sexual desire. Sexual desire is one of the major aspects of human life and is an absolutely sacred element, functioning to preserve the human race in perpetuity. Yet there is a tendency to forget its beauty, dignity, and absolute value, because people are unable to accurately recognize Nature's providence and principles as these pertain to human sexuality. Moreover, sexuality, as something common and possessed by all, is looked down upon. Its physical aspect is emphasized over its spiritual or moral aspects, and there is a tendency towards unbalanced, unnatural lifestyles in exclusive pursuit of pleasure, seeking random and excessive sex in an immoral and irrational manner. Our society, engaging in such acts that violate the providence of Nature, or in other words, pursuing sexuality in an unnatural manner, must accurately grasp the correct natural laws and essence of sexuality with its tremendous dignity and eternal value. In our sexuality, our sexual acts, we must work towards a normal sexuality, devoid of excesses or deficiencies, consistent with the laws of natural balance.

Such a lifestyle requires wisdom, and it means we must have achieved a balance, or a golden mean, which brings into harmony spiritual cultivation and a healthy personality. It is interesting to note that human beings, for over ten years after they leave the womb of their mothers, have absolutely no sexual feelings and do not engage in sexual acts. As mentioned previously, this period of childhood is a natural phenomenon as a person progresses from neutrality to the complete fruition of the complete um or yang nature. During this time, desire for food is emphasized in place of sex.

Material desire, desire for food. The instinct for material objects, in terms of human beings, begins with a focus on food. Among the various material substances that man needs in order to live in this world, food is thought to be the most important. Yet there is something we must keep in mind at this point. Although humanity's life is eternal, the material of this world has a limit. Ironically, the people of this world seem to have an infinite desire for material objects in scarce supply, while many people have only a limited desire when it comes to the spiritual, which is unlimited. This can be viewed as behavior in violation of the principles of nature. Those who follow such an irrational course are unfortunate, while those who live in agreement with nature can be called fortunate.

As a practical example, if we humans attempt to satiate limitless desires with our limited stomach and thus overeat, we inevitably get sick. On the other hand, if we don't eat or eat a poor or insufficient diet, we get sick from malnutrition and, in extreme cases, die. This is because such behavior violates the principles of Nature. For this reason, the ideal lifestyle is one that is rationally balanced without excess or deficiency, in accordance with the laws of equilibrium found in natural principles. In this respect, it is interesting to note that as soon as we leave our mother's bodies and are born into this world, though we have no sexual desires whatsoever, we have an innate desire for nourishment, which we unconsciously seek to satisfy as we begin sucking on our mothers' breasts. This isn't artificial but is rather a natural behavior that is innate. It is truly a wonder how mysteriously and rationally we are formed.

Desire for superiority. The desire for superiority is a term that I coined, and thus, many people will be reading it for the first time. The terms sexual desire or desire for food are well known. Yet there are also many times when people are moved by a desire for superiority. This is not something that they are being made to do or something artificial but rather a naturally occurring, innate behavior. The desire for superiority refers to the wish to be relatively superior, to be prominent above others, or to be ahead of others and happier than they are. With this desire, all mankind seeks fame and power. This natural competitiveness is a driving force behind individual and social progress and improvement. Yet, as before, this desire for superiority must be married to the rules of equilibrium found in the laws of Nature. Only then can man be happy and gain respect.

People often fall into a life of excessive greed as a result of their instincts. Those who pursue their desires in a rash and excessive manner end up being unhappy, while those who control their desires in accordance with the natural balance come to be content. Sexual acts and eating are required to sustain life. Nevertheless, those who are deficient or excessive in these areas are calling ruin and unhappiness upon themselves. Those people who live in accordance with the laws of balance based on the principles of the Do will enjoy happiness and health. In this respect, one's happiness or misfortune, depends on oneself.

Passage 5: Fundamental Defense

In order to protect and preserve life, human beings possess an innate ability to defend themselves. Of course, there are differences in individual ability. Nevertheless, man has from the very beginning been able to preserve the life he finds so precious by means of natural, unconscious action. This is true of all life; even microscopic animals are born into the world in innate possession of natural coloring used for camouflage or defenses in the form of toxins or noxious odors or some other unique means of defense or attack. Through such means, they have been able to survive.

With the progress of civilization, man has developed various weapons including the technologically sophisticated weapons of the present day. And man has adapted the unconscious modes of defense of primitive eras, gradually developing them into explicit martial arts beginning with forms of Soo Bahk, a traditional free form of martial arts. Man possesses the innate ability to justifiably defend himself, but when people take advantage of this ability with its inherent sanctity, and instead rashly misuse it to harm others, they call misfortune on themselves while committing a social evil. What's more, such actions run counter to the sanctity of Moo Do. If we respect our own life, then we must constantly respect and honor that of others. For this reason, we must work to become people who, instead of spitefully killing others, cultivate a life-giving spirit that seeks to protect the lives of others. This is the principle of balance in nature. By acting in this way, man becomes the source of life, which is happy and at peace.

Chapter 4

Regarding Acquired Nature

In the previous section I discussed man's innate nature, that which is *suncheon* or "before Heaven." Opposite to this is man's acquired nature, which is artificial rather than natural, *hucheon* or "after Heaven." The *hucheonjeok* element in man is virtue. He may adjust virtue according to time, place, and environment. I believe that virtue as a component of human life comprises the three elements: intelligence, balance, and Moo Do. These are what give humans mastery. Intelligence is equivalent to um, balance to neutrality, and Moo Do to yang.

Just as with the spirit (*shim*), spine (*choong*), and body (*che*) of innate nature, the three elements of acquired nature correspond in a like manner. Intelligence corresponds to consciousness as in the brain, balance corresponds to the spine as made up of vertebrae, and Moo Do refers to the body. In other words, the element of consciousness is Right Mind (*jeongshim*), the element of the spine is right determination or composure (*jeongjeong*), and the element of the body is Right Posture (*jeongja*). Right Mind is um, right determination is neutral, and Right Posture is yang. These three elements form the core of human life, just as human philosophy, the philosophy of balance, and Moo Do Philosophy form the basis for human life.

In terms of their essence, these three philosophies are the same. I have called this book *Moo Do Philosophy* since this work, written on the basis of experience, seeks to bring together a synthesis of human philosophy, the philosophy of balance, and Moo Do Philosophy while looking at life through Moo Do.

Chapter 5

The Logic of Good and Evil

In this world, people often speak of good and evil, or good and bad. While determining that which is truly good or truly bad might seem easy, in fact, this is not the case. This is because few people really know any precise criteria for good or the true meaning of evil. Judgments related to the concepts of good and evil are different according to one's subjective or objective standpoint, time, place, circumstances, emotional state, or ideology. Moreover, benevolent acts we do now can turn out to have bad results, while evil acts may have good results. Some things that are good in Korea might be bad elsewhere. This being the case, what is true good or true evil? The thing that I can state clearly regarding this issue is that actions in agreement with the principles and laws of Nature are good, and those actions that run counter to these laws are bad. Moreover, actions done out of truly good intentions are good, while those done for ulterior motives are bad.

Those who say that man is good by nature claim that man, as he appears in the world from his mother's womb, is originally pure and innocent. He becomes either good or evil gradually, with the passing of time, in accordance with his family conditions, education, and surroundings. According to advocates of the opposing view, man, when born into this world, is originally evil. They point to the fact that as soon as a child leaves the mother's womb, it sucks the mother's breast. This behavior, understood as the attempt to take that which belongs to someone else, is seen as evil. I would disagree. An infant's birth does not occur because the infant desires to come out into the world. At the same time, the infant is not born forcefully against his or her wishes. The infant simply comes forth from the mother's womb in accordance with the laws of nature; through the harmonizing of um, yang, and neutral forces, it moves from non-existence to existence. All the actions of the infant are unconscious, instinctual nature itself. No theory or doctrine can or need be added.

It is my opinion that the primal beginnings of all things in this world, are not um or yang but rather are neutral. Afterwards, in a gradual manner, these transform into a complete um or yang through a gradual process and the passing of time, in accordance with mysterious conditions and circumstances. Accordingly, the fetus, as simply an entity that is seeking to transform into either um or yang, is not good or evil but is simply nature as is. For the same reason, the infant sucks his mother's breast. This behavior was never taught: sucking his mother's breast is an unconscious, instinctual natural act. Moreover, breastfeeding an infant upon birth is done as the mother seeks to provide the infant with milk. Such a phenomenon, as a matter of course, is simply instinctual and natural. The infant does not exploit the mother by forcefully seizing the milk. Thereafter, the infant is imbued with good or evil as he or she is gradually influenced by family, society, education, and environment. It is a fact that all men, no matter who they are, love good and hate evil. So we must work hard to improve not just ourselves but also to create good families, societies, and nations. We must put forth effort to ensure that our societies and nations are governed by those who are good, so that they develop a world offering peace and happiness to all people.

As we live our lives, it is vital that we human beings act on an accurate discernment of good and evil. But we are not gods. We are not omnipotent, so we encounter many vague situations beyond our comprehension. For this reason, to distinguish between good and evil in our thought and actions, we need to live our lives on the basis of a philosophy that accords with the laws of natural balance. For this, we need to be conscientious.

True goodness first of all means striving to train one's character so as to develop in virtue. By doing so, one comes to be respected by others. In accordance with natural principles, one correctly recognizes the relative nature of things. One provides true help and benefit to others rather than harm, while working towards others' happiness in the spirit of service.

Evil in the true sense of the term is acting counter to the laws of natural balance and ignoring relativity. It means doing anything by any means for one's own benefit so as to bring harm and suffering to others' hearts and bodies or to material things. It means being crooked and devoting all one's thoughts towards satisfying one's instinctual desires, acting without any consideration of others. When we view history from the ancient past to the present, truly great figures worked to perfect their character and sacrificed themselves, working to serve others. Thus, the extent to which one perfects oneself and works for the sake of others determines the extent of a person's greatness. Concrete examples of this are Lao Tzu, Confucius, Shakyamuni, Jesus, and Socrates. Such greatness must include true honesty, benevolence, and freedom.

The equilibrium and principles of the Do dictate that there cannot be a totally good or totally evil world. A healthy world would be one in which good became the master and evil the slave. Moreover, good and evil based on the principles of the Do are eternally unchanging but human (artificial) good and evil change according to circumstances. For this reason, one should emphasize the discrimination of fundamental good and evil while de-emphasizing the distinction between that which is artificially contrived. Evil necessarily follows good, while good definitely lies latent in evil. If people have achieved the stage of goodness while yet unaware of the principles of the Do, they tend to become proud when confronted with the good and despondent or despairing when confronted by evil. We need to always walk the path of the correct Do in a humane manner, not becoming proud of goodness and not losing hope in the face of evil. For it is only when one is truly good that one can be a good guide to others.

The following words and actions accord with natural principles and with the dictates of man's conscience:

Do not hate evil or be self-righteous in regard to the good.

Instead of hating evil, the great man sees it in its proper perspective, reflects upon it, and does not repeat it.

The great man strives diligently with the understanding of the principle that good exists because evil exists.

The good means accord with natural principles, living honestly as an ordinary person naturally, and with good intentions. It occurs when each person is completely faithful to his individual nature. The person able to carry this out in practice is a "man of goodness."

A person who tries to be good in a forced and contrived manner or who is boastful of his good actions is not a "man of goodness." He is not good.

Goodness means to not think of good actions as being meritorious, but rather to see them as a matter of course. The person able to carry this out in practice is a "man of goodness."

There are cases in which evil is necessary to do good and good necessary to do evil.

Being ordinary is good. Being extraordinary is bad.

When it comes to good and evil, there are two kinds: that which is *innate* and that which is *acquired* and artificial.

Words and actions based on truly good motives are good, while those based on ulterior motivation are bad.

It must be concluded that man is fundamentally good.

Good and evil in man is determined by instincts and benevolence. For this reason, personal cultivation based on the principles of the Do is necessary.

The basic source of evil is excessive desire.

Chapter 6

The Theory of Being Ordinary

In this world, people often use the word "ordinary," but they do not seem to have a good grasp of the essential meaning of this word or what it means to act "ordinary." As this term's antonym, we have the word "extraordinary." The term "ordinary" refers to that which is general and not extraordinary, and is easy and not difficult, that which is not select or special. The extraordinary, on the other hand, is unique, special, difficult, outstanding, better than others, and superior. Among human beings, many seem to prize the extraordinary over the ordinary due to the desire for superiority. It is only natural that they should think this way. The problem is how this relates to one's position in life, abilities, conditions, methods, and validity. People think that living an ordinary life is easy and living an extraordinary life is difficult. With great urgency, they work towards an extraordinary life, which is difficult and arduous, rather than an ordinary life that is common and easy. In so doing, they take no interest in, and look down upon, that which is ordinary and common. Since everyone wishes for that which is extraordinary, this is what is deemed valuable.

Yet it seems to me that there need to be many people living ordinary lives and few living extraordinary lives for the extraordinary to truly be of value. This is according to the law that things that are plentiful become cheap and those that are rare become valuable. It can also be said that the ordinary is natural and the extraordinary is unnatural. The ordinary is the middle way; it is in accord with the philosophy of balance by which one conforms with the flow of reality. The extraordinary leans towards one extreme. In other words, it is unnatural—not the middle way and not balanced.

If people really want to be extraordinary, rather than living their lives greedily seeking the extraordinary, they should work to realize and maintain a lifestyle that is ordinary. By doing so, they will in fact bring the extraordinary to fruition. In other words, the ordinary and extraordinary are different theoretically and in terms of their essence, but as an actual phenomenon within this world, the truly ordinary is extraordinary. This is an inevitable phenomenon based on the principles of the Do.

The following serves as an example. Everyone in this world wants to go to heaven when they die instead of to hell. In heaven, they have thrown open all the doors and stand waiting to let in all of the good people, but in spite of this, the place is dead quiet. In hell, planning on a low turnout of evildoers, only one door has been opened, but people have crowded through this door into the infernal regions where they squabble like hungry demons. This is based on the same principle as that above. It applies to all people of the world, but the Korean people need to especially keep this in mind so as to achieve authentic happiness and the development of their nation.

In this world, there are the normal and the abnormal. Societies in which the former is the driving force are normal (healthy) societies, and those dominated by the latter are abnormal societies. In other words, normal falls into the category of good, while abnormal is in the category of evil. In philosophical terms, normal (healthy) societies refer to those that accord with the principles of the Do, while those that run counter to these principles are abnormal. A normal, healthy society is moral, ordered, principled, and establishes a harmony between good and evil. An abnormal society is immoral, unordered, and unprincipled with no balance between good and evil. Naturalness and artificiality play a part here. A good society is based on trends of the era and changes in nature, while a bad society, as something artificial, bases itself on the actions of man. In other words, societies are distinguished by whether men follow the truth of the Do. The good society spoken of here is not an issue; rather, an evil society is the problem. We therefore need to work towards creating a good society. Nature continually changes without resting for an instant. Society also continually changes, as does man. These changes form our history.

We human beings want to change ourselves, going from good to evil or from evil to good. In human society, if we were only able to manage the harmonization of good and evil in a rational and ideal manner, we would enjoy eternal happiness and tranquility. The problem is that man innately possesses the three instincts. For this reason, I must repeat that the solution is for man to live a rational and natural life based on the principles of balance as found in the natural way. A healthy society is one where:

People know to love nature.

Human life is valued.

Principles of balance guide men's lives.

People are honest and have good intentions.

Those with good character and ability are well-treated and respected.

Public morality is maintained.

There is trust.

People get along with others.

People get fair rewards for their efforts.

People understand their indebtedness to others.

People sweat, investigate, and put things in practice.

Chapter 7

Heaven and Hell

Words such as paradise, heaven, and hell have come down to us from the religions of ancient times. It is said that those men who, when alive, were good and kind will, upon death, ascend to heaven or paradise where they will live eternally enjoying peace, happiness and tranquility. Those who live in the opposite manner, committing numerous evil acts during their lives and causing others to suffer, will, upon death, enter hell where they will experience suffering, unhappiness, and torture. When seen from a realistic or scholarly angle, this idea is a bit nebulous and hard to prove. No doubt, a belief in such things is sometimes helpful or beneficial in our everyday life and serves to prevent unfortunate things from happening.

The motivation for creating such a belief, it seems to me, was so that people would abstain from evil and do good. It was part of a movement towards purification of society's practices, customs, and trends. It is a great conception, which has played an important role. Even so, I don't agree with it. Such a belief may have been helpful to mankind, but it has failed to instill in man a sense of reality and sincerity. I predict that in the future, as human knowledge and science advance and there is more focus on practical ways of thought, the number of people believing in such things will decline.

In place of a belief system with an abstract heaven or hell after death, I claim that heaven and hell occur in the present life. People who suffer severe mental or physical shock, who suffer extreme pain or are in extreme physical need, have no way of knowing whether they will go to heaven or hell in the future. They believe that death is the end, or even if they believe they will go to hell, they feel that this is something to worry about after death. So there is an increased tendency for such people to commit evil acts in response to their suffering or vanity, or as a means of satisfying instinctual desires. If human beings were to witness good people going to heaven and evildoers going to hell, no one would commit an evil act in normal circumstances. But this is not the case.

When we look at history or at informal legends, we find many examples of ancient rulers who held absolute power, calling themselves emperor. But their violent reigns were short-lived. Wielding absolute power and enjoying all sorts of delights, they may have fashioned themselves as the happiest of all people, but if we look beyond the facade, we see this wasn't true. In many cases, their lives ended in misfortune even before they were able to live out their full life spans. These violent rulers believed they would win the respect of all people. Yet history proves the opposite to be the case. The meritorious actions of the sage ruler, on the other hand, remain even after his death, and the people continue to cherish and respect him.

The same principle applies to ordinary families and individuals. If a person commits numerous acts of evil during his life, that person or his offspring pay the price for the crimes during the present life. Though there are occasionally those who do not pay for their evil, they are found only in one or two out of ten cases, and it is often due to the accumulation of good acts performed by their grandparents before them. Even in these cases, when great evil has been committed, there seems to be no getting around paying the price for it. The same is seen in our families. This is the way of Nature.

In my own life, I have closely observed how people pay for vicious crimes in exact proportion to the crime. In those cases in which one only pays for half of the crime, one later receives retribution for the rest of it through untimely death, or one's close descendants end up paying for it. No one who chooses to do evil can be happy or make progress. The same holds true for families and nations. This is the way of Nature. On the other hand, the close descendants of a person who does much good when alive tend to enjoy good fortune. In other words, such actions ensure that not only oneself but even one's family enjoys happiness. And the same holds true for nations.

According to the words that have come down to us from tradition, those families with a great accumulation of good deeds definitely prosper. This is a reality. The experience of those who do good is a mirror image of that of those who do evil. This is a naturally and necessarily occurring phenomenon as a principle of Nature. Valuing such principles, a wise person should devote his energies to the accumulation of good through an authentically benevolent mindset instead of striving for power, fame, or riches.

Power, fame, and riches, instead of giving man true happiness, often bring on misfortune. Man's desire for such things is an attempt to satisfy his instincts, the satiation of which leads to man's unhappiness. As one practical example of this, there are those who, in order to satisfy their instinctual drives, drink or eat excessively, engage in immoral behavior based on a desire for fame, or engage in excessive and random sex. Such behavior causes them to become ill or creates other misfortunes. These actions lead not only to their personal downfall but to that of their families and societies as well. This necessarily follows from natural principles.

I want to emphasize: heaven and hell are not floating in space in the distant future, they are right here in the present life. Moreover, man and the myriad things should only be devoted to harmonizing um, neutrality, and yang in accordance with the fundamental principles of Nature, producing offspring and preserving life into the future. With death, the fundamental essence returns to the One. Whether one goes to heaven or hell after death is unknown. Life, for all of us, is a profound reality. Those who spend their lives doing good in accordance with Nature will receive happiness during their life, or will ensure that their offspring enjoy happiness. Those who spend their lives doing evil will definitely pay the price of unhappiness, and if they don't, their offspring will.

Man is completely free in his thought. According to some people, even to think an evil thought is a sin. I do not think so. After all, since the thought has not been expressed outwardly, it does not influence or harm others. And if one's conscience is activated, an evil thought can provide the impetus to do good.

In conclusion, I suggest that if our goal is to encourage people to be good, we should instill a practical awareness of heaven and hell in the current life as it exists this very moment. I believe that such an emphasis will lead not only to the happiness of the individual but would also be practical and effective in the movement to purify society as well. In the end, the question of whether heaven and hell are to be conceived as existing in this life or in the afterlife is not really the issue. The goal is how to most effectively encourage people to live lives based on goodness and avoiding evil. People are typically interested in what they can see and unconcerned with that which is invisible. Even if heaven and hell do exist, clearly it will be those people who, being good, reap the reward of happiness during the current life who end up going to heaven after death, and it will be those who, committing evil acts, reap the rewards of unhappiness in the current life who end up going to hell. Such is the truth of Nature. In this sense, when looked at from a logical standpoint, the doctrine of heaven and hell in this life and that of heaven and hell upon death are the same.

IV

THE PHILOSOPHY

OF BALANCE

The Philosophy of Balance

Balance, the ultimate law of Nature, is an absolutely necessary aspect for the normal maintenance and preservation of the natural world's myriad images, forms, and entities as they are produced from the Great Ultimate. The various astronomical bodies of the solar system, Earth, Mars, Jupiter, or Saturn, each revolve ceaselessly in a specific orbit at specific times. This is nothing less than a manifestation of the law of balance operating in Nature. If this law of balance were destroyed, each planet would go any which way, hurtling chaotically through space, and the solar system would be destroyed. Nature's law of balance maintains the stability of the solar system.

This same law of balance is more difficult to understand as it operates in the world of man. The term "balance" has been used in our everyday lives since ancient times. It incorporates the concepts of levelness and equality; it means not falling over towards one side. Balance is the most important issue in our daily lives, yet there is a tendency to disregard it. This tendency is the source of misfortune for human beings. Few seem to truly consider balance as a philosophical concept based on the fundamental principles of Nature. Because I believe this is important, I wish to introduce my "*philosophy* of balance."

As we live our lives, we do not always feel the direct or indirect influence of balance. This is because Nature is so vast and unlimited.

As the fundamental *mo che*, this sacred and profound phenomenon acts towards all things with kindness, love, intelligence, and sacrifice with complete fairness and impartiality, asking for not a single thing in return. Yet human beings are not even interested, much less grateful. This forms a tremendous paradox. The principle of balance is so vast and transcendent that it is hard to understand or be aware of through human intelligence and is difficult to apply in everyday life. I emphasize it here in the hope of making people aware.

The principle of balance is the natural manifestation and sustained existence of the phenomenal realm in accordance with the principle of harmonization of um, yang, and neutral forces, which in turn are grounded upon the basic principles of the Do. The philosophy of balance is comprised of um, yang, and neutrality, the basic aspects of Nature's Do, and these have the unique characteristic of constantly harmonizing with and transforming one another. The term "balance" used here can be likened to the use of a scale, the everyday implement utilized to accurately measure the weight of objects.

As everyone knows, at the midpoint of a traditional scale, there is a central support with parallel arms going out in both directions. Empty bowls are suspended from the two arms. The left bowl corresponds to um and the right one to yang, while the central support, corresponding to neutrality, carries out a centralizing effect. If these three elements of the scale each do what they are supposed to do, the two arms become parallel and the scale thereby functions. If we truly reflect on the laws of the universal principle through this analogy with the scale, we can use the understanding to maintain and develop clarity, happiness, and health within our daily lives.

The balance of the scale can be destroyed if one side is heavier or lighter, causing the arms to shift to one side. When this happens, the scale cannot maintain its balance. In the same way, when man or other entities lose their center or identity and follow extreme theories or engage in extreme actions, the natural order is damaged and misfortune results. The positive expression of this principle is the "middle way" (*choongyong*) of Eastern philosophy. Of course, if one wants to truly understand the middle way in its philosophical dimensions, it may be difficult, but it is not obscure if one seeks to understand and correctly cultivate its principles in one's daily life. There will be much more discussion of the middle way in the chapters that follow.

People understand the middle way to mean the center, which is neither in excess or insufficient. But it is hard to find an explanation that is easy to apply. It is said that the middle way is neither this nor that, neither white nor black. In many cases, the concept is misused in a vague or opportunistic manner. For this reason, to properly understand the middle way—that most valuable treasure of human life—we need to engage in authentic spiritual practice in the spirit of the Korean term *suyang*. *Su* means to wipe off or shine something, while *yang* here means to grow or develop. *Suyang* therefore means spiritual practice or acts carried out to improve oneself. I would like to talk of the philosophy of balance and the issues surrounding this philosophy with the idea of helping people actually to put this philosophy into practice.

The essential element promoting healthy and wholesome development of this world's myriad phenomena and entities is balance. When a change occurs in the balance, things break down or become diseased, and in extreme cases, cease to function or die. In order to maintain this balance, centeredness, a sense of identity, and effort are required. In this respect, the degree of balance is determined by the extent to which man has perfected himself in all ways. In the next section, we will see the importance of man's center or fundamental nature in the filtering of stimulus and reaction.

It is a natural principle that stillness elicits movement and movement elicits stillness. Neutrality serves to adjust and harmonize um and yang. By means of the action of harmonizing um and yang, Nature's myriad images, forms, and entities maintain and carry on life while constantly undergoing change. This is the basic law of the world. In the natural world, neutrality plays the role of adjustment and harmonization. In the human world, it functions as the middle way, the balancing support, and one's sense of identity. The middle way, a key element in Eastern philosophy, means to properly maintain the center without becoming excessive or deficient.

The problem is that when it comes to real life, this may all sound logically valid, but it is hard to put into practice. Part of the difficulty is that many people do not properly understand the need to maintain the center and find the idea wishy-washy or unclear. But it is also true that people can be opportunistic and, in extreme cases, actually hinder the middle way while failing to establish a clear sense of identity. Or they can engage in selfish, immoral, inhumane behavior because they are most aware of their instinctual desires. In Western philosophy as well, there is a fault in the overemphasis on everyday reality and an obsession with things. Here too, people possess instinctual desires; they forget the middle way and instead follow egotistic and materialistic lifestyles that are ignoble and immoral.

V

MOO DO PHILOSOPHY

Chapter 1

Introduction

Statues of a scholar (left) and warrior (right) representing "mun" and "moo"

When I entered this world from my mother's womb, I was born into the socially and politically unstable, terrifying, and turbulent era of the late Yi Dynasty (also referred to as the Chosŏn Dynasty). Early on, my mother passed away and I spent my childhood suffering from loneliness, hunger, and disease. Later, when practicing Moo Do, I personally suffered bitterness, betrayal, threats, blackmail, and severe and unjust oppression, and even had a few near brushes with death along the thorny and dangerous course of my life. Even amidst these adverse circumstances, I maintained to the end a sense of justice, hope, and boldness. As I passed my years seeking peace and harmony, I had the honor of teaching students throughout the world and meeting people; and as I traveled, I also had an opportunity to experience the various world cultures and encounter different worldviews.

Within these difficult circumstances, I never let go of my sense of self-dignity, good-heartedness, and boldness. I didn't despise others and held the belief that I was born from nature, would live a natural and wholesome life, and would eventually return back into nature. Perhaps it was this conviction that kept me from sinking into despair or hatred throughout my life. I have spent my entire life solely as a martial artist. So here I am, setting down my view of life based on what I have learned of its ideology and what I know directly based on my own experiences. This is Moo Do philosophy. Moo Do and *moodoin* (literally "martial Do person") refer to someone who walks the authentic Moo Do.

So what is Moo Do? This has been dealt with in numerous books since ancient times, and everyone is familiar with it. However, I have yet to hear anyone speak of a Moo Do Philosophy. Many people in the world regard Moo Do as nothing more than a style, method, or technique for fighting against an opponent. This idea is even found among martial arts practitioners. People have forgotten that the essence of Moo Do was originally to protect one's own precious life and by extension, a way to promote one's health and happiness through training. Instead, people package it to make money or learn it as a way to beat other people up. This isn't the "way," but rather the "way of evil."

My intention here is to make martial artists and ordinary people aware of the true identity of Moo Do so that it can be taught better. I would also like to encourage martial artists to reflect and become more aware, and by doing so, find something here of use in their everyday life. Moo Do in the true sense of the term means to not only train one's character, but also to strive in one's attitude and actions to serve and help others through personal sacrifice.

To explain this in more linguistic terms, the *moo* in Moo Do refers to actions to fight or defend externally, and at the same time to suppress the fight against one's opponent internally. Hence, moo is active and productive, or yang. The *do* (Do) in "Moo Do" is the source of Nature, replete with the absolute power and ability that created the myriad images, forms and entities of the universe. In other words, it is philosophy's mother-image, which gave birth to um and yang in the primal beginnings, and as such is the source of *mun*. The original meaning of *mun* was "pattern," which is now differentiated by putting the radical for "thread" to the left of the original character. The character eventually took on the meanings of culture and civilization (the patterns of society) and literature (patterns on paper). Traditionally, scholarly or cultured people were known as *munin*. Moo Do refers to the dual training in *mun* and *moo*. *Mun* is um while *moo* is yang, so Moo Do comprises the Do, um, and yang.

Moo begins with action and culminates in a doctrine of balance. And *moo*, being primarily focused on the physical, is external yang. The source of martial arts (*mooye*) is a person's innate defenses, while *Moo Do* is the expression of physical action that accords with the laws of balance as found in the basic principles of Nature.

Mun begins with study and culminates in theory. And *mun*, being primarily focused on the mental, is internal um. The source of *munhak* (academic study) is man's innate nature, the nature bestowed by Heaven, or individual nature. It is an expression of the philosophy of the image.

Moo Do Philosophy is based on pure natural philosophy. Though I have written much about the Do and Nature, I have chosen to call my book *Moo Do Philosophy* for three reasons. First, it is because this book has been written on the basis of ideas and experiences that I have undergone as I have lived out my life as a martial arts practitioner (*moodoin*). Second, it is because I have synthesized the features unique to Moo Do with the fundamental principles of Nature, transforming this synthesis into philosophy. Third, with the book I hope to contribute to the understanding of authentic Moo Do via philosophy—the basis of academic study. I would like to prevent the decline of the sacred Moo Do while stimulating the Moo Do spirit (which has been on the wane) and the morality and vitality of Moo Do practitioners. The book aims to promote awareness of true Moo Do and promote the development of students with a truly humane character.

Chapter 2

Sip Sam Seh and Moo Do Philosophy

Passage 1: Introduction

The *Song of the Sip Sam Seh* is only familiar within the Moo Do world, yet even here the number of those who don't know it probably exceeds that of those who do. I have included it here since it is a key philosophical element forming a basic condition in our everyday lives, and as such, is an important and inseparable key philosophical element in the realm of Moo Do as well.

The history of the term is as follows. If we take the number 8 from the eight trigrams and the number 5 from the five elements and combine them, we get the number 13 (*sip sam*). The final syllable *seh* (posture) has important significance as a term used in respect to the practice of martial arts. When added to the number 13, it gives us the term *Sip Sam Seh*.

The eight trigrams and five elements, the Sip Sam Seh, are so extensive, lofty, and full of philosophical import that I can only provide an overview here. To discuss the Sip Sam Seh in detail, one would have to explain numerous philosophical texts, beginning with the *Chou I* (*Book of Changes*). Here, I will try to provide an explanation of only the essential points of the Sip Sam Seh that form the core of Moo Do and are expressed in the *Song of the Sip Sam Seh*. Song lyrics or lines of poetry are often abstract and full of exaggeration and metaphorical impressions. For this reason, it is difficult for anyone other than the original writer to express the meaning accurately or completely. However, I have emphasized the Sip Sam Seh in this work because of the tendency of most modern men to place excessive importance on that possessing form and image while neglecting the formless and imageless.

The eight trigrams of the Sip Sam Seh indicate the directions and include the "Four Propers" and the "Four Corners." The Four Propers refer to accumulation, as in the accumulation of elements such as consciousness, sensations, etc., that make up a human being. The Four Corners refer to position. The Four Propers refer to the north, south, east, and west and the Four Corners to the northeast, southeast, northwest, and southwest. If the Four Propers are viewed from the perspective of physical position, the east is left, the west right, the south to the front, and the north to the back. Seen in terms of *shim gung* or spiritual training, the east corresponds to um, the west to yang, the south to equilibrium, and the north to ki. If the Four Corners are viewed from the perspective of physical position, the northeast is the diagonal direction to the left and back, the southeast to the left and front, the northwest to the right and back, and the southwest to the right and front. In terms of *shim gung*, the northeast corresponds to virtue, the southeast to force[12], the northwest to mind, and the southwest to action.

In Moo Do's hand strikes and *shim gung*:

1. The um of the Four Propers, as the um nature, corresponds to stillness.

2. The yang of the Four Propers, as the yang nature, corresponds to movement.

3. The equilibrium of the Four Propers, as balance, corresponds to fullness.

4. The ki of the Four Propers, as the atmosphere, corresponds to emptiness.

5. The virtue of the Four Corners, as morality, corresponds to the basis.

6. The heart of the Four Corners, as the rectified mind, corresponds to an honest mind of goodness.

7. The posture of the Four Corners, as correct carriage or proper posture, corresponds to one's autonomy or identity.

8. The action of the Four Corners, as a discipline, corresponds to

shim gung or actual practice.

The five elements are metal, wood, water, fire, and earth.

1. Straightness, which belongs to metal within the five elements, refers to honesty. It thus corresponds to stimulus.

2. *Hyo*, which belongs to wood within the five elements, refers to filial piety. It thus corresponds to reflex, reflection, and kindness.

3. Love, which belongs to water within the five elements, refers to love and respect. It thus corresponds to judgment.

4. Trustworthiness, which belongs to fire within the five elements, refers to faith, belief, and righteousness. It thus corresponds to distinction and discrimination.

5. Decisiveness, which belongs to earth within the five elements, refers to centeredness or stability. It therefore corresponds to the middle way's *bujungbyungjuhang*. *Bu*, in the term *bujungbyungjuhang*, means one should not do something; *jung* means to lean towards excesses; and, *byun* means to fall short. *Ju* means to maintain proper distance and refers to judgment and control. *Hang* signifies revolt and means that one should not go to great excesses. *Bujungbyungjuhang* means that one should do one's best not to be excessive or insufficient in all of one's thoughts and actions and should work to maintain adaptability and appropriateness.

The eight trigrams and five elements, the Sip Sam Seh are a basic element of the philosophy and practice of not just our particular way but of all Moo Do.

The Sip Sam Seh is a precursor to the development of our system, and so we need to investigate it deeply and extensively. The *Song of the Sip Sam Seh* is a lyrical composition praising the key points and core of the Sip Sam Seh. Below I will give a translation of the song, which was composed in classical Chinese.

Passage 2: The Song of the Thirteen Influences

十三세에 대한 노래가 있다. 원문 그대로 소개한다.

十三勢歌　十三勢總勢莫輕視　命意源頭在腰隙

變轉虛實須留意　氣遍身軀不小滯　靜中觸動動猶靜

因敵變化示神奇　勢勢揆心須用意　得來不覺費工夫

刻刻留心在腰間　腹內鬆淨氣騰然　尾閭中正神貫頂

滿身輕利頂頭懸　仔細留心向推求　屈伸開合聽自由

入門引路須口授　功夫無息法自休　若言體用何爲準

意氣君來骨肉臣　想推用意終何在　益壽延年不老春

歌分歌分百卅字　字字眞切義無遺　若不向此推求去

枉費工夫貽歎悟

Passage 3: Translation and Explication of the Song of the Sip Sam Seh (Thirteen Influences)

Translation: *Never neglect any of the Sip Sam Seh.*

One must not neglect any of the Sip Sam Seh. One should not take lightly any part of it and should instead regard it as important.

Translation: *The source of the will is in the waist.*

The basic starting point of establishing one's will is to take the head, which fundamentally forms the meaning and vitality of the Sip Sam Seh, and control one's waist so as to concentrate the power of ki.

Translation: *Pay attention to the slightest change from full to empty.*

One must definitely keep in mind the transformation and change of the empty and full. Explained in more detail, it means that one must always work to investigate the change and operation of emptiness and fullness, key elements to Moo Do.

Translation: *Let energy flow through the whole body continuously.*

If ki pervades one's whole body, there is not the slightest imprudence. Explained in detail, it means that if the force of ki evenly fills the entire body, one has no cause for worry; if one's mind and body are healthy and wholesome, one is able to live a happy life.

Translation: *Stillness embodies motion, motion stillness. Seek stillness in motion.*

This is similar to the statement "There is movement amidst stillness and stillness amidst movement." Translated literally, it means that within stability, one maintains movement, and even while moving, one maintains stability. This is an expression of a key aspect of Eastern philosophy.

Translation: *Surprising things will happen when you meet your opponent.*

One manifests change and the marvelous to one's opponent or the enemy. From the standpoint of Moo Do, it means that one employs stunning and novel techniques in response to the situation or to change in one's opponent or the enemy.

Translation: *Give awareness and purpose to every movement.*

In response to all poses, one activates the mind, establishing the will. In one's actions and thought, one must concentrate the mind and ki on the entire Sip Sam Seh and be in agreement with principle.

Translation: *When done correctly all will appear effortless.*

In mastering the Sip Sam Seh, if one practices with diligence over a long time, one can gain good results, coming to realize what one did not understand previously.

Translation: *At all times pay attention to the waist.*

One must concentrate one's mind on the waist every moment. More precisely, it means that when one performs a martial art, one must never forget to focus one's ki on the waist.

Translation: *Relaxed clear awareness of abdomen, the energy can be activated.*

If one extends and cleans the abdomen, ki naturally rises. If one appropriately controls the breath so that it is stable, the abdomen is purified and the ki force naturally becomes complete. It means to focus the will on the danjun.

Translation: *When the base of the spine is erect, energy rises to the top of the head.*

If one properly sets one's backbone in the center, one's consciousness extends up to one's crown. Put more simply, if one always correctly aligns one's spine, one's consciousness circulates up through one's neck to one's head, making the mind clear and promoting health.

Translation: *The body should be flexible. Hold the head as if suspended from a string.*

With the whole body cheerfully light and highly sensitive, one feels as if one is suspended from the crown of the head.

Translation: *Keep alert and seek the meaning and purpose of your art.*

One strives in the pursuit of the method, paying attention to even small details.

Translation: *Bent and stretched, open and closed, let nature take its course.*

One freely bends, extends, opens, and combines. By practicing the Sip Sam Seh martial arts, all of one's movements become free and unrestrained. This passage and the four preceding ones are related.

Translation: *Beginners are guided by oral teaching.*

When guiding the beginning student in the way (martial arts), one must use words to guide him.

Translation: *Gradually one applies himself more and more. Skill will take care of itself.*

If one practices and strives without taking breaks, the Sip Sam Seh practice will be learned naturally.

Translation: *What is the main principle of the martial arts?*

What will be your focus, the words or the body? Explained simply, this is asking where you should focus, which is on consciousness, energy, or the body.

Translation: *The mind is the primary actor and the body is the secondary one.*

Consciousness and the force of ki serve as the master when practicing the Sip Sam Seh. The bones and flesh of the body become the servants. This passage is connected with the one above.

Translation: *What is the purpose and philosophy behind the martial arts?*

Where do you think the ultimate significance of the Sip Sam Seh practice lies?

Translation: *Rejuvenation and prolonging of life beyond the normal span.*

It is in gradually extending one's life span, living a long and healthy life, not getting old, and always maintaining one's youth. This passage is connected with the one above.

Translation: *So an eternal spring.*

Let us sing, let us sing, the more than 150 characters. This means to always sing the Sip Sam Seh that is comprised of over 150 characters and cheerfully practice the spiritual dimension.

Translation: *Every word of this song has enormous value and importance.*

Each character true and frank, there are no mistakes in its meaning. This means that in the entire text of the Sip Sam Seh, nothing differs from the truth. It is all genuine without any mistakes to the correct meaning.

Translation: *Failing to follow this song attentively.*

If one does not make progress pursuing this or…put simply, this means if one does not pursue the true practice of the Sip Sam Seh,

Translation: *You will sigh away your time.*

If one wastes time for practice, one will have regrets. If one is lazy in one's practice or wastes time practicing in a flawed manner, in the end, one will be filled with regrets. This passage is connected with the previous two

Passage 4: The Five Elements and Eight Trigrams Comprising the Sip Sam Seh

In conclusion, the *Song of the Sip Sam Seh* contains the complete basic teachings of Moo Do. The Four Propers and Four Corners are methods based on the doctrine of the Sip Sam Seh. There are also the basic movements (forms) of the Sip Sam Seh, the basic training techniques and the *haenggongshimhae*. These represent further analysis and added descriptions of the contents of the *Song of the Sip*

Sam Seh. Since they are not so necessary in the practice of our art, they have been omitted here.

Composition of the Five Elements and Eight Trigrams Comprising the 13 Influences Described by the Song of the Sip Sam Seh.

Five Elements (Form)

earth	fire	water	wood	metal
decisiveness	trust	love	filial piety	straightforwardness
middle way	distinction	judgment	reflex	stimulus

Eight Trigrams (Formless)

Four Propers

north	south	west	east
back	front	right	left
ki	equilibrium	yang	um
empty	full	movement	stillness

Four Corners

southwest	southeast	northwest	northeast
right front	left front	right back	left back
action	force	mind	virtue
practice	master	force[12]	base

Passage 5: Rise of Munhak from the Standpoint of Philosophy

The origins of *mun* correspond with knowledge, while knowledge corresponds with *munhak*, the study of literature. During primitive times, *munhak* did not exist. People had feelings based on their innate instincts and then gradually developed intelligence. For a long span of time, knowledge was passed down through speech and oral traditions, but finally men developed writing. Initially, this consisted solely of symbols, but writing eventually developed into separate glyphs depicting animals and material objects. This eventually became more systematic so that grammar and sentences could be expressed. However, written script and literature have not existed for much more than five millennia.

Written literature has played an important role in maintaining man's position and sense of identity as the master of all things. Writing contributes to developments in history, philosophy, and literature itself, and in so doing, has made a decisive contribution to the development of human civilization. In other words, the development of writing was nothing less than a sweeping revolution for all mankind. Human intelligence and literature are intrinsically connected.

There are two types of human knowledge, *innate* and *acquired*. Lao Tzu and Chu-hsi, the leading figure in Chinese Neo-Confucianism, called innate knowledge "the luminous" (*myeong*) and acquired knowledge as simply "knowledge" (*ji*). The "luminous" or *innate* knowledge corresponds to innate nature and consists of instincts that cannot be altered through one's surroundings, habits, or education. Innate knowledge comprises the fundamental aspects of man that are unaffected by experience. In contrast, acquired knowledge (*ji*) emerges from acquired nature and is created by man. It may be altered or influenced by the environment, habits, and education. Thus knowledge or literature (*munhak*) has an inextricable connection with philosophy.

Knowledge (*ji*) and literature (*munhak*) are inner things, and as such, belong to um. Some people think that *mun* has a higher status and *moo* a lower status. This may be because in traditional Korea of the Yi Dynasty (1394-1910), among the ranks of the upper class (*yangban*), the government ministers who were classified as civilian scholar-officials were of higher status than the military officials. Yet it need not follow that moo has a lower status than *mun*. In our lives, we first decide to do something and then, based on this decision, we move our bodies to accomplish the task. This is simply an order of our everyday lives. There is no need to choose one aspect of the phenomenon as superior or inferior. Both innate and acquired characteristics help man to harmonize *moo* and *mun*.

Looking back on history, we can see many cases in which misfortune for countries and peoples resulted when there was excessive emphasis on either *mun* or *moo*. In severe cases, this excess caused some nations' downfalls because the extreme imbalance violated the basic principles of Nature. We must harmonize *um*, *yang*, *mun*, and *moo*, maintaining a balance so as to be able to enjoy a life characterized by health, happiness, peace, and freedom. This is the dual cultivation of *mun* and *moo* that I always advocate.

H. C. Hwang demonstrating a movement from the Moo Yei Do Bo Tong Ji with active physical characteristics.

Passage 6: The Rise of Moo Do as Seen from the Standpoint of Philosophy

I have come to a full understanding of Moo Do Philosophy and wish to share this philosophy. The first reason for undertaking this is that Moo Do contains a philosophical element. Second, it is because it is based on my own practical experience. Third, it is because it takes its form based upon philosophical concepts such as the eight trigrams and five elements of the *Sip Sam Seh*.

I would like to explain in concrete terms the character moo that occurs in the word Moo Do. The character for moo is a combination of the characters *gwa* and *ji*. *Gwa* means knife and *ji* means to stop. Put together, they mean to not use a knife. This explanation is familiar, and it has already been stated in my work *Soo Bahk Do Dae Kahm* and in other writings. At this point, one might object that this seems to be in disagreement with the meaning of *moo* (martial). This is because moo, is an expression of external action taken to preserve one's life from an attack, or on occasion, action in the form of a counterattack. For this reason, most people, when they hear the term moo think of attacking, punishing, or murdering an opponent through the use of violence and weapons such as knives or guns. The character moo, considered in isolation, means to not use a knife, but moo's essence is to defend one's life or to counterattack. The Chinese character moo therefore refers to physical techniques and forms used for defense and attack.

Next, I would like to talk about the *do* in Moo Do. Do, as mentioned previously, means path and is the fundamental principle of Nature and the source of all images and things. Since the Do is the source of the myriad images and concrete entities as well as philosophy, it necessarily serves as an important aspect of human consciousness and morality. If moo is viewed simply as a physical means or a technique used for defense, attack, and violence, it is degraded into something with no spiritual or moral value. Practiced in this way, it is clear that it would eventually result in man's downfall. The characters moo and do have thus been combined to form the term Moo Do, with the idea of preventing man's evil course towards self-destruction and encouraging people to train their bodies and minds so as to live happy, healthy, and peaceful lives. We must harmonize our physical bodies and spirits, as we harmonize um and yang.

Passage 7: History of Moo Do's Development

Back in the days when our ancestors possessed no weaponry, they had to fight with their bare hands. It is this fighting that has undergone development up until the present and can be classified as follows:

Dosu
    unregulated bare hands
Yu sool/jujitsu
    unregulated (no holds barred)
Yudo/judo
Other
    regulated - hapkido
    wrestling (highly regulated)
    boxing (regulated, competitive)
    clubs, spears
    swords, daggers, knives
    throwing techniques, archery, combined techniques
    technological, scientific weapons

East entrance to the side room of Anak Tomb No. 3 from the Koguryo Dynasty (37 B.C.E. - 668 C.E.) depicting figures engaged in Soo Bahk Ki (right side) (Kim, 2004).

The various barehanded fighting forms are all ancestors of Moo Do. The forms that have come down to us with gradual developments are *soo bahk, tang soo* and *kwon bup.* Jujitsu developed out of barehanded fighting, but it was dangerous to perform in everyday life. It was therefore developed into judo in Japan by making it more oriented to physical training so that it would appeal to the public at large. The various forms of hapkido appeared, employing twisting techniques. Wrestling actually began as a form of entertainment.

Eventually, objects were employed as weapons against aggressors. Initially these were very primitive, but they gradually developed to become the nuclear bomb used today. In using an external object, it is impossible to be completely self-dependent, and the fundamental issue remains unsolved. Countless numbers of external objects can be employed, but when the object is not available, one ends up being extremely vulnerable. An even bigger problem is that external objects owe their discovery to human consciousness and their use to the human body. Put another way, they cannot be useful for a human society in which men fail to maintain healthy spirits and bodies. If external objects are misused, they lead to misfortune.

Training to establish a balance among these factors is our calling on this earth, our duty, and our right. Sometimes people come up and ask me which is better, boxing or judo. I would like to ask such people where the true intent of their question lies. If such a person's question is to simply find out which is useful for conquering an enemy, I would like to tell him that the true significance of the training of our art does not lie in such an immature purpose. Its fundamental ideology is simply to train the mind and body. Defense against external enemies is not its fundamental significance; this is nothing more than a byproduct. Today, when the nuclear bomb is in existence and even greater weapons are in the works, people who go on and on about what works against external attacks must be seen as foolish. When we reflect on that fact that we created nuclear weapons, we must work to develop people who are truly human, training ourselves so that we can harness such forces as nuclear power to contribute to the happiness of mankind. Suffice it to say, that if someone asks such questions from the standpoint of training of the mind and body, I can explain from what I know as a specialist in this field.

Passage 8: Relationship between the Philosophies of Nature, Balance, Life, and Moo Do

Up to now I have discussed the philosophies of nature, balance, life, and Moo Do. It may help to think of the philosophies of nature and balance as existing within the realm of Nature, grounded in the basic principles of the Do and transcending the human world. The philosophies of life and Moo Do, on the other hand, fall within the realm of man. While the term *Do* is a symbol for the metaphysical, the latter two philosophies have a direct relationship to man and are centered on concrete issues in man's everyday life. In this sense, the four philosophies mentioned above may be divided into the metaphysical and the physical.

Yet the philosophies of nature, balance, man, and Moo Do all have their source in the philosophy of the Do. The philosophy of life is a general and all-pervasive field extending the principles of the Do to each class and sector of the entire human race, while Moo Do is an associated philosophy emphasizing that the goal and results of action control man's life. Moo Do's movements are to protect one's own life or to make a lethal attack on an opponent. This being the case, a *moodoin*, in addition to protecting his own life, must become a human being capable of recognizing the dignity and value of all life in the world. He must become a person who knows how to truly love nature and peace in accordance with the basic principles of the Do.

Passage 9: Theory of Change

The principles of the Do such as time and space and the neutral, um, and yang natures do not change. They remain the same eternally. But according to these unchanging principles of the Do, the world's myriad images and entities change constantly. The speed, method, and form of this change vary, but the myriad entities undergo ceaseless, interminable change. The world's myriad images and entities change and appear as phenomena in direct proportion to their material qualities and quantities. When night passes, day comes; with the passing of day comes night. Spring comes but soon gives way to summer, which then turns to fall. Such transformation occurs. This is the principle of Nature and is absolute.

There is nothing in this world, and surely not man, that is able to counter change or stop it. As a result, the stars, sun, and earth will definitely undergo destruction at some point, and it goes without saying that the myriad images and entities that exist upon the earth will undergo the same fate. We human beings will all die around a century after appearing from our mothers' wombs. It doesn't make any difference whether we are powerful, strong, or rich.

In accordance with the laws of change, even difficult things can be achieved through the steady application of effort, and even the long can become short through the speed of a moving force. That which is in front does not stay in front forever, but falls behind when superseded by something faster. Therefore, the sage does not go to one side of a pair of conflicting opposites. Instead, he resides in the realm of the natural Do, which serves as the basis for everything in the world. He does not seek to teach people by words only, but instead provides a silent example through his actions. The people of this world believe that the beautiful is always the beautiful, and the good always the good. However, when beauty, goodness, and power reach their peak, they decline, and after declining to their lowest point, ascend once again. This is according to the laws of Nature.

We should not fear change, but instead try to understand the principle. Moreover, imagination gives birth to actuality, while actuality gives birth to the imagination. As we will see, change is manifested through the stimulation, reflection, and repeated functioning of the imagination and the actual.

Chapter 3

Energy

Energy clearly exists in our world. It has an inextricable connection with all the myriad images, forms, and concrete entities of the universe. As such, it is a core element of our lives. I am of the opinion that the *mo che* of energy is clearly the Do. The reason I believe this to be so is that all things in this world are full of energy, and they have been produced from the Do. As mentioned previously, neutrality is the Do, and the Do gives birth to um and yang, and functions to rationally control and harmonize these forces, based on the necessary principles of Nature.

Within this scheme, um is stillness and yang is movement. The point to be observed here is that the fundamental quality or essence of yang is energy. Nothing in the universe is able to move without a source of energy. Even if movement would seem to be a substantial characteristic of something, natural law states that it will not move until the proper conditions, function, and stimulus are present.

Neutrality is neither um nor yang. Instead, it possesses a mandate to create balance, to make adjustments and centralize. Neutrality corresponds to the concepts of balance.

Um corresponds to stillness and possesses the distinguishing characteristic of eternally tending towards calm. It elicits its opposite (movement) while having an affinity for other um elements. However, it does not thereby create a synthesis.

Yang corresponds to movement and possesses the distinguishing characteristic of eternally tending towards movement. It elicits its opposite (stillness) and draws things towards movement. It has an affinity for other yang elements but does not thereby create a synthesis.

Consequently, um (stillness) and yang (movement) are not two opposing entities but rather have a positive tendency to harmonize. In this process, neutrality plays an intermediary role. According to the laws of Nature, as this harmonization occurs, heat (energy) is emitted, and there is an accompanying flash of light. This represents the origin of energy emission or its origin.

Through this phenomenon, the laws of balance are manifested, electricity is emitted, and there is an accompanying gravitational and magnetic force. All heat, the energy of the universe, is produced through such a process. This is the principle of Nature, and this is the great principle of the Do. All of Nature's myriad images, forms, and entities necessarily possess their respective attracting force. The relative strength of this force, known as gravity, is in direct proportion to an entity's mass. To state this more simply, all things have a gravitational pull. Um and yang also have this gravitational force, pulling on each other to make energy, which is the principle of Do. Therefore, Do is the source of energy. I define this energy as being innate ki.

Diagram from Soo Bahk Do Dae Kahm (*Hwang, 1970*).

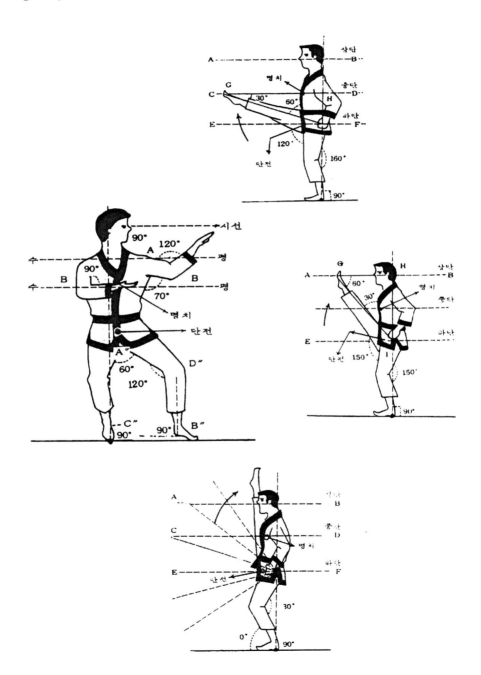

Chapter 4

What is Ki?

Chinese character for "ki" (also referred to as "qi," gi," or" chi")

We human beings often talk of ki. If we analyze the Chinese character for ki, we find that the top portion represents steam, that which exists but is not visible to the eye, has no form, and is empty. The lower portion is an element representing *mi*—the rice that human beings consume. The combination of these two elements forms the character for ki, which signifies power, force, or primal energy. In the terminology of physics, F=force, m=mass, and a=acceleration. Ki is energy, the force in the physics term F=ma. Force may in general terms be equated with power (the application of force over time), and then physical energy.

The character for ki is particularly common in the realms of Moo Do and Asian medicine. Moreover, the philosophical concept of ki as existing within the realm of nature refers to the natural and mysterious source of energy. In Korean, ki appears in many words dealing with energy, for example *kiun* (vigor), *ungi* (transport energy), *daegi* (the atmosphere, literally great ki), and *gonggi* (air, literally empty ki).

Lao Tzu's concept of ki is as follows. The term "desolation" refers to that state before ki has transformed into concrete entities, when things are in "the form of the formless" and "the image of the imageless" (see Chapter 14 in the *Tao Te Ching*). This is to say, *mu* is nothingness but it is from this nothingness that entities are produced. And although it exists, its form cannot be seen. "Ki is independent and unchanging." All things in the universe definitely die if ki leaves them, but even when these things disappear, ki itself is not affected at all. "It traverses universally without deficiency." This means there is no place where ki does not exist; no matter how big or small something is, it exists within the boundaries of ki. As a result, all things in the world are produced having *ki* as their source, and in this sense, ki is the mother of the cosmos or "all things under Heaven" (see Chapter 1 in the *Tao Te Ching*). Pure ki as it exists apart from things cannot be defined in terms of concepts, language, or writing. This is because when one defines something saying "This is that," one still has not defined the antithesis, "This is not that."

In other words, that with an image or form can be defined, but regarding that which is without form, no definitions can be given. If, for the sake of expediency, we artificially express *mu* through human concepts by words, we describe it as the Do, or as great, as ki or empty (see Chapter 25 in the *Tao Te Ching*).

If we describe the modern term "energy" in metaphysical terms, it is what Lao Tzu describes as the Tao, primal ki.

When this is described in physical terms, it is um and yang ki. Um, as stillness, is negative, whereas, yang, as movement, is positive. Moreover, the tension between um and yang ki does not represent a denial of the other or an antinomy, but rather a positive and harmonious relationship in which they support and supplement as they oppose one another. I repeat that the *mo che* of the celestial sphere is the Do. And the Do is totally neutral. Regarding this, it should be kept in mind that this world's principles demand that if two or more things are to last forever within a cooperative relationship, there must be regularity, order, and synchronicity among them.

That which mysteriously forms in a self-regulated manner from the stage of completely empty obscurity is neutrality, the Do, the central source or the central pivot. And this plays a rational, impartial, and ordering role as it mediates between um and yang, giving rise to their harmonization and transformation. It is from this harmonization that energy is produced. In other words, neutrality is the Do, and the Do, being neutral in nature, can also be called central ki or empty ki; it is eternal without limit, the enigmatic *musang* (imageless).

The universe's myriad images, forms, and entities are strong or weak, and have other such differences, but they all possess ki. The space within the universe is completely filled with ki, and this ki is eternally flowing along with time. Man is born into this world in innate possession of ki within his body. I call this *saenggi* (birth ki). This birth is a basic element of life. Man's body is comprised of gases, liquids, and solids. Man takes in *daegi* (great ki--the air in the atmosphere), food, and light, so as to maintain and preserve his life and his body. In this sense, air, food, and light are acquired ki, or fuel for the production of energy, which is absorbed into the body. Through the actions of the heart, these are harmonized and transformed into ki, and through the functioning of ki circulation are brought down to the *danjun*, where they are concentrated. The danjun is therefore the focal point of ki. I call this acquired yang ki.

The synthesis of innate birth ki and acquired yang ki is primal ki. It is what people generally refer to simply as ki. In the above explanation, I have explained ki—which is generally discussed in vague terms—in a philosophical, systematic, rational, concrete, simple, and logical manner. That which supervises and adjusts all the functioning and circulation of ki is the mind, and that which is transformed and produced through the spine is the refined ki or vitality. This vitality is the source of the production of life.

Since this issue is of the highest importance, I would like to reiterate it. Birth ki is the source of man's innate ability to maintain, preserve, and pass on life, but this, by itself, is not sufficient to sustain life. In the maintenance of life, the three essentials--brain, heart, and spine--each play a central role based on the functioning of natural birth ki. Air passes through the lungs to the heart, food passes through the stomach—the digestive organs—to the heart, which manifests heat as energy, which passes through the brain, which in turn rationally harmonizes the innate birth ki with the acquired yang ki. And that which is produced and transformed as a person's unique ki is controlled through the natural laws of balance descending into the *danjun*, where it is concentrated. And this forms what is commonly called ki or primal ki.

The electrical energy that appears due to the Do, the mysterious harmonization of Nature's um, neutral, and yang forces, is the source of energy. Mechanical energy is chiefly which is referred to as energy by science, while man's ki is the mysterious energy manifested according to the process discussed above.

Thus, the core elements controlling man's health and that most precious of all things, life, are the principles of the Do, the laws of balance, innate birth ki, the control and functioning of acquired yang ki, and ki circulation.

Chapter 5

Moo Do Practice Through Reflection on Principles of Do

Passage 1: Stimulus, Stillness, and Movement

I would like to set down a rational philosophical theory of the movements used by those training in Moo Do based on actual practice.

According to the fundamental principles of Nature, a stimulus is the starting point of action for the myriad forms and entities. There are stimuli related to the natural, the artificial, the image, and the material. Furthermore, there are internal and external, as well as mental and physical, stimuli. The movement towards the opposite, which necessarily occurs with stimuli, is essentially the same as the movement towards reversal mentioned previously.

In accordance with natural laws, within each stimulus, stillness and movement necessarily accompany each other so as to become the elements change and non-change.

The essence of stillness is always stillness: its original character is to eternally move towards stillness. Although stillness is unchanging, it manifests a movement inducing change. Since it leads that which is moving toward stillness, its stilling influence is, in a sense, inducing change and movement.

The essence of movement is always to move: its basic character is to always strive towards movement. In this sense, movement is always changing but has unchanging stillness as its proximate cause.

Giving is movement, receiving is stillness; hence, giving is yang and receiving is um. And due to giving and receiving, reflex and reaction occur, and so through giving and receiving, transformation is manifested.

Stimulus is the beginning point of the changing and the static, and it arises in accordance with the eight trigrams and five elements, the Sip Sam Seh. That which is stimulated is led from stillness towards movement. At the time of stimulus, it is stillness, but afterwards, movement appears. After movement arises, stillness returns. And once a stimulus is received, a reaction or reflex necessarily arises in accordance with natural law. Man makes good use of stimuli. When used in a rational manner, stimuli are used to create happiness; but when misused, they bring on misfortune.

The use of this reaction and reflex determines whether or not man is able to successfully complete a rational harmonization of luminosity, knowledge, and ability, as mentioned in Chapter 2, Passage 5 above. There is no doubt that the environment and experience exert an enormous influence on man; however, they are unable to reconstruct him, but instead, exert a significant influence.

Let me explain stimulus and reaction. When one senses something with the mind or via sensations, this first passes through one's center (one's subjectivity, sense of identity) on its way to one's innate nature and then goes back through one's center as it is outwardly expressed. Such a sequence represents sound action and movement that is natural, right, and conscientious. However, in certain circumstances, mental or physical sensations received externally do not pass through one's center or one's fundamental nature; or they are directly expressed outwardly without contact with one's internal fundamental mind; or they do not initially come in through one's center but instead are directly expressed as they make contact with only one's fundamental nature.

The important condition determining man's ability to manifest natural and sound action is whether or not he is able to correctly and accurately preserve his Heavenly-endowed innate nature. Man must strive to train and develop his basic nature. Furthermore, his ability to manifest his actions accurately, naturally, and in a sound manner is determined by the extent to which his center or sense of identity is righteous, conscientious, and in agreement with natural principles. This is to say that man, in his everyday life, must work to acquire and train himself in the rational, natural Do and virtue while perfecting his knowledge. Indiscriminate acts are immoral; as actions that violate the laws of balance, they will necessarily call forth misfortune. Discriminate actions, on the other hand, are moral. As actions in agreement with the natural and sound rules of balance, they will necessarily lead to happiness.

Stimulus, reaction, and balance are a direct, basic condition for the performance of martial arts. The detection of a stimulus and reaction immediately before the reception of that stimulus is defensive action in martial arts, whereas response immediately after receiving a stimulus is a counterattacking movement. And response directly before receiving a stimulus is frequently a direct attack in martial arts. The former is often internal while the latter is often external. The above actions are passive. Direct martial arts movements based on the manifestation of one's internal fundamental mind or knowledge are internal, active actions.

In martial arts, stimulus, reflex, and reaction become practical defensive measures. In martial arts, we therefore talk of the repeated and continuous stimulus and response, or of stimulus and reaction.

Furthermore, in terms of the performance of martial arts, those actions that manifest via one's internal basic nature or luminosity are generally sound, and when they are not, it is normally due to development or training. On the other hand, those actions that manifest according to external stimulus or the environment are generally abnormal, and when they are not, this is generally due to development or training. Therefore, in order to develop as a correct and authentic *moodoin*, we must strive to achieve a rational and balanced synthesis of internal and external actions in accordance with the fundamental principles of the Do.

Put in more simple terms, in our Moo Do training and movements, it is important to train rationally so as to harmonize stimulus, response, and change in accordance with the laws of Nature and balance.

Passage 2: Things that a Moodoin Should Maintain

I must stress once again that a necessary prerequisite for those training in Moo Do, or for that matter, for ordinary members of society as well, is a healthy and happy lifestyle. In order to protect, maintain, and pass on life, man possesses instincts and the ability to defend himself. This is called *mooye* or *Moo Do*. Since the martial arts implied by the term Moo Do have tremendously important repercussions on one's own life or on the life of one's opponent, this is an area that we must approach with great sincerity and care.

The true essence of moo is to come to the aid of those who are weak but are in the right, and to not take the side of those who are strong but evil. A person of moo lives a life of great principles—the authentic and greater significance of moo. This is a representation of the authentic *moodoin*.

As discussed in Section III, the mind is um, the spine is neutrality, the body represents yang. The mind corresponds to intellect, the spinal cord corresponds to balance, the body to Moo Do, to action. The brain corresponds to the mind; the spine corresponds to balance; and, the body to the heart. When these are viewed from the standpoint of general everyday life in Moo Do, they are the Three Essentials. Man's effort to develop habits and an environment supporting correct awareness and practice related to these Three Essentials is an absolute prerequisite to human health and happiness. The correlates and basis for developing these Three Essentials are: Right Mind, Right Composure, and Right Posture.

Right Mind is the mind being applied to spirit. Right Mind means having the correct attitude. Right Mind is expressed by the eyes.

Right Composure is composure of the spine being applied to balance. Right Composure refers to a center that is correct and firm. Right Composure is manifested in the spine.

Right Posture is posture being applied to the physical body. Right Posture refers to correct carriage. Right Posture is expressed by the waist.

The spine and balance are connected to the waist, the *huri*. The center of the waist is the spine, while the left and right represent um and yang. The center serves as the base point of centrifugal and centripetal force. For this reason, the power of Soo Bahk Do movements is derived from the *huri*. Man's spine is directly connected to a central pivot with the universe above and the earth below. For this reason, as one learns to perform the movements in Soo Bahk Do, beginning with the basic forms, one learns the principles and methods of opposing along with techniques employing stimulus and reaction, defense and counterattack, repetitions and changes between a number of forms, such as attacking and springing.

Furthermore, the Seven Essential Elements of health that are necessary to maintain and preserve human life are: spirit, balance, atmosphere, temperature, environment, food, and movement and stillness. The balancing and regulation of the physical body, in terms of the Seven Essential Elements, is called *un-gi* (ki movement) or *gigong* (ki circulating through the body).

Martial arts practice is required for the sake of *un-gi*. When the ki flows smoothly through the body, one enjoys disease-free health. When this happens, there are, in some cases, certain natural physical responses.

VI

PRACTICE OF MOO DO

MIND TRAINING

Chapter 1

Mind Training

Moo Do's distinguishing characteristic is that all theory and ideology must be accompanied by rational practice or action. Up to this point, the explanation of Moo Do has been chiefly centered on theory, thought, and philosophy. In this section, my discussion will be centered on actual practice, the essence of Moo Do.

The traditional form of this practice is today's Soo Bahk Do. It appears in ancient works such as the *Moo Yei Do Bo Tong Ji* (Martial Arts Diagrams General Record) and can be seen on the wall mural of Goguryo-era tombs from 1700 years ago. This term is the source for all later martial arts terms. For this reason, I have determined that Soo Bahk Do is most representative of Moo Do, and thus my discussion of the actual practice of Moo Do is chiefly centered on this art.

Soo Bahk Do consists of mind training, inner training, and outer training. Mind training is a method of training in which the mind and body are centered on one's spirit or consciousness. In inner training, the mind and body are centered on the internal organs. Outer training, on the other hand, is a method of training the mind and body centered on the external. These have been divided up artificially for the sake of instruction, but in actual practice, consciousness, internal organs, and the exterior all come together to form a human being.

As a microcosm of the universe, man has the spine, spirit and physical body. In other words, man practices the martial art Soo Bahk Do as neutrality, um, and yang. In accordance with natural principles, this practice naturally incorporates the corresponding centrality, stillness, and movement, as well the stimulus and reaction these engender. In addition, the practice also requires Right Mind, Right Posture, and Right Composure as necessary conditions.

The outer training has already been dealt with in the *Soo Bahk Do Dae Kham*, published in 1970 (Hwang, 1970). As for the inner training, I have already prepared a manuscript for a separate publication. For this reason, in the present work I will concentrate on mind training.

Breathing techniques and postures described and depicted in the Mu Yei Do Bo Tong Ji.

Passage 1: Mind Training (*Shim gung*)

The essence of mind training is the pure mind/heart. This consciousness or spirit is the source of all things relating to man. It is without limit and is pervasive, and its form does not appear to oneself or others. It is completely free. Naturally, there are enormous differences in the manner in which consciousness is manifested, depending on a person's innate nature and on their knowledge and ability.

Yet there are certain aspects that are the same regardless of person, place, or time. Consciousness does not violate the fundamental principles of the Do; it is in agreement with the laws of balance; it accords with luminosity; it agrees with the principles of virtue; and it is in accord with the Three Bonds (sovereign and subject, father and son, husband and wife) and the Five Relationships (closeness between father and child, loyalty between sovereign and minister, distinction between husband and wife, order of seniority between elders and younger people, and trust between friends). In general, consciousness can be understood in terms of the general themes of tradition, common sense, and principles.

Passage 2: The Significance of Mind Training

Mind training means to calm the mind within the body and perform training centered on consciousness and the nervous system by means of the mind's ki so as to promote mental health.

Passage 3: The Goal of Mind Training

The purpose of mind training is to establish and regulate the mind on the basis of training so as to stimulate spiritual development and thereby promote spiritual health.

Passage 4: Mind Training's Three Essential Elements and Great Necessities

Three Essential Elements

Right Mind (*jeongshim*)

Right Posture (*jeongja*)

Right Composure (*jeongjeong*)

Three Great Necessities

Mind Ki: the Do, virtue, and balance

Inner Ki: innate nature, (*bonsung*), instinct (*bonneung*), original defenses (*bonbang*)

Outer Ki: acquired nature, the external atmosphere, environment, movement/stillness

Passage 5: Man's Three Cognitions, Five Senses, and Seven Emotions

Man is born into the world in innate possession of the following:

The Three Cognitions—chiefly internal

Spiritual Cognition: spiritual awareness

Precognition: feeling or sense of something beforehand

Sixth Sense: unconscious feeling that arises naturally (intuition)

These are purely internal and refer to each person's imaginative capacity. People share these essential cognitions, but there are differences in the extent or nature of each person's abilities. These forms of cognition exert a major influence on philosophical thought.

Man is born in innate possession of the following five senses:

Vision: seeing with the eyes

Hearing: hearing sounds with the ears

Smell: smelling odors with nose

Taste: tasting food and other things with the mouth

Touch: sensation that occurs when external objects come into contact with the body.

These are related to the environment.

As man receives life at birth, he comes into innate possession of the following seven emotions:

The Seven Emotions—both internal and external

heui: joy

no: anger

bi: sadness

u: to be concerned or worried about something

gyung: surprise

gong: fear

sa: to seriously ponder something

When these Seven Emotions are excessively activated, they damage one's health, and in extreme cases, lead to illness. For this reason, one must be particularly cautious in one's daily life.

Some would say that the Three Cognitions, Five Senses, and Seven Emotions control man's life. But even though man is influenced by these, he should not allow himself to be controlled by them. To the contrary, man should be in control of them. After all, man is the master of all entities and is the microcosm of the universe, and if controlled by these things, man is sure to suffer breakdown or misfortune. Man is happy when he possesses the capacity, wisdom, and self-confidence to be in continuous control of himself in any situation that occurs anytime and in any place.

In addition to the qualities mentioned above, there are such qualities as good-heartedness, justice, hope, experience, bravery, spiritual cultivation, reading, and investigative effort that serve as the mind's nutriment.

Passage 6: Theory and Praxis of Mind Training

Mind training is chiefly concerned with the pure mind. The mind is the source of all human events and corresponds to virtue. In other words, one should properly speak of "the mind, which has its source in virtue." Virtue, on the other hand, corresponds to the Do.

Prior to this, I have explained a number of theoretical principles, including the Do, virtue, the principles of balance, and um and yang. These are all directly related to mind training, and in terms of content, are mind training. But no matter how good a certain philosophy, theory, or piece of academic writing may be, if the principles do not find their proper expression in our actions, they are of no value whatsoever. Just as the diamond is the most valuable and precious gem in the world, it must be carved and polished in order to display its exquisite luster. Only then is it able to truly function as a precious stone and be recognized by people as something of great value. The principle is thus the same: the natural, philosophical, and theoretical are put into direct practice in the form of training and development. The methods and procedure for this are called "mind training," and putting this mind training directly into action is called "mind training praxis." The training and praxis (discipline) serve as the two prerequisites necessary for maintaining a healthy spirit.

We find it difficult to do mind training, unify consciousness, and concentrate. This is because of the natural principle that notes that changes necessarily occur in time and the environment, and as they do, adaptive change also necessarily occurs in human consciousness and the body. During my time in various Western countries and during my long stay in America in particular, I have observed that people seem to have a very difficult time doing mind training or mentally concentrating. It goes without saying that there is little effort put into this, but there doesn't even seem to be much interest. For the most part, Western people seem to think that if a person is to become great, authentic effort towards a personal goal is more important than concentration.

The principle of the Do is one, but among humans who live within nature, there are those who follow this principle and those who oppose it. Man's instincts are based on nature, and as such are neutral in theory. But this does not hold true in man's everyday life. There seem to be many people with excessive greed who manifest a mind that runs counter to reason, and who try to act on such a mentality in an effort to satisfy their desires. In my view, this phenomenon appears in accordance with the laws of relativity with the manifestation of um and yang, which are produced by the Do. And this is in agreement with the principle of the relativity of good and evil that forms one of the most practical and important aspects of human life.

However, because we encounter instinctual desires as an actual aspect of our human fate, this is not to say that we should merely despair and lose hope, succumb to pessimism, or just allow anything to happen as it may. On the contrary, we must put forth all our effort to wisely and rationally harmonize these instincts in accordance with Nature and the principles of the Do, so as to develop a virtuous character. After all, human beings, as the spiritual head of all entities, have both the calling and the ability to induce these forces to work towards our happiness, peace, and freedom. I am completely confident that the way for us to wisely solve and deal positively with this important issue is the principle of the Do, the principle of balance, and Moo Do.

There are two basic rules for training and developing the spirit. One is the Accordance with Principle Method (*sullibup*), which involves following the fundamental principles of the Do in order to achieve mind training (*shim gung*). The other is the Opposition of Principle Method (*yungnibup*), involving situations in opposition to Nature's principles of balance.

The first method, as a practice of mind training that accords with the principles of Nature and the Do, is a natural and conscientious method that needs little additional explanation here. The Opposition of Principle Method, however, is problematic. Intuitively, we know that a theory or action running counter to the principles of Nature is not good. Yet in actual circumstances, such situations are unavoidable. When we reflect on the undeniable reality of that which runs counter to principle, we clearly need to face up to this honestly with cool judgment and discrimination. We must take it upon ourselves to bravely and sincerely thrust ourselves into adverse circumstances and directly feel, intuit, and experience the truth, essence, and fundamental character of adversity to principle. By doing so, we can come to a correct, accurate, and rational understanding of its essential nature and can thereby alter such circumstances in a positive manner in our actual lives and transform them so that they accord with principle.

This is the path toward realizing happiness, peace, health, and freedom in human life; it is the restoration of "accordance with principle" (sulli). This is the fundamental principle of battle expressed in the classical work *Sun Tzu: Military Methods*. If one wishes to vanquish one's opponent, one must first accurately understand both oneself and one's opponent. In short, this ability to deal with situations that involve opposition to principle is necessary as man works to perfect his character.

The practical method and praxis of development by which man goes beyond affective and theoretical knowledge and acquires this ability experientially is mind training. It is vitally important that we sincerely take an interest in mind training and put forth sincere efforts towards putting it into practice. The activity to rationally apply the law of balance, the principles of the Do, and the principles of calm and movement to the human body is Moo Do mind training, along with inner training and outer training.

Passage 7: The Five Levels of Mind Training and Praxis

There are five levels of mind training and praxis.

1. In the first level, one must make a sincere effort to acquire a complete understanding of the Do, space, time, um, neutrality, yang, balance, virtue, and philosophy. As a preparatory stage, this level is characterized by stillness.

2. The second level involves direct experience, grueling training, the training of fortitude, outer training, inner training, and training to overcome one's self. These are primarily active forms of training, and this level, as the stage when actual practice begins, is characterized by movement.

3. The third level is a stage of quiet practice aimed at calming the mind and removing all wandering thoughts. While pacifying the mind and body, one develops Right Mind, Right Posture, and Right Composure while avoiding all greed and excessive work. If one is overworked at this time, one needs to immediately recover with sufficient rest and adequate sleep. This level represents the beginning of still action.

4. During the fourth level, one calms the mind and practices

gigong, sometimes spelled "kigong" because it is a method for manipulating ki within the body and is used as a healing art in Korea and China. One "enters the mountains to practice," an idea that is associated with Buddhist monks, since most temples are in the mountains. One engages in practice without speaking so as to unify consciousness, and undertakes spiritual cultivation. At this time, reciting poetry and reading effective books are important. This is a process involving still action. And I would like to add that even though the fourth stage is associated with entering the mountains, the *gigong* technique, as the most important technique for training the mind, can be applied anywhere. There are numerous methods and types of *gigong*[13]. In the next section, I will introduce the light dregs technique (*yunsubup*) and unfolding ki technique (*pogi bup*), since these have a direct connection with mind training.

5. In the fifth level, there are special forms of training and spiritual cultivation such as the hundred-day prayer retreat (*baegil gi do*), fasting and prayer, meditation, and stage of non-self technique (*muagyung bup*). In actual practice, these techniques are quite difficult. For this reason, they are best practiced after a person has spent a long time in actual practice and has made good progress. These techniques are highly effective, but this should not lead one to think that a person without any general knowledge or experience is able to make use of them to achieve his goals. In fact, if practice of these techniques is undertaken too rashly, they can even have a negative effect. A practitioner undertaking training in these techniques must pay close attention to his own abilities and level, and be mindful of the proper time, place, and environment. It is best if the training is undertaken with much guidance from someone with direct experience or a more senior student.

Mind training begins with stillness, goes through movement, and back to stillness where it reaches its terminus.

Passage 8: Methods of Mind Training and Praxis

1. The silent thought technique (*mungyum haenggong bup*) is a training in which one first calms the mind and then establishes Right Mind, Right Posture, and Right Composure. One controls the breath and holds the body in a natural manner, free of tension. Dispelling all stray thoughts, one focuses on one's future objective. The training thus has an association with mind training, but for the main part, it is employed in specific circumstances to train the latent aspect of one's consciousness.

2. The consciousness unification technique (*jungshin tong-il bup*) means to unify or concentrate the mind into a single whole. The preparatory phase for this is the same as that of the technique mentioned above, but the concentration discussed here is different. The first type is the technique of concentrating the mind in order to attain a specific goal. The second is to simply bring together the refined ki of one's whole body and mind without any other objective. This technique is not designed for specific cases, or a particular time, place, or circumstance, but is characterized instead by purity, freedom, and naturalness. This method also forms a precondition for achieving the highest goal of mind training—the stage of non-self (Korean: *mua*, Sanskrit: *anatma*).

3. Fasting, prayer, and the hundred-day prayer retreat (*baegil gido*) are techniques by which one concentrates one's mind into a unified whole and prays for the achievement of a goal by relying on the power of another, a spirit or god. The concentration of prayer is to make one's mind come into unity with something outside oneself. The *baegil gido* gets its name from the hundred days (*baegil*) during which the technique is continuously practiced. Because the technique of fasting and prayer is performed without eating anything, special caution is necessary to avoid extremely adverse effects.

Something I would like to add at this point is that Westerners have a hard time understanding techniques such as silencing of thought, unification of consciousness, and meditation as they are practiced by

Eastern people. Instead of focusing on the more logical and formal aspects of the East, Westerners tend to emphasize the practical. They seem to continuously focus all their efforts and energies on definite objectives. In other words, they concentrate their minds upon the practical.

4. Meditation is to completely dispel all goals, wishes, obsessions, and stray thoughts one may have as a human being and reach the stage of the non-self. Many of the preparatory activities and attitudes necessary are the same as those needed in the previous techniques, and there may be differences in form depending on the time, place, environment, and person. When it comes to the principles involved, however, there is no difference. While maintaining one's body and mind in a natural manner, one allows the refined ki and mind to become empty. If one gently allows the eyes to relax in a natural and light manner, they will close of themselves. If this condition is maintained, one will initially enter the stage of no-thought no-imaginings. This condition is not achieved by anyone at any time or any place simply as a result of doing a certain amount of mind training. It is only possible after a great deal of time and sincere effort.

The complete, pure attainment of this condition is the stage of non-self. This is the highest goal of mind training. If one intends to recover the spirit within the human body, to discover the refined ki and the mind's purity, one should first establish one's mind, posture, and center, and sit in a meditation posture in a quiet room. Discarding all imaginings, one single-mindedly concentrates on the breath. Breathing forms the waves that carry the mind. As these waves gradually become calm, the mind likewise calms down. When this happens, it is like the clear surface of water that reflects all the images under Heaven.

If one keeps training using the breathing technique, one grows accustomed to it. The refined ki and spirit return to their natural state and the gates to human nature and luminosity open. After further mastery of the technique, one is able to harmonize the mind at will so that it accords with all things, and one thereby enters the state of no-thought no-imaginings. The mind as the "celestial sovereign" becomes very settled and the entire body follows course. One establishes one's intent to be fully aware and leaves behind all daydreaming, then closes one's eyes or shuts them half-way while staring at the tip of one's nose. If one then turns the light of the mind inward with all one's energy, a great light appears from within this darkness. The light disappears and then reappears countless times only to disappear again. At this point, one's body and mind become ecstatic. If one continues to practice, a form begins to take shape within this light, and even though one's body remains in the room, one possesses supernormal vision and supernormal hearing[14]. However, these are not the goal but just the beginning.

When the subtle brilliance amidst darkness becomes more stable, and as one continues to put effort towards training, a large screen appears within the mind and countless things begin to appear on this screen. At first, the form that appears on this screen cannot be distinguished due to the numerous other figures that become chaotically intermingled with it. But if one keeps practicing, something singular and clear can be discerned from amidst these forms. Continuing on from this point, one becomes aware that the thing one is looking for is mixed in with the multiplicity of forms. If one keeps practicing from this point, one develops, for the first time, foreknowledge, permeating vision, and "through-walls permeating vision," which is the ability to see past an obstruction. One is thereby able to know tomorrow's weather beforehand or know who will visit.

If one continues to practice, demons, tigers, beautiful maidens, and other images will appear and attempt to seduce the meditator or interfere with his practice. One must drive these away in order to reach the stage of completion.

In other words, through this practice, one becomes cognizant of the *samjae*—Heaven, Earth, and man—and looks down clearly at the *samsaeng*. Here, the term *samsaeng* refers to man's current life, the past, and the future. One passes through the various stages of training, the first of which corresponds to the five elements (golden cultivation training, wood test skill, water reception steel, fire entrance ledger, and earth ascending level[15]) and many more until one attains the recovered stage of purification[16]. One becomes able to see one's previous lives and see into the hearts of others[17]. Spiritual luminosity appears from within oneself, as do the demons. That which drives away demons is also one's self.

The Korean term used for purification, *kyejae*, helps to define the process. The character for *kye* is glossed as, "That which prevents suffering is *kye*," the prevention of misfortune or calamity. The character for *jae* is glossed as, "Cleansing the mind is *jae*," purification or cultivation of the mind. Thus, *kyejae* refers to the cultivation and practice of mind training that prevents illness and leads to a life of health, tranquility, and happiness.

5. *Yunsubup* and *pogi bup* are two techniques with a direct connection with mind training. *Yunsubup* is known as the light dregs technique and is used to correct certain conditions. There are a variety of human diseases that occur due to worsening of ki circulation as a result of mental discontent and chaotic change. These disorders are generally called *hwabyung* (fire disease). Since fire originally has the quality of rising, the mind ki—the cause of *hwabyung*, rises just as fire does. Diseases caused by this sort of deterioration of the mind ki cannot be cured through diet, medicine, internal medicine or surgery, medicinal liquors, or even simple inner practice (*neh gung*) or outer practice (*weh gung*). There are three methods that can cure such a disease: calming the mind, calming the body so as to bring back down the mind ki that has risen, and practice of the yunsubup.

The *yunsubup* or light dregs technique is used to bring the ascendant mind ki back down into the lower abdomen, legs and arms and thus regulate ki circulation and cure hwabyung. There are three stages in the practice of the *yunsubup*.

1. Preparatory Stage
   a) Straighten the spine.
   b) Relax, removing all tension from the torso.
   c) Sit in a meditation posture.
   d) Close the eyes.

    e) Calm the mind.

2. Actual Practice
    a) Visualize a mysterious elixir falling from heaven onto the top of your head.
    b) Visualize the mysterious effectiveness of this elixir as it permeates your head and infuses your entire body.
    c) Visualize the elixir gradually permeating your body from the head downward, into both shoulder and arms, into the chest, lungs, heart, liver, stomach, abdomen, lower body, sexual organs, all of the legs, the back side of the body, the spine, waist, and every part of the body. Visualize it cleansing the body of disease, toxins, and bad ki as it flows downward.

3. Results
    a) If you carry out this form of mind training several times in succession, you will feel as if there were a liquid remaining in one's lower body.
    b) If you grow proficient in this technique, you will smell a mysterious fragrance that is impossible to describe.
    c) You will be able to hear the sound of the visualized elixir as it flows down into the body.
    d) Your head will feel cool and refreshed.
    e) Your waist and legs will feel comfortable and warm.
    f) Pain and stiffness will disappear.
    g) You will feel ecstatic to the point that you are unaware of the body. You will reach a condition approaching the stage of non-self. You will become blissful.

Pogi bup is a special mind training technique associated with others, such as *sunshim gongbup* (pure mind technique) and *sangdaejuk haenggongbup* (relative training technique), that are used by experts to help cure other people. Many diseases occur due to rash mental or physical behavior, or due to irregularities in environment or diet. Because the mind controls the physical body, these illnesses can be cured using the three methods of calming the body and mind; having faith, unifying the mind, prayer; and the practice of the *pogi bup*. There are many people who suffer because they are unable to cure an illness by themselves. *Pogi bup* is when another capable and expert person cures the disease through ki.

The principles of *pogi bup* are in keeping with the Do. Ki flows from the strong to the weak, moving from areas of abundance to the areas of least concentration. Just as the universe is formed through the harmonization of um and yang, the natural movement to restore harmony that has been lost is based on the same principle. The practice of the *pogi bup* occurs as the fundamental ki from a person with an ample amount of mind ki and refined ki is absorbed into the body of the patient who has weak mind ki and weak refined ki. By supplementing the patient's ki, the patient's natural ability to cure himself is restored.

To practice the *pogi bup*, the ki donor must be conscious of the following techniques: the ki donor's mind is calm, honest, and conscientious; the donor's body is calm and neat; and the mind is focused without any stray thoughts. There are preparation and practice steps for both the ki donor and the ki recipient.

1. Preparatory Phase
    a) Preparatory phase for practitioner
        (1) must have complete faith
        (2) pure body
        (3) completely healthy mind
        (4) completely healthy body
        (5) complete removal of all miscellaneous thoughts
        (6) must not engage in any idle chatter whatsoever

    b) Preparatory phase for patient
        (1) calming of mind, honesty, conscientiousness
        (2) calming of body
        (3) meditation to unify consciousness
        (4) complete faith
        (5) complete removal of miscellaneous thoughts
        (6) must not engage in any idle chatter whatsoever

2. Actual Practice
    a) Method for practitioner

  (1) Use mainly the palms.

  (2) After preparatory phase is completed, take in great ki.

  (3) After inhalation, hold ki.

  (4) In some cases, care must be taken to not hurt nasal passages when breathing

  (5) After holding ki, circulate it.

  (6) After circulating it, expel it.

  (7) Rub palms together, making them warm.

  (8) Lightly touch diseased area or place hands just above area.

  (9) While beginning to breathe out, visualize one's abundance of mind ki and refined ki flowing out through one's palms into the body of the patient.

b) Practice for patient

  (1) After preparatory phase is completed, calm the mind and have firm faith in the practitioner's ability to heal the disease. Mentally prepare oneself to accept the mind ki and refined ki of the practitioner.

  (2) Faith of both the practitioner and patient must completely harmonize.

  (3) Only when this mutual faith is in full operation can the mind ki flow between practitioner and patient.

  (4) If complete faith and trust is lacking at this time or if the practitioner's and patient's minds are at odds, or if they engage in idle chatter, the transference of ki will not take place, and as a result, the disease will not be cured. In other words, both practitioner and patient, emptying their minds and abiding in the state of non-self, must have complete faith.

Chapter 2: Sun Do

In the East, one often hears the terms *sun* or *sun do*. *Sun* is also known as *shinsun* and s*un bi*. Korea is historically and traditionally very advanced in the practice known as *sun*. Since *sun do* has many points in common with Moo Do Philosophy, I would like to briefly explain some of its key points.

The character for *sun* consists of the radical for "person" on the left and the character for "mountain" on the right. *Sunin* means mountain person and refers to the Taoist school in which people clearly and sincerely cultivate the Do. In ancient times, there was an inextricable connection between *sunin* and mountains because the deep and remote mountains have fresh air and good water. It was therefore only natural that people would leave the secular world behind and seek out the natural environment of the mountains. Just as in Moo Do, the Do in *sun do* is the Korean pronunciation of the character for Tao.

Sun do is the path of cultivating the Do, and it refers to practice for the sake of *muwi* or non-action in the sense of spontaneous action without selfish motives and non-desire. There are many aspects of sunin and sun do that modern people find hard to accept.

Sunin train their hearts and minds while living a free lifestyle in their own particular manner within a natural environment. The method and form of their lifestyle varies according to person, and the way that they procure food, clothing, and lodging varies according to their environment, circumstances, and each person's individual character, but they all have some things in common. They all seek to live like people of primitive times, and they practice the Do and live their lives in agreement with the basic principles of Nature.

Sunin lives center upon the spirit rather than the body or other material aspects of life. Sunin describe the spirit as originating in Heaven, just as earlier chapters in this book have referred to man's innate nature and luminosity. For the sunin, the spirit is the source of everything having to do with man. It follows that since man's primal essence, primal drive, and primal spirit are the same as Heaven, these things represent man's Three Gems. Man's harmonization of these

Three Gems (primal essence, primal drive, and primal spirit) is called *gyung* (vigor); gyung refers to the body; and the body is believed to be free. These delineate a philosophy centered upon the self.

The renunciation of excessive instinctive desires, selfishness, and hatred and the practice of cultivating and training the mind and body are the principles of *sun do*. Man's freedom develops his essential force and enables him to unify mind and body. Within *sun do* training, there are three essential elements. The first is *jeongshim* (Right Mind), the second is *yunjin* (determination—literally, swallowing one's saliva), and the third is *heupyeol* (taking in heat) or *heupki* (taking in ki) and this refers to the *gigongbup* described in the previous chapter.

The first essential element, *jeongshim*, belongs to mind training. The second element, *yunjin*, and the third element, *heupyeol*, belong to inner training. Whereas in many sects, there is talk of human nature, the *sunin* tends to talk of *myung* or mandate of Heaven. And whereas many people advocate goodness, the sun school tries to awaken luminosity. In addition, breathing techniques and the "original image" technique are mysteriously combined to become the sun school's *myungmyungbup* (technique of expanding luminosity). Considered a secret transmission coming down via tradition, these principles and techniques could be called a Heavenly device.

Parts of these beliefs are contained in the following statements:

> *The mind is the lord of the body and the source of all things; therefore always be mindful of the mysterious gate constantly guarding one's honesty.*

> *One is sincere, without self-deceit.*

> *The joyous development of the celestial sovereign is the Way to be traversed by men.*

> *The ancients say the reward of good and evil is created and received by oneself. It is thus possible for man to take wickedness and evil and transform it into good. So shouldn't we transform evil into*

good?

Hell, full of cries, has no gate yet people struggle to enter. Heaven has a path to it but few people come. Is this not a great cause for concern and trepidation?

When encountering circumstances, one must deduce, through one's experience, that which is true and that which is false. It is possible to completely understand this on one's own.

So whether walking, standing, sitting, or lying down, everything must be rectified and made straight.

The *sun do* inner training is also practiced with bold determination. Ki techniques are continuously practiced with utmost sincerity. This is the great principle of the *sunin's* revitalization breathing. When this practice is brought to perfection so that one practices with the mind and body as a unity, one is able to do this in a superhuman manner, gathering together and blending the refined ki at will. This refers to the expelling of old, dirty ki and the breathing in of the fresh great ki.

While assuming a good posture, one begins to exert energy in the area of the *danjun* below the navel. In other words, one takes in a deep breath. One gathers the ki into the *danjun*, and then slowly expels the ki. The amount expelled must be less than that taken in. This is called the *danjun hoheupbup* (cinnabar field breathing technique) or the *yungibup* (training ki technique). When mastered more fully, the technique can develop into a variety of more advanced techniques, including *hwanjungbup* (transforming essence technique) and *taeshikbup* (fetal breathing technique).

In short, *sun do* is a method of training centered on mind training and inner training. In conclusion, Moo Do Philosophy and *sun do* naturally have much in common, and thus *sun do's* key points have been dealt with here.

VII

EDUCATION FOR

CHARACTER DEVELOPMENT

Chapter 1

Introduction

In addition to his innate nature, man needs knowledge in order to develop. I would like to discuss those aspects related to Moo Do that are necessary for man. The proper growth and development of acquired knowledge is an issue with direct implications for one's fate. Acquired knowledge comes from one's environment, experience, and academic learning. But the problem of knowledge as a spiritual issue is limitless.

A poignant example is provided by the mother of Mencius, the famous Chinese philosopher and interpreter of Confucius. Although she lived as a widow, she moved three times in order to provide her son with an education that would make him fully human. Mencius thus rose to become one of the great philosophers of ancient China through the efforts and utmost sincerity of his mother. Among the expressions to come down to us from the past, we find reference to habit as the "second endowment," a reference to that which one receives in addition to one's fundamental nature as endowed by Heaven. Mencius's mother did what she did so that her son would acquire good habits, or a "second endowment."

Why is an acquired intellectual education necessary? For man to live a natural, happy, and peaceful life, it would seem to be unnecessary. But in reality this is not so. Due to excessive desires and a desire for unnatural material things, man ends up creating misfortune for himself. He pollutes the precious atmosphere and water and creates terrifying technological weapons, which not only harm man but threaten life on the entire planet. Today, man is rashly seeking his own destruction without a hint of remorse or conscience. It is hoped that man, based on his intellectual civilization, will immediately cease his violation of the principles of Nature, return to the proper Do where he can live a natural life, and eventually return to nature (pass away) with dignity.

In other words, living in accordance with the laws of balance is man's shortcut to happiness. When it comes to acquired education, it is important to research more ideal and beneficial ways to conduct family, societal, and school education. However, the issue that takes precedence over this is the development of an authentic and conscientious humane character in possession of the Do, the true intellectual virtue that is grounded in the fundamental principles of Nature.

According to Lao Tzu, true knowledge is automatically aware of virtue and goodness and completely comprehends the Do. In order to acquire this sort of true knowledge, one must properly understand that the Do—the good-heartedness and fundamental nature of things—lies within (see Chapter 19, *Tao Te Ching*). In our quest for authentic knowledge, we must not get caught up in the evil and unnaturalness that lies on the exterior of things. The more we look for knowledge on the outside, the more our knowledge tends to veer off into unnaturalness or evil. Lao Tzu also said that we must arrive at true knowing by being aware of the limits of knowledge and transcending judgments. Lao Tzu calls the arrival at true knowledge "ignorance," but it is clear that this "ignorance" that Lao Tzu advocates so strongly does not refer to a state of stupidity in which one does not know anything.

Judgments that are formed through perception are called knowledge. Man's perception can only grasp visible phenomena. For this reason, if we obstinately insist on solely those judgments made via perception, we are unable to fully comprehend the Do. It follows that the first step towards authentic knowledge is the realization of the limits of knowledge. I believe that the life of all things in the universe is brought forth from the Do, and among these things, only man is self-aware. It is because of knowledge that man can speak of good and evil in regard to instincts. I have been discussing this concept of knowledge by means of the ethics expounded by Lao Tzu.

Chapter 2

Virtue

In Korea, we often hear people talk of *dodeok*. What does this term mean? Do is the fundamental principle of Nature and the source of the world's myriad images and entities. *Deok* is the *mo che* of Nature and the human manifestation of the Do as fundamental principles. The Do of pure Nature is without limit, eternal and vast, the image of transcendent purity, fair and impartial, willing to sacrifice itself for others. But *deok* is grounded in man and therefore cannot play a role like that of the pure Do of Nature. All we can do is work towards this ideal. After all, if we view man from a realistic standpoint, we must concede that he has instincts, and these become the starting point for all problems in human society. To put this all another way, *dodeok* refers to the human character in complete possession of the Do.

Regardless of the outstanding qualities a person possesses, if he does not work to train and develop his mind and body and strive to acquire knowledge and virtue, he cannot become a truly human person, a person of greatness. If you choose a particular country, and then select ten people at random, eight or nine might be great. It might seem to follow then that the country in question, with such a large number of people of good character, will be the greatest nation, but this is not in fact the case. This makes sense from the standpoint that whatever is common in the world becomes cheap, whereas that which is uncommon comes to have value.

People of true ability in this world do not show off or pretend to know. But people who lack ability or have very little of it—those who are empty like a balloon—often show off and put on airs. I wish that the world had a few less superior people and more inferior ones. By "inferior" person, I mean people of character who had true ability instead of vain pride and show, people who were humble instead of showy, people who could take a cool look within and see themselves accurately and could play their proper role in society. In our everyday lives, we must live in a conscientious and ordinary way, have good manners, and know how to yield to others. We must know how to serve others and have a sense of sacrifice that allows us to live with others without selfishly inflicting harm on them.

What I would like to especially stress here is that these characteristics are not simply to be understood or verbally parroted forth—we must develop the habit of putting them into actual practice. In the end, a happy, healthy, and free society is the path that is best for each one of us. If we take a cold look at our current situation, we see many people who advocate individualism or freedom, thinking "Why should I sustain a loss and forgo gains?" "I have grown up on my own with dignity; why should I humble myself before others with no consideration of benefit?" This is egotism and libertinism. People who think like this do not understand the true meaning of individualism and freedom. Seeking to live their lives according to their whims, they seek the temporary and small benefit, ignorant of the greater benefit. For this reason, such people never manage to become great; they are never able to take off the mask of the petty man.

Here, the term "great man" is the wise man of virtue who lives in accord with Nature, the sage. He is inwardly wise and outwardly regal. As a sage, he is benign. The term "petty man" refers to a person who takes life, who violates the Heavenly ethic, who denies the maintenance and continuation of life, who deceives his conscience, who lies, is not straightforward, and does not keep promises, who is lazy, who brings on fear, hunger, and disease, and who steals.

At the moment when man is born, he is a completely natural entity, totally innocent and undefiled by this world. He is a sacred entity with a pure mind who transcends good and evil. Beginning as that which is imageless, man acquires form before reverting back into the formless. This is to say man is born of Nature, lives naturally, and then returns to Nature. This phenomenon is described as "Coming empty-handed, leaving empty-handed," or as "returning to the One." As the offspring of God, one goes back to God. This is natural law. It is absolutely impartial, applicable to all.

Once we are born into this world, the question of how we are to live is the most important and pressing. The main point is to "live naturally." This seems simple and clear, but in actual practice it is the most difficult and complex question. There is a saying, "When a tiger dies it leaves its hide, whereas a man leaves his accumulated deeds." Man, living his life in a natural manner, creates a legacy in accordance with his Heaven-given nature, and it is this that he leaves to the world when he passes away. In creating a legacy, it is better to create a good one than a bad one, and better to leave a formless one than one with form.

Historical legacies possessing form include the ruins of ancient Greece and Rome, the palaces and Great Wall of China, and other such monumental remains. Yet only the frameworks of the ancient Greek buildings still stand and the elaborate palaces of ancient China have completely disappeared. On the other hand, the formless legacies, such as Lao Tzu's philosophy of the Tao, Confucius's philosophy of human-heartedness, Shakyamuni's philosophy of compassion, Christianity's philosophy of love, Socrates' philosophic methods, and Newton's principle of gravity, are perennial legacies for all time.

The greatness of a legacy is determined by the extent to which it represents a sacrifice of one's self for the good of others. As man attempts to live his life in an authentic manner, the most important role is played by instinct and virtue. The extent to which man's consciousness is defiled or pure is determined by the training of his instincts and the extent of his virtue. Man is the lord of all things. To be lord in this sense means to be a true guide to all life in this world. For this reason, it is important that man leaves behind a great legacy when he dies. Although man may surpass animals in terms of intellect, when it comes to the principles of Nature, he is far behind. This is because he fails to live a life according to the principles of the Do.

Man cannot live through consciousness alone, nor can he live solely with the human body. The right Do is for man to walk the path of the middle way in which spirit and body are in a harmonious balance. This is in accord with the myriad things that are formed through the rational harmonization of um and yang. This path allows man to enjoy good health and acquire practical skills. In order to help others, we must possess health and ability. In order to help others, we must avoid being deficient ourselves. Yet often, we have infinite greed. We desire to do well and become wealthy irrespective of how others do. In attempting to live well, we hurt others. Needless to say, this violates the principles of the Do and virtue.

It is impossible for us to live by ourselves in this world. People, no matter who they are, want happiness, peace, and long life. And the opposite is also true; everyone fears famine, hates terror, and suffers when sick. If these three things could be eliminated, human society would be happy and cheerful. Imagine for a moment that we achieved perfection. Since there would then be no further room for progress, this would mark the end, after which we could only decline. This is, after all, the principle of the Do. The wise solution is for man to train and cultivate his body and mind in accordance with the principles of balance found in Nature. If we are mindful of the Three Essentials discussed earlier and the Three Esoterica outlined below, we may attain lives of virtue.

Three Essentials
  Right Mind: brain
  Right Posture: heart
  Right Composure: spine

Three Esoterica

  Three "No"s
    No Hunger
    No Fear: stillness
    No Disease

  Three Moderates
    Sexual Desire
    Material Desire: centrality, balance
    Desire to be Superior

  Three Practices
    Mind Training
    Inner Training: yang, movement
    Outer Training

There are three additional keys to daily life. The first is reflection. Reflection is truly one of the absolute conditions necessary for human improvement. No matter when we do something, it naturally forms part of our experience. Some things make us happy, others we regret. There will always be something we did out of ulterior motives. We therefore need to reflect on the past, looking at it objectively as a mirror. As we do so, we can strive to improve ourselves by repeating that which we have done well in the past and by not repeating our mistakes.

The second is judgment. As we directly encounter things in our lives, it is important that we intuitively judge, from an objective standpoint, whether something is right or wrong. If we decide things in a rash and blind manner, we will definitely fall into error and bring calamity upon ourselves.

Third is discrimination. This rational analysis takes the judgment mentioned above and decides whether or not it should be carried out, if it is possible to carry it out, and if acted upon, how it is to be done.

For these elements to have a proper direction and effective results, the following three basic conditions must be met. First is *dodeok*, virtue that accords with the fundamental principles of nature. Second is ethics, the principles to naturally be carried out as a human being in accordance with natural principle. Third is a true mind of goodness, balancing man's subjectivity and instincts so as to moderate desires. We must put all our efforts into actual experience, spiritual cultivation and development, and education. This is not achieved through power, money, position, fame, or mere slogans. It is only completed through the middle way in accordance with the philosophy of balance. It can only be realized through Moo Do philosophy based on the most precious of all things in the world—human happiness, health, freedom, tranquility, and Nature.

Chapter 3

Man's Mind is God

Does God exist? If God does exist, it is the mind of the Do and myself. The Do is the basic *mo che* of all the world's myriad images and things. In this sense, my mind is God. God is my mind. God can do whatever he wishes with anything in this world. And God is known to reject evil and praise goodness. In other words, God is believed to be able to solve at will those problems that man cannot deal with. Yet it must be remembered that man has a special ability, the ability to awaken. For this reason, man, if he single-mindedly applies all his energies to a task, will definitely accomplish it at some point. The human mind is without limitation and absolutely possesses all capabilities, so if man has firm determination, he can definitely succeed in whatever he sets out to do. For this reason, man's mind is equivalent to God.

Man is identified with God in being able to do all things. This does not mean that man, with godlike capabilities, is able to accomplish anything without training and effort. For man to be like a god, he must be in accord with the fundamental principles of Nature with truly good intentions. He must engage in sincere efforts and continuous investigation of discipline in action (praxis), experience, and training in order to develop his intellect and sincerity. At the same time, these efforts must be accompanied by accurate judgment regarding beliefs, focus, good, and evil, in accordance with the laws of Nature. When these things form a proper synthesis, man can use his birthright, his ability, to be spiritually awake to naturally overcome space and time.

Modern people often say, "Try and you will succeed." This is equivalent to what has been said thus far about the mind being God. However, this must never be taken to mean that we will succeed in all our goals simply by repeating certain slogans, or through power, position, wealth, or coercion, or that we can reach our goals via temporary enthusiasm, lies, unjust attitudes and motives, sly stratagems, or unnatural behavior. The reality of our world clearly indicates that these things do not work. Such unnaturalness does not achieve anything; it merely contributes to social evils in the form of immorality, chaos, and disorder. It has no value, does not achieve its objectives, and brings misfortune upon one's self.

Chapter 4

The Do that Avoids Both Extremes

In his discussion of concrete things, Lao Tzu refers to the transcendent inner entity. Lao Tzu and Chuang Tzu described how the various entities of the world tend towards polar opposition and are thereby in an antithetical relationship. These two philosophers felt that if we pick up one side of an argument and insist that we are right, we end up falling into a contradiction (see Chapter 2, *Tao Te Ching*). They therefore advocated adhering to neutrality, the middle way based on the way of the Do. In the Taoist school, this is called "the technique of forgetting the two and adopting the center" (*mangyang yongjung bup*).

Chapter 5

Do as the Function of Mu

In philosophy, we often hear mention of the terms *che* (essence) and *yong* (function). *Che* refers to fundamental essence, while *yong* refers to phenomena perceivable by man. However, Lao Tzu employs the word *yong* to mean "use." Lao Tzu frequently employs the word *li* (benefit, profit, or advantage) to discuss existence (for example, in chapters 8, 11, 19, 36, 53, 56, 57, 73, and 81 in the *Tao Te Ching*). Yet he uses *yong* to discuss non-existence, or *mu*. Thus, according to Lao Tzu, existence is profitable but non-existence is useful (see Chapter 11 especially). The people of the world understand those things that appear before their eyes, but do not understand the use of non-existence, which lies hidden in the background. In the Confucian school, the Do and ki are seen in terms of existence and fullness, whereas the Taoist school sees Do and ki in terms of non-existence and emptiness. The Confucian school advocates *yuwi* (action), whereas the Taoist school advocates *muwi* (non-action).

How can we understand non-action as useful? This term *muwi* is translated in various ways. Although it literally means "not doing," it does not really signify "doing nothing" but rather refers to a type of action that is natural and is not based on selfish desires. The Taoist school even takes this a step further and says, "By doing nothing, nothing is left undone." When the Taoist school mentions study, it also refers to it in the conventional sense, claiming that academic study means to acquire knowledge whereas the way of Do is to daily remove knowledge. By constantly dispensing with knowledge, one arrives at the point of completely understanding the Do's essence. The Do's essence, being the source of all things, "Does not act but leaves nothing undone." In other words, non-existence becomes the function of existence. This also applies to the middle way. For example, good and evil represent two extremes, but the middle way is the source. The middle represents the world prior to manifestation, whereas harmonization occurs within the phenomenal realm.

Chapter 6

Virtue as Generator of the Generated

A related concept refers to the phenomenon of the transformation of things. The content of the concept "transformation" is that existence is comprised of concrete entities, whereas non-existence is comprised of ki. The passage from existence to non-existence occurs as a concrete entity transforms into ki, whereas the passage from non-existence to existence occurs as ki becomes a concrete entity. Virtue transforms things by means of the principle of harmony. Therefore, the generation of the generator is called the Do; and the generator of generation is called virtue.

The work known as the *Doctrine of the Mean* (*jungyong*) is a synthesis of the philosophies of Confucius, Mencius, Lao Tzu, and Chuang Tzu by anonymous Confucian scholars, compiled during the Chin and Han periods. Harmonization (*hwa*) does not refer to a synthesis of things that are identical. The concepts of harmony and identity are distinct. When we speak of harmonization, we do not refer to a mutually negative, contradictory relationship, but rather to a positive harmonization of a contradiction. In simpler terms, A does not negate B, and B does not negate A. Rather, both A and B negate themselves to form a mutual harmony, bringing C into being. As mentioned before, Do is indeterminate ki, one is the transformation of ki from the Do, two is um and yang ki, and three is the empty ki produced from um and yang ki (see Chapter 21 of the *Tao Te Ching*). The highest principle governing the myriad things of the universe is that when they arrive at their highest point, they necessarily descend.

Chapter 7

Theory of Intuition

As we observe things, there are basically two reactions. We can ask questions of existence, such as, "What is it?" or "How is it that it exists?" Or we can ask questions dealing with becoming, such as, "What becomes?" "How does it become?" In academic terminology, the former path of inquiry is that of ontology, while the latter deals with origination philosophy. The former is the main interest of Western philosophy, while Eastern philosophy is chiefly interested in the latter. The former is best represented by Plato's philosophy, which perceives the actual essence of things to be fixed, and the latter is best represented by the thought of Lao Tzu, who perceives things as being in flux. The former sees reality as possessing form. Although its essence cannot be perceived via the senses, it can be completely understood through thought. It thus forms the ground of perception. In the latter system of thought, reality is always moving. It cannot be known via the senses but it can be felt. It thus forms the ground of intuition. The things we can know or intuit are merely phenomena— not the actual essence.

We must ask, "What is knowledge?" "What is intuition?" The Western philosopher Immanuel Kant defined the relationship between intuition, knowledge, and reason and said that intuition synthesizes the material provided by the senses, and the understanding synthesizes intuition, creating experience. Reason synthesizes empirical judgments so as to create metaphysical knowledge. However, Kant set a limit, saying that man was unable to know "things in themselves" (*Ding an sich*). Lao Tzu, in contrast, said that by eliminating acquired knowledge, one could know the Do. The things that we can know and intuit are only those forms and activities that occur within the phenomenal realm.

Chapter 8

The Image as the Object of Intuition

Intuition is a form of knowing. Whenever we observe an object, two mental functions come into play. One of these alters nature so as to create an abstract concept. The other takes the image in its primal form, directly intuiting it. This intuiting function requires an objective entity. In other words, intuition occurs between a subject, which intuits, and an object, which is intuited. The goal of intuition is simply to be sincere and objective. The issue is to find out what the object of intuition is. Lao Tzu said it was the formless form, the imageless image.

"Form" refers to the appearance of entities whereas "image" refers to its behavior. This being the case, for every object, there is a form and image that we may intuit. The Korean word for intuition, *jikgwan*, literally means direct (*jik*) seeing or observation (*gwan*). In the word *gwansan*, *gwan* means observation while *sang* refers to a movement. *Gwansang* means to intuit the movements and changes of an object. The "study of the changes," as in the *Chou I*, is a kind of philosophy of intuition, or a philosophy of *gwansang*. A phenomenal entity must transform before it moves, and must move before it takes on form. Image, used in this sense, is the object of intuition in the philosophies of Lao Tzu and Chuang Tzu and in the philosophy of change set forth in the *Book of Changes* (*Chou I*).

I have stated that the object of intuition (*jikgwan*) is movement (*sang*) in Taoist philosophy. As it works its objective, intuition has a "discarding of form" function, by which we do not pay attention to an object's outward characteristics when we observe it. Intuition also has an "adoption of the image" function, which refers to the attention towards an object's movement or direction. "Adoption of the image" as it pertains to the movements of an individual object is called *dansun chwisang* (simple adoption of image). We may also intuit common movement among multiple objects. This movement that encompasses numerous movements is called general movement. When adoption of the image is carried out regarding general movements, this is known as *bokhap chwisang* (complex adoption of image). Examples of this include the observation that all things are fluid in nature, that living things must die, or the observation that all things come into being, grow, go into decline, and then are destroyed. With the above in mind, it is clear that intuition must involve both discarding of form and adoption of the image. This is because we are unable to directly see the true image of an object if it is distinguished as a spatial phenomenon.

Chapter 9

Limitations of Intuition

Objects that are beyond the range of the senses cannot serve as the object of intuition. For example, the Do is unimaginable, is without image or form, and is devoid of artificial striving (*muwi*), hence, it transcends intuition and knowing. As a result, it cannot become the object of knowledge, let alone intuition.

Chapter 10

View of Man

Confucius and Mencius did not view man in terms of God or Nature. They simply wanted man to be truly human. They emphasized the realities of everyday life. According to their thought, man is to be developed into the superior man, someone who is inwardly wise and outwardly regal. Inwardly, such a man is like a sage and outwardly is seen to possess the character befitting a king.

Neither did Lao Tzu and Chuang Tzu see man in terms of God. They had a natural view of man. They want to transform man through ki. The central aspect of ki is emptiness. As touched on previously, the virtue they advocated does not require that man be true to the self; rather it is empty, vacuous ki. In this respect, the views of man in the Confucian and Taoist schools differ. In short, the human ideal in the Confucian school is positive, while that of the Taoist school is negative. In the Taoist view of man, man appears from ki at birth in the same manner as the four seasons in accordance with natural law and is later transformed back into ki at death.

Chapter 11

Human Types

According to the chapter entitled "All Under Heaven" in the *Chuang Tzu*, men are of five types. The first is the Heaven-man who never departs from the Do—the ancestor of all things. The second is the spirit-man who never departs from the refined ki of the Do. The third is the superior man who never leaves the truth of the Do. The fourth is the sage who regards Heaven, Virtue, and the Do as a foundation, a basis and a gate and thus obeys the laws of change. The fifth is the regal man (*gunja*, also translated as superior man in the Confucian *Analects*), who bestows kindness upon the people through benevolence, righteousness, rites, and music.

The first type of person, the Heaven-man or authentic man. has achieved the highest stage of unity with Heaven. The second type, the spirit-man, has not achieved the level of the authentic man but has been transformed by ki. The third type, the superior man, does not have the attainment of the spirit man but has within his heart the logos underlying the transformations of Heaven and Earth. The fourth type of person, the sage, regards Heaven as his foundation, virtue as his basis, and the Do as his gate and accords with nature in matters of right and wrong or birth and death. The fifth type of person, the regal man, is said to show kindness to the people through benevolence, righteousness, rites, and music. But if anyone regards Heaven as their foundation, virtue as their basis, and the Do as a gate and harmonizes with change, he can achieve any of these levels. The authentic man, spirit man, superior man, sage, and princely man are nothing more than artificial designations of people according to the respective level of their character.

Chapter 12

The Way to Become a Natural Person

I have stated that the goal of the Taoist school is to have man be natural. How, then, is man to become natural? This is done by discarding knowledge and emotions, reducing desires, and transcending birth and death.

The first method to be employed by man when seeking to become natural is removing knowledge. As touched on before, in the Taoist school the technique for arriving at the highest stage of knowledge—also known as stage of Heaven and Earth—is to discard knowledge. This is because knowledge, contrary to what one would expect, actually serves as a hindrance to our attaining a complete understanding of things. The result of discarding knowledge is natural ignorance. However, this ignorance is an ignorance that comes after knowledge and is therefore very different from the ignorance of the caveman.

Lao Tzu, in reference to politics, spoke of an *umin jungchaek* (literally, "foolish people policy"). This does not mean to engage in foolhardy governance of the nation's citizens. Rather, it means that the politicians, in their governance of the nation and the people, should not resort to stratagems and schemes but should instead govern with virtue so that the people become good human beings and, consequently, support the nation and follow its leaders of their own accord. This is to say, there is a knowledge lying within ignorance, which forgets preconceived notions regarding facts and values, and grasps the Do as the source of things.

In the "Discussion on Making All Things Equal" chapter of the *Chuang Tzu*, it is written that when the debate is over, true and false become overly precise, the Do is obscured, and contrary to what is intended, one's words end up giving rise to contradiction. This problem occurs when things are viewed from a limited perspective. Seen from a high and unlimited perspective, there is nothing so great in itself; everything is relative. Thus, truth is not eternal truth, falsity is not eternal falsity. And if there is the true, there will definitely be the false; where there's right, there is sure to be wrong. True knowledge, the knowledge of ignorance, is obtained only after one has transcended discriminations of true and false or right and wrong. This is the method of making all things equal.

The second method is the elimination of emotion. In the Taoist school, the method of mastering the stage of Heaven and Earth is to eliminate emotions. In his discussion of the elimination of human stimuli and emotions, Chuang Tzu wrote that when we talk of form it makes sense to speak of human form, but when it comes to emotions, we should not look for "human emotions." Instead, we should strive for non-emotion, meaning "great emotion" or *daejung*. We should not harm the body with feelings of like and dislike. Instead, we simply entrust ourselves to Nature and experience emotions that transcend the limited perspective of the ego. Our minds should not be ensnared by feelings of pain and pleasure.

The third method is the reduction of desire. Man's desires are unlimited, but the material goods of this world are limited in nature. If our unlimited desires get out of hand, they become unbalanced with respect to the limited material goods, and this leads to unnatural consequences, which bring misfortune in their wake.

The fourth method is transcendence of birth and death. To attain the highest stage of the Do, one must transcend birth and death. Man's death and life are nothing more than natural phenomena based on the laws of nature; they cannot be altered through the power of man. From the standpoint of the Do, the arising of the Do is birth and the entering of the Do is death. According to the "Discussion on Making All Things Equal" chapter, man's life arises like Heaven and becomes one with the myriad things. So, even though man's body dies, his life does not disappear. Man's life is nothing more than alterations in ki. It is only when man does not get caught up in notions of birth and death and personally realizes that these are nothing more than transformations in ki that he can become a Heaven-man, who has realized the stage of unity between Heaven and man.

Returning to the question of "What is it?" versus "What becomes?"

we find that in philosophy, one can exclusively take up existence and discard becoming, or alternatively, take up becoming and discard existence. In the former case, transforming substances are brought into the realm of knowledge where they are made into abstract concepts and defined in a fixed manner. Even the fundamental essence of the universe is seen as a fixed entity. In the latter case, transforming entities are brought into the realm of sensation where they are perceived as "images" (patterns of behavior) prior to their becoming knowledge; and their pure behavior is extended into a continuum so that even the essence of the universe is seen as a production that is in flux—the imageless image of Lao Tzu.

It is clear, then, that to grasp things as fixed entities, the faculty of knowing is naturally required. On the other hand, to grasp things as a fluid becoming, the faculty of intuition is required. As I suggested early in the book with my arguments as to why the egg precedes the chicken, my explanations are centered on the doctrine of becoming. Some scholars distinguish between existence and that which exists. They say that the field of study dealing with that which exists is science, and the field dealing with existence itself is philosophy. Existence is said to be manifested through time.

The ancient Chinese philosopher Lieh Tzu divided things up into production and the produced. Regarding production and change, he said that there was the born and the non-born, and the transforming and non-transforming. He furthermore said that the non-born can give birth to the born, and the non-transforming can transform the transforming. He said that production itself can produce entities, the produced, while transformation itself can transform entities, the transformed. He called the producer "the unfathomable and solitary" and the non-transforming "returning." These two spirits, which never died, were called the mysterious female. These formed the root of Heaven and Earth. It seems to continuously endure, and is never exhausted no matter how much it is used (see Chapter 6 in the *Tao Te Ching*). In this way, that which gives birth to things is not born. That which changes things does not change.

Chapter 13

Explanation of Vitality

The manifestation of human life is vitality. Moo Do is the path that man must walk in order to maintain and pass on life in accordance with the principles of Nature. The martial moo in Moo Do signifies vitality, and vitality is moo—the manifestation of a truly human life. What then is true moo or true vitality? *Moo* is capable of controlling all humans and life, but it does not take life but instead revitalizes things. In Moo Do, *do* is the source, and pertains to the physical body, activity, and technique.

Chapter 14

Guidance for Training in Soo Bahk Do

Passage 1: Introduction

The goal of training is vitality. In other words, it does not stop at being able to attack or defend, but extends to life. Even if someone is an enemy, the goal is to keep him alive. Based on the principles of Nature, we establish the following pointers in order to achieve the objective of vitality. Emphasizing beauty, goodness, and speed, the following contributes to scientific training.

Passage 2: The Ten Articles of Faith of Martial Virtue

Below are listed the "10 Articles" with an explanation of how they pertain to martial virtue, Soo Bahk Do, and training.

1. Loyalty to country

   Based on the spirit of the ancient Silla knights, we are committed to the great principles of the nation and the people.

In ancient times, one was loyal to one's sovereign. In our modern democratic society, we all receive benefits from the nation, but people rarely have a sense of gratitude. We should therefore be thankful to our nation, and out of gratitude, we should be willing to sacrifice ourselves for the sake of our country.

2. Filial piety between parents and children

   Children serve their parents with filial respect; parents cherish their children.

This is an issue involving the logos of Nature. As a matter of course, children should repay their parents' kindness with filial devotion. In ancient times, only filial piety towards parents was stressed; parents' love towards children was not emphasized. Parents' love of children is such a natural and innate ethic that it was apparently viewed as needing no mention. However, this is not necessarily the way children see it. To counter this one-sided tendency, in modern times, stress has been placed on the importance of the loving words and actions of the parents. Love, used in this sense, is distinct from romantic love, referring instead to compassion. More important than words, is that the parents serve as good examples and models of behavior.

3. Feelings of love between husband and wife

   The two sexes harmonize through affection and love, becoming the mo che for the happy development of mankind.

A married couple, coming from different families with no blood relationship, must join their two bodies into one whole. To do so, they must form a harmony based on sexual fidelity and romantic attraction. By doing so, they can create a happy household and a harmonious and happy family and contribute to a sound basis for the happiness of mankind. The husband and wife must always remain aware that their relationship is the foundation for the life of the household and society.

4. Mutual cooperation between siblings

   Siblings stand united in the spirit of mutual cooperation and harmony.

Born of the same womb, siblings have a natural blood relationship, which cannot be sundered under any conditions. Because of this, they mutually cooperate and aid each other for mutual benefit, so as to become a significant force for the development of happiness.

5. Respect and protection of old and young

   One acts with respect and humility, and protects the just cause of the weak.

The elderly, in so far as their strength allows, must make use of their past experience to protect and develop the young. After all, the young are the pillars of our future. The young, on the other hand, must be courteous and humble, and sincerely respect the elderly as they become lonely and weak. As they do all they can to help them, out of an attitude of true respect, our society will become full of joy.

6. Loyalty between teacher and disciple

One learns truth through a sense of righteousness.

This means the teacher, with a sincere mind, develops the disciple, doing all he can do to ensure that his disciple becomes a truly humane person. This training of the disciple's character and body will enable him to be active as a good and able worker in society, so that he can contribute to making our society into a good place to live. The student, for his part, feels gratitude and a sense of indebtedness to the teacher who, though originally a stranger, has created a personal connection with him, helping him develop his character, intelligence, and skill so as to live in a dignified manner.

7. Trust between friends

Through a sense of trust and harmony between not only friends but all of mankind, there is peace and happiness.

The reality is that we cannot make it through life by ourselves and must, therefore, always have a social nature. Our associations with people should always be based on a sense of honesty and trust. A lack of trust will prevent a relationship from lasting long and eventually lead to unhappiness. The closer a friendship becomes, the harder it is to maintain without honesty, civility, and trust. When these things are missing, society tends to become corrupt.

8. Discrimination in the taking of life

One distinguishes between right and wrong in a just and fair manner.

In our lives, we must always appeal to our own good conscience, judging fairly and justly between what is truly right and wrong.

Human virtue, character development, refinement, and independence must definitely be part of this process. This is one of the five precepts of the knights of Korea's Silla kingdom.

9. When advancing into battle, one does not retreat

    Able and brave, one sacrifices oneself for righteousness.

Meaning that one must never turn back once battle has been enjoined, this is one of the five precepts of the knights of Korea's Silla kingdom. The true meaning of this is that, when engaged in training the mind and body, we must abide by higher principles of just and noble action while manifesting a humane character, ability, and righteous courage. It does not mean to rashly fly into battle without caution when there are clearly fatal hazards and no chance of surviving.

10. Definitely put things into actual practice

    With a sense of hope, one definitely carries things out in practice.

This means that no matter how good an opinion or theory may be it is of no value whatsoever if it is not carried out in practice. For this reason, in any undertaking, effective achievements are only realized when one does not stop at mere consideration or words but instead takes positive action. Of course, this action still needs to be accompanied by reflection, judgment, and discrimination, and must reflect true character, virtue, experience, spiritual development, refinement, and conscientiousness. In particular, I would like to point out the need for sound theory and sound praxis (discipline) as necessary components of Moo Do.

Passage 4: Main Elements of Soo Bahk Do Training and Points of Emphasis

1. Five Key Elements and Points of Emphasis in Mental Training
    a) Elements
        (1) contact with nature

(2) environment
(3) experience
(4) conscientiousness
(5) educational refinement/culture

b) Points of Emphasis
   (1)   love and protection of nature
   (2)   ki pressure
   (3)   propriety
   (4)   humility
   (5)   gratitude
   (6)   sacrifice
   (7)   courageous cultivation
   (8)   sexual faithfulness
   (9)   inner strength and outer flexibility
   (10) patience
   (11) love of reading

2. Five Key Elements and Ten Points of Emphasis of Physical Training
  a) Elements
     (1)   contact with nature
     (2)   environment
     (3)   appropriate nutrition
     (4)   appropriate exercise
     (5)   appropriate rest

  b) Points of Emphasis
     (1)   ki pressure
     (2)   gaze
     (3)   movement from center to center
     (4)   expansion and retraction of body
     (5)   strength and weakness of force
     (6)   tempo of ki
     (7)   precision of ki
     (8)   adjustment of distance
     (9)   breathing technique
     (10) training techniques of hands and feet

Passage 5: Emphasis on Cultivation of the Way over Physical Technique

Most people know Soo Bahk Do as the weaponless weapon, as a fierce method of barehanded attack used to overwhelm an opponent during a sudden, violent assault. When abused, this is extremely dangerous, but it is of great value when used for the good. For this reason, in the training of our art, much emphasis is put on mental/spiritual training. However, there are some lesser-informed people who take up training thinking that the only way to make improvement is to use their training in actual fighting. They make pretentious statements that the training has value only if it enables them to win in fights. Such attitudes are truly regrettable. Anyone studying Soo Bahk Do should emphasize its spiritual aspects over its technical aspects.

Passage 6: Points of Caution when Practicing Soo Bahk Do.

1. The goal should be true training of mind and body.

When first learning, it is nice to have hope, expectations, and aspirations. However, if these feelings become too blind and excessive, with the student thinking that he will somehow learn to brilliantly defend himself against all attacks within the span of two or three months, he generally does not last even a month, let alone two or three. This makes perfect sense, since the student's expectations are not realistic. Nothing in this world is attained so easily, and if it were, it would be of no value whatsoever. Therefore, pass through the first gate of practice with an empty heart, without excessive ambition.

2. The need for sincerity

It is said that, "Sincerity moves Heaven." But sincerity goes beyond this. Through sincerity alone, one can do anything. In other words, forget all your stray thoughts and practice with all your energy.

3. Need for effort

Even a precious diamond will not shine until it has been polished. No matter how much you like this art, if you do not practice hard, you won't be able to realize its value. With this in mind, you should strive with full effort, overcoming all difficulties, until you achieve your goal.

4. Need to see things through from beginning to end

This means to maintain your initial goals, hopes, and courage to the end. If you do so, you are sure to achieve your objectives. As you continuously put things into practice, you will need great courage as you encounter difficulties that others are unaware of. To make it through adverse circumstances and difficulties, even to find time within your busy schedule and overcome the cold, heat, and feelings of laziness, requires extraordinary courage. Steadfastness in the face of such adversity is true courage. Yelling in a loud voice, boasting, violent acts born of conceit, and like actions are not courage.

5. Need for training with fundamental spirit of Soo Bahk Do

Although this hardly needs to be reiterated here, it must always be kept in mind that it is the person who understands the true spirit of the Do and practices day in and day out with techniques and training that reflect this fundamental spirit who achieves rapid progress and well-ordered development.

6. Regular practice

This refers to continuous, everyday practice, but since it isn't possible to devote every minute of the day to practicing, it is important to set a fixed time for it. Through regular practice, it is possible to achieve good results in each area, and the development of such good habits are sure to have positive effects on other areas of life as well.

7. Listen to what your teacher and senior students say and learn from watching.

Your teacher and senior students, by definition, have a great deal of experience. You should actively seek to learn by observing how they do things as well as from their theoretical knowledge. This will be a great benefit to your practice. Although you might feel that you are more aware of your strong points and faults than anyone else, there is a great deal that is unconscious. For this reason, it helps your progress to have the teacher and senior students aid in the development of your strong points and, especially, to fix mistakes as soon as possible so as to assure your effective development.

8. *Do not be impatient for results*

No one forgets completely about results or does not hope for them. You must realize that if you don't dwell on them and practice with sincerity, results will naturally be forthcoming. Impatient for results in the beginning, people sometimes overdo things in practice until they injure themselves. Their enthusiasm then tends to wane as they are often unable to keep it up. In the end, they are unable to achieve their objectives. Even during their practice, they are so impatient for results that they are unable to focus on their movements. In an attempt to achieve something beyond them, they end up achieving nothing. So do not be impatient. Through steadfast practice, you will make progress step by step.

9. *Unique strengths and weaknesses*

Just as everyone has unique facial features, they develop special techniques in accordance with their body type and physique as well as the extent and type of training they have undergone. Even so, this is not something that beginners should be overly concerned with, but is rather an issue to be taken up after some time has passed. If you have strong arms and therefore concentrate on arm movements to the exclusion of all else, you will be unable to properly carry out the movements and develop your body in the proper way. This does not agree with the basic principles of our art. Of course, while training in all areas, certain skills become particularly developed. It is perfectly reasonable that you will naturally discover certain unique strengths in accordance with your particular body type and interests and seek to employ these.

10. Order of practice

During practice, we find some things difficult and other things to be easy. We should therefore practice steadily in a set sequence, starting from what is easy and moving towards what is difficult, from the simple to the complex and from the big to the small.

11. Teaching method for new forms or new techniques

When learning a new form or new technique from one's teacher or a senior student, you must adopt an earnest attitude and fully understand the major points. You should not approach it superficially (what is called "licking the outside of the watermelon"), thinking that you just need to move your hands or feet a certain way. For example, when learning a new form, you divide it into two phases: initially you learn the easier aspects and then gradually move on to the more precise elements, paying attention to posture, the method of exerting force, tempo of the technique, expansion and contraction of the body, visual line of sight, breathing, and so on. Having acquired the essential aspects of the form, all that is left, is to repeatedly practice it. All training techniques can all be acquired in this manner.

12. Method of overcoming laziness

Although this usually doesn't become a major issue, it is of vital importance. Laziness is not something that is intentional or due to a lack of sincerity, but is simply a phenomenon that naturally arises after a certain amount of time has passed. The first thing you must do to overcome this phenomenon, which occurs from time to time, is firmly establish habits of practice. And most important of all, you have to take interest in what you're doing. Without this, the final goal can never be reached.

13. Need for cleanliness after practice

I would like to particularly point this out as an issue that needs attention following practice sessions. If you relax and are not careful following a grueling practice session, it is easy to catch a cold. For someone without direct experience, it is hard to imagine how important it is to keep one's body clean and pure after practice and take proper rest. The body does not develop during activity or exercise but while taking adequate rest afterwards. Anyone interested in health and physical condition should be aware of this, and not focus exclusively on exercise periods. You need to always remind yourself that the period afterwards is even more important.

VIII

PERSONAL REFLECTIONS

Chapter 1

Lao Tzu's Political Philosophy

Below I will take a look at the political thought of Lao Tzu and other Taoists. These philosophers classified political rule into four types. The most ideal type was when the sovereign ruled the people through natural non-action (*muwi*), resulting in people not knowing if the sovereign existed or not. The second was when the sovereign ruled through virtue and was therefore loved by the people. The third was when the sovereign ruled through laws and punishments and the people therefore feared and despised him. The fourth was when the sovereign lost the trust of the people and the people therefore no longer had faith in him and did not obey him. The greatest ruler is said to teach without words, letting things be self-regulating. He speaks with gravity and never says anything flippantly. Under his rule, when the common people succeed in their work, they think, "We have done it all by ourselves." It should also be mentioned that politics is frequently mentioned in the *Lao Tzu* text (the Do *Te Ching*). I believe that this was in response to the political and social chaos of the time.

Lao Tzu and the Taoist school took non-aggression (*bujaeng*) as their political ideology. They regarded *ki* as that which is supremely flexible and weak and believed it was attained through emptiness. *Ki*, in this context, referred to power. The Taoist school thus regarded the power of non-aggression as the basis of politics. By being flexible and weak, the *ki* they spoke of was able to overcome that which is strong. In conventional terms, politics means power. In other words, politics, as normally conceived, is inseparable from conflict and struggle, and so it is believed that one can win in politics only through aggression. With this is mind, there is the notion that whoever wins is just; whoever loses is branded a rebel. However, power is not synonymous with struggle and conflict. When it comes to power, there is the power of aggression, but there is also the power of non-aggression. Moreover, victories achieved through unjust aggression lead to misfortune. This is because aggression is not a principle of the Do. Confucian thinkers, beginning with Confucius himself, viewed *ki* as being supremely great and strong, and so believed it appeared with the accumulation of righteousness. As the ideals of sagehood, knowledge, benevolence, righteousness, and talent became increasingly stressed, the Confucian thinkers gradually forced man into an unnatural state where he was mechanical, as if a slave to virtue. In spite of their objection to this tendency, the Taoist school does not say that one should not be benevolent or righteous or that one should not acquire knowledge. They simply stated that in a world in which the great Do was in operation, these things would not be necessary. They advocated the philosopher-rule approach by one who is inwardly a sage and outwardly a king. In other words, a king who carries out a natural rule of non-action (*muwi*) for the sake of the people, edifying them without words, so that the people only know that he exists, but regard him as completely unconnected to their lives. In short, since this type of rule is non-authoritarian, the people do not feel any pressure. In the "rule of the wise sovereign," the sovereign, unable to rule through natural non-action and uplift the people without words, carries out a benign government of action (*yuwi*). In the case of the sovereign who rules with laws and regulations and uses authoritarian measures to rule the people, the people fear and avoid him. When the sovereign cannot even rule the people through laws and regulations but must resort to so-called "wisdom," tricks, and stratagems, the people no longer obey his commands and look down at him with distrust.

During the non-acting (*muwi*) rule of the philosopher-ruler, an ideal society is formed as the people break free from their delusions and all their erroneous desires for property, power, and fame. The people living in such a society can enjoy happiness, but they do not play a central role. In this respect, Lao Tzu emphasized the tremendously important mission of the philosopher-ruler. The people loved the ruler but did not see him as the architect of the ideal society. In fact, the country prospered to the extent that people did not understand him. Lao Tzu put forward a policy of keeping the people ignorant (*umin ujungchaek*). During the ensuing Chen and Han kingdoms, this ideal was used as the theoretical background for authoritarian rule, but this was not really the political concept as envisioned by Lao Tzu. This represents nothing more than a misappropriation of the idea. I would agree that the phrase *umin jeongchaek*, understood literally, means "making the common people foolish, powerless, and ignorant so that the ruler can rule in an authoritarian, dictatorial manner as he wishes." Of course, this ideal, understood in this way, can be applied to benign dictatorships. But Lao Tzu's true intention was something quite different. Lao Tzu was saying that as the amount of knowledge grew, instead of being put to good use it became misused due to greed arising from man's instincts, and this could harm both the country and its people. People should therefore undertake spiritual cultivation to gradually forget what they already know until they arrive, through ignorance, at the stage of non-action and non-desire and thereby become people of nature. In short, Lao Tzu's political philosophy can be summarized as non-action, non-desire, and non-aggression based on the concept of *umin ujungchaek* "a rule that makes the people foolish." I have no objections to the overall political philosophy stated above, but in order to give my personal political thought, I will need to add a few things.

Chapter 2

My Political Philosophy

The ensuing discussion of politics will not be conducted from the standpoint of the government or political science, but instead will treat the subject from a philosophical perspective. As mentioned before, man is the ruler of the myriad entities. As such, he is the strongest entity in this world. For this reason, there is nothing that can attack human beings. But in the real world, this isn't always the case. Authority and those who occupy positions of authority exist (and must necessarily exist) for the sake of the people. Even so, history is full of examples of people who seize power and then conspire against political foes, arresting, suppressing, and killing them. At times, they go so far as to slay their relatives and family members. When all is as it should be, those in authority are the servants of the people, but often rulers use the people to further their own individual ends and enslave them. In modern times, there is another issue, namely, material goods. Material goods are nothing more than extra items useful to us as we live our lives. And there is a worsening trend for man, the lord of all things, to be the slave of money—something created by man to avoid the complexity and inconvenience of carrying around large objects.

Born naturally into this world at the head of all things, man has become a virtual slave to money. In this way, money and power are increasing usurping man's position of spiritual leadership. In the world today, we see people murdering and robbing others for money. Some of these cases even involve the murder of spouses or parents! This is truly regrettable. We need to accurately understand human beings and the fundamental essence of life, recovering our identity so as to return as quickly as possible to a natural lifestyle. This is, after all, the law of balance found in Nature.

I would now like to take a look at Korea's early modern history. During the five centuries of the Yi Dynasty, there were some periods of good government, but bad government was more common. Let's look at a few examples. First, there were many cases in which the sovereign or ministers performed acts violating the natural order so as to seize power. Second, there is the example of government, caught up in a bureaucratic mentality that ignored the common people. In other words, human dignity, value, and ability were evaluated on the basis of bureaucratic rank. This pernicious habit of mind is still present, even today. As a result, the problem of corruption among public officials is still a major social issue. Until Korea, or any other country for that matter, puts an end to unjust bureaucratic cronyism, it will be difficult to establish true democracy.

At some point during the Yi Dynasty, a system of fixed aristocratic classes known as the *yangban* was put into effect. This naturally gave birth to a corresponding underclass. This system is reminiscent of the system of slavery in effect in America at the time of its founding. It is a mystery why the rulers of a cultured people like the Koreans, who boast a 5000-year history, would choose such an immature, primitive, and shameful system. Even up to the time when I was young, this immoral and inhumane system existed. Fortunately, it has completely disappeared.

Personally, I think that the true meaning of the term *yangban* (nobleman) refers to the balance between both (*yang*) sides (*ban*) of phenomena. Seen in this way, a true *yangban* is someone who possesses both virtue and character. This is someone whose spiritual development is complete, and who has completely trained their body. Such a person of character, possessing a healthy physique, has established a balance between *mun* (academic learning) and *mu* (martial training). The *yangban* system may have originally been established with the vision of creating such people to contribute to the advancement of the nation. But its original intention was perhaps distorted as rulers, ministers and other leaders sought to manipulate the system and misuse authority for their own personal benefit. Of course, this interpretation of the term *yangban* is based solely on my own speculation.

I am not a politician and am not engaged in political work. My intention here is simply to discuss political ideas from the standpoint of philosophy and virtue. Even when I was young, the trip from Seoul, the capital of Korea, to Tokyo in Japan took two or three days. But since 20 or 30 years ago, it has been possible to eat breakfast in Seoul and lunch in Tokyo, and it won't be long before we find ourselves eating breakfast in Seoul and lunch in New York. As progress continues unabated, we will someday approach the era of space travel.

In the future, even though man's knowledge and science make infinite advances, we will never be able to ignore the principles of Nature, the Do, neutrality, um, yang, space, time, laws of balance, life, production and absolute laws. At the same time, we must continue to be content with those things that form the core of our everyday life including virtue, the Three Bonds[18], and Five Relationships[19].

If man's knowledge and science were to make infinite advances in the future so that man achieved all his desires, man's essential essence would be lost in the process. Man would become a slave to his science. When man becomes faster than the speed of light, he will have brought on his own destruction. This is because the application of infinite desires to a finite world runs counter to the principles of Nature.

In the future, there will be many changes in the area of politics. I foresee our political system going through a chaotic phase in the future followed by absolute dictatorship. This, in turn, will much later be followed by a system of moral government based on an ideal democratic system of small communities.

In the vast span of time stretching forward from the present, mankind will undergo unimaginable changes and encounter unimagined suffering and difficulties of great complexity.

We must seriously take interest in these issues, bringing to bear our best efforts, intelligence, and virtue for the sake of human happiness.

The fundamental element in this should be an all-out effort to establish, and put into practice, a lifestyle based on Nature involving wholesome virtue, based on the laws of balance present in the fundamental principles of the Tao. And we are in dire need of political leaders who are "inwardly a sage and outwardly regal."

In concrete terms, this means that the people of the world must all focus on spiritual training to develop their own individual natures and develop into truly humane people. At the same time, they need to properly undergo the correct training to develop sound bodies. Political leaders need to develop ideal character, adopt correct political views, and carry these out in actual practice. If we conclude that politics is complex and difficult, it will be so. On the other hand, if we look at it from the standpoint of the correct Way (Do), we find it is not so difficult as long as one possesses the key elements of a developed human being.

One simply needs to engage in natural politics, free of desires, based on the philosophy of the Tao. Based on the laws of balance, one is truly fair and impartial, working for the welfare of the people. One carries out politics in a way that enables people to live in peace and inspires trust. When this is done, there should be no difficulties. In other words, the political leader must be inwardly wise and outwardly majestic, while adopting the true Do; being, truly fair and impartial based on the laws of balance. He must not let this remain mere theory. This must be accompanied by practical application.

Chapter 3

Lao Tzu's Economic Views

The economic structures of the current era can be divided into two types: systems of free competition based on the satisfaction of the desires of most people, and economies under strict control that distribute products created primarily through labor. However, Lao Tzu rejects both of these alternatives, advocating an economy of non-desire with no private property.

Man creates material goods in order to satisfy his desires. In order to produce things, labor and machines are required. But human desires are limitless, whereas materials are limited. In other words, labor and machines are limited, which means that there aren't enough goods, a situation that leads to conflict. With this in mind, the Taoist school advocated an economy of non-desire. What exactly does this entail? Lao Tzu said that the production of economic goods should be limited to man's abilities and left at that, and that people should get rid of excessive desires and be satisfied if they had the necessities for everyday life. When people try to satisfy desires beyond their needs, when they acquire a lot of goods, they cease to work. In extreme cases, their minds become scattered as they live extravagantly or turn to stealing. In order to prevent this from happening, people need to get rid of their desire for possessions and eliminate domination from the realm of politics. This is to say, for mankind to live in peace, it must take the system of property ownership and political domination and transform it into a system free of these elements. In other words, even though goods are produced, they should not be possessed, and, even though one assists in production, there should be no domination.

Moreover, according to Lao Tzu, if valuable and good articles are not produced and if profits are not sought, there will be no theft in the world. For this to happen, he said that one should not let people have many goods but should instead suppress their desires, encouraging them to be satisfied with what they have. Endless dissatisfaction with what one has and the desire for more things is viewed negatively by an economic system based on non-desire. Such attitudes are said to lead to the ruin of both families and nations. Lao Tzu went on to say that those upper-class people who enjoy sumptuous foods and don fancy attire in extravagant palaces are nothing more than thieves. The lives of the royalty are extravagant, while the farmers and common people suffer from deprivation. High officials wear silk and carry sharp swords on their waists, eating whatever they desire. Lao Tzu called such behavior "the actions of a great enemy," since it violates the natural Way, which seeks to share that which is in excess with those who don't have enough. The reason people face starvation is because the upper class takes in too much in taxes. And the reason people are difficult to rule is because the ruler governs through individual will and desire. People take death lightly because of excessive desires. Lao Tzu noted that all of the beneficial instruments and machines created from desire are weapons of evil. In short, he rejected technological civilization. He did so because he believed that these things, contrary to their purpose, harmed man's original humanity.

According to Lao Tzu, if a country is governed according to the principles of the Do, it becomes peaceful; but if it is governed with righteousness, there will be wars utilizing bizarre methods, creating chaos in the world. If there is a government of non-action and non-desire, everything under Heaven will be regulated. This is explained by the fact that when there are many prohibitions, the people can't be free; when taxes are high, the people grow even more destitute; when people think only of their own benefit, the government loses its authority; and when technology advances, fantastic products are created in abundance leading to an increase in theft. In this case, there is a failure to control man's unlimited desires. When people have many desires, these become disruptive to everyday life, and thus the nation creates many laws. As a result, there is an increase in theft. This happens when man's desires are not held in check but are instead allowed to expand infinitely. These problems are solved by the leader who is without desire for possession or control, one who is inwardly a sage and externally a king, who carries out a government of non-action, non-doing, and non-desire, giving prominence to that which is fundamental. In short, this is the economic doctrine of non-desire.

Lao Tzu's ethical doctrine is non-action (*muwi*); his political doctrine is non-contention; and his economic doctrine is non-desire.

At this point, one has to wonder, "Without action, how can one lead an ethical life? Without fighting, how can one govern? Without desire, how can one lead an economic existence?" However, ethics are not something manmade, but rather represent something natural. Politics is allowing things to assume a natural order. And economics is the limiting of desires. This does not mean telling people not to eat when they are hungry or not to wear clothes when they are cold or not to live in houses. People need to eat, wear clothing, and have a place to live. After all, these things are all only natural. It is when people are excessive, take others' things, live beyond their means, and exploit the fruits of others' labor that this becomes unnatural. In reference to such people, Lao Tzu said that those who know how to be satisfied with what they have live lives of abundance, whereas those who are unsatisfied feel like they are lacking something. As a result, they desire others' belongings and thus fight with them, and this tendency eventually leads to nations going to war with one another. When people know how to be satisfied, they cease to be greedy and concentrate fully on the inner dimension of their lives. In Lao Tzu's ideal society, horses are no longer needed for travel or for war, so they can be employed effectively in farming. On the other hand, when everything is in a state of chaos, people become full of greed and cease to focus on the inner dimension. Exclusively focused outwardly, they engage in wars and foreign invasions. Lao Tzu is therefore anti-war. This naturally follows from his advocacy of non-action, non-aggression, and non-desire. Struggle and war are the most unfortunate events in human society and represent a social malady, which has its roots in the desire for domination and possessions.

Chapter 4

A Brief Account of My Economic Views

Lao Tzu's economic views as outlined above represent a coherent doctrine based on rational and philosophical principles. However, in the modern era, economic theory has undergone extensive and far-reaching changes as a result of materialist and capitalist thought and the advances of science. Even so, when it comes to fundamental principles, things do not change. The current economic trends will continue throughout the world for the time being. This is to be explained by the fact that many modern people have an ideological bias towards economics that involves materialism, which has caused them to lose their reason and believe that the material world is all-powerful. As a result, they are completely ignorant of the principles of balance that are inherent in the Tao, the principles governing the myriad entities and their intrinsic behaviors. If this trend continues it will lead to disaster and, ultimately, to man's demise. With this in mind, we must do all we can beforehand to prevent this from happening.

Correct understanding of the fundamental problems of economics, as well as practical measures to bring about normalcy, are needed. However, it is my opinion that what is even more urgently required is a thorough-going realization of an economic lifestyle grounded upon the laws of balance in accordance with the principles of Nature. I believe the basic conditions for world economic stability to be as follows:

1. Development of economic ideals founded upon desirelessness, in accordance with the principles of the Do.

2. Development of economic ideals based on the laws of balance.

3. Natural and rational population control for all of mankind.

4. Natural and rational distribution of goods to all of mankind.

5. Establishment of rational and fair social welfare for all of mankind.

6. Establishment of a rational, free, and open economic system for all of mankind.

7. Worldwide unification of currency and currency value.

8. Rational and fair worldwide distribution of foodstuffs.

9. Fair compensation for the hard work of everyone in the world, and a system that guarantees the rights of ownership of this compensation.

10. Understanding of the principle that goods drop in value when overabundant and rise in value when scarce.

11. Efforts towards rationalization of production demand and consumption and a solution to energy problems.

12. Worldwide elimination of violence and war; cessation of limitless desires for limited material goods.

Chapter 5

Military Doctrine

I would like to discuss my observations regarding America's national defense, the military. I am neither a military expert nor a soldier, and this book is not a work specializing on military topics. I will therefore not attempt to discuss the topic in a specialized or detailed manner as there is no need to do so. I will limit my comments to a simple statement of my philosophical views as a person involved in martial arts. In the famous classic by Sun Tzu, *The Art of War*[20] the forward states, "The first is the Tao; the second is Heaven; the third is Earth; the fourth is the general; and the fifth is method."

These are the five great principles of national defense and, specifically, the military. Expressed in more concrete terms, "The first is the Tao" refers to the fundamental principle of Taoist philosophy. "The second is Heaven" refers to the principle and phenomena of the universe and nature. "The third is Earth" refers to the principles and phenomena of the planet where we all live. "The fourth is the general" refers to human beings themselves and, specifically, to military personnel. "The fifth is method" refers to general law and to military regulations in particular. These are basic principles of national defense, applicable anywhere at any time. My observations of the American military are based on these. American soldiers' ability to follow rules and not get out of hand, yet behave in a natural manner is in agreement with the basic principles of Taoist philosophy. In Lao Tzu's *Tao Te Ching*, it is said that the secret to warfare is to win wars without fighting. A practical example of this was America during the Cold War. It seemed destined to fight the other major power—the Soviet Union, but instead of waging war, it paved the way for the transformation of Communist states into democracies. This is in agreement with the spirit of Moo Do. The *Tao Te Ching* also states that taking one's enemy lightly will surely lead to defeat. I think America follows this principle in the way that it refuses to make an unprovoked attack on any nation, to include even those that are weak. This agrees with the essence of Moo Do spirit, which is centered on defense and does not attack first. These examples show the many ways that American military policy is in agreement with Taoist philosophical principles.

For the readers' reference, I would also like to list some differences between Moo Do and the military. The objectives pursued by Moo Do practitioners in terms of physical and mental training as well as techniques and forms are different, but their basis is much the same. Yet they differ in the sense that each Moo Do practitioner, acting in the true spirit of Moo Do, has as his goal the training and development of the mind and body, whereas the military, as an organization, has as its goal the defense of the nation.

Lastly, in my personal observations, the general social aspect (cultural and economic aspects) of American society has developed based on Western philosophy.

Chapter 6

Some Concluding Remarks

As I bring to a close my thoughts on these matters, I should note that having been born in Korea, I have spent most of my life there, but have also lived about 20 years in the U. S. and 10 years in China. I would like to discuss my direct experiences in these places in philosophical and practical terms.

Philosophy is generally classified into Eastern and Western philosophy. Eastern philosophy primarily consists of two schools of thought. First is the philosophy of the Do originating in the ancient thinker Lao Tzu, a philosophy of production and balance based on um, neutrality and yang, which in turn, has its source in Nature. The second involves Confucian moral philosophy which originated with Confucius involving a philosophy of benevolence and virtue that has, as its source, the humanistic ideals of the Three Bonds and Five Relationships. In the East, these are the two main streams of thought. Besides these thinkers, there are those in the East who advocated ontological systems and other philosophies but their influence has been minor.

The former system of thought, Taoism, has not achieved much practical development in the East. According to my objective observations of America during the time I have lived here, it is clear that the principle ideology of Taoism has been consistently applied in the U. S. from the country's foundation to the present, particularly in the field of politics. In general but concrete terms, the ideal of freedom and democracy, as advocated by Lao Tzu, seems to have achieved its practical realization not in the East, but rather in America. About 20 years ago when I went to Philadelphia, which served as the capitol when America was first founded, I visited the capitol building (currently a museum). Once inside, the first thing I saw was a bell, the Liberty Bell, that had been passed down as the symbol of freedom from earlier times. For some reason, I was deeply moved. Surprised at my reaction, I took a closer look. On one side, there was a crack. The bell was silent, yet it was able to provide me with a valuable lesson. Although the bell didn't have a very long history, it was an expression of the American people's frontier spirit and arduous struggle as they encountered this new continent where they established, with much sweat and tears, a great nation of freedom. I had to bow my head. Then I went farther into the museum and looked more closely. What impressed me even more at this time was that the legislative, judiciary, and executive branches were already completely separate at this time. This was something that had been unimaginable in East Asia in the past. It was especially impressive to see that this division was not just in theory or form but had been realized in actual practice. It occurred to me then that America's present status was not an accident or a miracle, but rather had been brought about with this division of powers as its fundamental cause. I could see that the American people and leaders had fully digested the ideals of freedom and democracy that are basic principles of the philosophy of the Do in the East, and had been true to these ideals, rationally putting them into action so as to create America as the great nation it is today. In this sense, so many of the practical policies of American politics are consistent with the principles of the Tao. With this political foundation, America's progress has occurred as a matter of course.

The Confucian school, which began with Confucius himself, advocated a moral philosophy, which spread extensively into the various countries of East Asia. In the process, it was transformed into a religion[21] and in this form it attained great popularity. It was mentioned previously that Taoist philosophy never really bloomed. In my opinion, the reason for this is that the various nations of East Asia were monarchies, and the leaders sensed that if Taoist philosophy, with its emphasis on freedom and democracy, were ever to become widespread, it would deal a fatal blow to the absolute power of the monarch. As a result, they used their absolute power to suppress Taoism. Confucian moral philosophy, on the other hand, was a philosophical ideology that benefited them in every way.

While I believe that Confucianism had its good points, it seems to have placed excessive emphasis on theory and form while neglecting actual practice. In this sense, it was negative. Although Western thought has a few common points, it has not had much impact by and large.

Chapter 7

The Ideal Society as Envisioned by the Taoist School

What is the ideal society as envisioned by the Taoist school? Lao Tzu stated that in order to suppress the strong and support the weak, excess goods should be shared with those who do not have enough. This was the ideal society, which was in accord with the Heavenly Tao, the essence of natural principles. Lao Tzu would have us dismantle authoritarian government structures and capitalist city-states with their civilizations based on desire for knowledge, domination, and possession. In their place, he would have us establish small, cooperative agricultural societies. These would have no need for war or weapons. They would not develop technological civilization that would harm nature. They would neither launch invasions nor be subject to invasion. Enjoying tranquility, the people would have no reason to travel to other places. Living a simple, primitive life, the people would be happy with simple clothes and food. They would regard their backwards agricultural lands containing the bones of their ancestors and the sweat of their labors as a paradise, which they in turn could pass on to successive generations of their grandchildren. They would be happy with their traditions and customs; and with an abundant inner life, their external requirements would disappear, so that no one would want to leave the place where they were born. At first sight, Lao Tzu seems to be calling for a return to a primitive lifestyle, but this is not really the case. In Taoism, the method of obtaining the highest knowledge and highest level of attainment is the discarding of knowledge. The discarding of knowledge results in ignorance. But this ignorance, having passed through knowing, is different from primitive ignorance. It is an ignorance that comes after experience. Primitive ignorance is the realm of nature, whereas the ignorance subsequent to experience is "the stage of Heaven and Earth." It is the universal stage.

Post-experience ignorance resembles primitive ignorance just as the stage of Heaven and Earth resemble the stage of nature. People in a natural stage do not know how to bring discrimination to bear on phenomena, but in the case of those in the stage of Heaven and Earth, it is not that they do not know how to discriminate—rather, they forget it.

In the realm of metaphysics, Lao Tzu regarded the Do as *mu* (nothingness) and regarded virtue within the phenomenal realm as *muwi* (non-action). His views on man are framed within the discarding of knowledge, emotion, and desire and the transcendence of birth and death. In terms of social outlook, he advocates *muwi*, non-aggression, and non-desire. This being the case, what kind of society did Lao Tzu envision? Before we answer this question, it should be noted that Confucianism views a person unable to discriminate as not having attained the stage of discrimination, and someone who "forgets it" as having knowledge transcending this stage. In Taoism, this isn't properly understood. In Taoism, whenever individual religious cultivation is mentioned, there is praise for the infant, the child, or the fool. This is because primitive people, children, and fools are simple and ignorant and thus resemble the sage. And in terms of society, primitive society resembles the Taoist "unity of Heaven and man" and "the realm of Heaven and Earth." According to Chuang Tzu, in a society of the highest virtue, mountains have no paths; rivers have no boats or bridges; and people have no hometown, just like the birds and the beasts. Without the discrimination of the petty man, everything is like the era of primitive barbarism. How is it possible, when living in the world of established knowledge and set forms of virtue, to live like people in primitive times? While the Taoist would maintain some of the advances in terms of social environment, when it comes to their practical response, they equate the natural realm with "the realm of Heaven and Earth."

Chapter 8

The Ideal Society of the Confucian School

Let's now take a look at the ideal society as it appears in Confucianism. I have looked at this issue in terms of two phrases that appear in the work called the *Great Learning* (*Daehak*) including governing of the nation and pacification of everything under Heaven. The achievement of "governing of the nation" leads to a world of minor tranquility, whereas "the pacification of all under Heaven" leads to a world where all prosper similarly. In the former society, the people adopt family and national ideals for their own benefit. In the latter society, on the other hand, in addition to having great respect for family and national ideals, the people take the ideals normally associated with self-benefit and adopt them to the society at large.

The citizens in a society where all prosper similarly do not extend filial responsibility solely to their parents or parental affection solely to their own children. They instead seek to create completely adequate facilities for social welfare and make it so that everyone has a job. Women take care of the family at home and do not have excessive desires for things. People do not seek to dominate or harm others. There is such a lack of criminals and thieves that people can sleep with their doors open. This represents a society where man's politics, economics, and culture have attained their highest form of expression.

Chapter 9

Doctrine of Return

Space is filled with the endless flow of time and the *ki* image, the fullness of the *ki* essence. As for the behavior of *ki*, it transforms as a fluid image changing into a fluid form, from which it transforms into a *ki* image, an image of nothingness.

Human beings follow the same pattern. They transform from *mu* (non-existence) to *yu* (existence) and then return back to *mu*. The human body is comprised of gases, liquid, and solids. Life is maintained and passed on through the maintenance and harmonization of the equilibrium of these three things. After this, one is transformed, becoming a *mu* image and thereby returns to the One via *mu*. In this way, man, as an animal and one of this world's myriad entities, while in existence eats primarily vegetable matter to maintain life; but when his time comes, he dies, becoming dirt and thus becoming the food for vegetation. This is nature's phenomenon of returning and represents a principle of Nature.

Chapter 10

Human Insensitivities

Human feeling is sensitive to the external, but there is a lack of interest in the internal. Put simply, people are interested in what they can see with their eyes instead of that which is invisible. The following insensitivies should be avoided:

1. Ignorance of nature.

2. Lack of exact knowledge of one's individual nature.

3. Ignorance of one's authentic conscience.

4. Disregard of one's sense of autonomy.

5. Ignorance regarding what authentic human nature is.

6. Ignorance regarding true instincts.

7. Lack of gratitude towards one's nation, parents, and teachers.

8. Disregard of one's enslavement to money.

Within this world, there is the imageless and that with image, the formless and that with form. Moreover, there is theory and reality. In addition, there is the manifestation of um, neutrality, and yang, of stillness and movement, of emptiness and fullness as well as cause and effect. In this world, it is the endless transformation of these things that creates the formation and flow of history.

The ego, the "I," exists as one of this world's myriad images and entities. One could even say that it is because this entity called "I" exists that the myriad images and entities of this world exist. If one imagines oneself disappearing from the world, nothing remains. Everything seems empty and in vain. For this reason, we need to recognize that the ego is highly important, mysterious, and absolute.

And we need to recognize the need to live in a natural and sacred manner. Man, as a microcosm of the universe, corresponds to a single particle, in other words, the nucleus. This was put forward by Zhu-xi[22] in ancient times, and it is an idea with which I agree. With this in mind, we must live lives of wisdom characterized by harmony and change in accordance with the laws of balance based on the principles of Nature. At the same time, we need to live in harmony with the myriad images and entities of this world in accordance with the principles of relativity.

Chapter 11

The Difference between Hope and Desire

Hope, as an aspect of pure consciousness, is without limit. Yet hope is generally taken lightly. Desire, on the other hand, is generally an aspect of the material. In other words, it involves that with limitation. Even so, people tend to place much importance on it. One reason for this is that people tend to be interested in that which they can see. The invisible, on the other hand, is often neglected. Hope, as something purely spiritual, does not cause any harm even if it is excessive or insufficient, but desire, as something chiefly materialistic, is problematic when it is excessive or lacking. This is one of the paradoxes of human life.

Chapter 12

Man, as the Spiritual Leader of the Myriad Things, Cannot Become a Slave

While allowing himself to be enslaved to his own instincts and knowledge, man is constantly worried about, and detests the very thought of becoming a slave to others. In short, he is unconcerned about interior matters and sensitive only to things on the outside. This is because of the strength of instinctual desires. The degree of man's reactions corresponds to the strength of the instinct. If man's aim is eternal advancement and development, he must not become a slave to anything in this world. Man must realize that he is an important particle in accordance with the principles of the universe, and that he is the spiritual master of the myriad things.

Chapter 13

Regarding the Statement "Life is War"

When we hear it said that "Life is war," as we look back on past history and our present situation, we have to agree. Along a similar vein, we often hear about the "law of the jungle" by which the strong devour the weak. This is essentially the same as equating life with war. It is also said that war spurs on the advancement of civilization and gives birth to new civilizations.

I would have to disagree with all of this. In fact, I reject it completely.

This attitude is opposed to the laws of balance based on the principles of Nature, but it is also fundamentally inconsistent with the Three Bonds and Five Relationships based on human morality. The statement "life is war" reflects an attitude that comes from human instinct. Human beings fail to accurately realize the true nature of their *a priori* instincts. This attitude especially arises as people try to satisfy their instinctual drive for superiority over others. The only thing that is able to create, transform, evolve, or send back man or any of the other myriad entities is the infinite, unlimited, infinitely unchanging Do, which is the source and basis of the universe. Needless to say, man is unable to do any of these things. Throughout my life as a practitioner of Moo Do, as I have traversed through the many vicissitudes of life, I have come to see this Do as Moo Do's ultimate goal. I have become firmly convinced that authentic Moo Do is absolutely necessary if we are to live our lives naturally in a truly human manner, for this path is in accord with Nature's laws of balance. For this reason, Moo Do (Soo Bahk Do, mind training, inner training, and outer training) is a practice necessary for everyone in the world. The body and mind training in this practice, in terms of both training and practice, transcends national borders and, matters of race and religion. This is something that people are capable of doing. Since the human race spread forth from a single human being in the distant past, I claim that we are all clearly brothers and sisters, so this practice is part of a movement to bring the entire world together as siblings within the same family. The ultimate goal is to eliminate war, violence, and envy, get rid of hatred, and cooperate in a spirit of harmony so that all of mankind can enjoy happiness, peace, health, and freedom. I continue to work towards this goal even now.

I believe that man, and of course the universe, myriad images, and entities, must simply submit unconditionally to that which creates the absolute, impartial, and natural principles. These principles are absolute, immutable rules, which no one and nothing in the universe can modify, change, oppose, complain of, reject, or disobey.

It is clear then that man, for whatever reason, must not lightly disregard human or other life or commit murder, for this is the most heinous of crimes, absolutely unacceptable whether viewed from the standpoint of natural law or morality. In spite of this, ignorant and incompetent leaders create wars under any plausible pretense. Past history provides a grave testament to the cruelty of such immoral leaders. I therefore reject war.

I would now like to say something about the law of the jungle. In my opinion, this is different than the issue of war discussed thus far. People, of course, do not directly hunt and eat one another like animals. Rather, this refers to a certain type of behavior, such as when people threaten someone who is weak with knives or weapons, when they cause them physical or psychological harm, or kill them in order to rob them of their goods, when those in power abuse their power to cause them suffering or oppress them, demanding goods or bribes, or when people abuse others or enslave them. Such actions are clearly unnatural, inhumane, and immoral.

When we take up this issue from the standpoint of the other animals instead of from the standpoint of man, the situation is quite different. In the animal world, it is true that the strong openly devour the weak in order to survive. It may then be asked, if this is in violation of the principles of nature, how these animals, which openly violate these principles, live and prosper without any problem. Murder, in itself, is clearly an unnatural and evil act, but in this case, this natural principle is countered by an opposing principle. The principles of Nature are truly strange and mysterious. At this point, let's take a look at a concrete example involving animals. There are almost no animals that will turn and eat their own kind, even though one is stronger than the other. However, the strong do eat the weak of other species of animal. It is interesting to note in this respect that the stronger animals tend to have fewer offspring, while the weaker species tend to reproduce rapidly and exist in larger numbers. And it is a natural condition of life that all life forms in the world must eat to survive and reproduce. Since weaker species have a higher rate of reproduction and exist in higher numbers, if nothing is done, their numbers will expand beyond their supply of food, leading them to become extinct. The strong, by devouring the weak, naturally keep the size of the population in control, allowing them to survive. Let me give just one example. In one place, there were numerous deer. Since the deer caused no problem and were beautiful to look at, the local villagers liked having them around, but a tiger appeared and started reducing their numbers, so the villagers shot the tiger. After this, the deer population increased again. This made the villagers very happy. But at some point, the population ceased to grow. Since there were no tigers hunting them, the people thought it strange and conducted an investigation to see what was happening. They discovered that the local environment didn't provide enough food for a larger population. Nature therefore has a rational means of maintaining the balance of life.

For this reason, the law of the jungle, as it operates within the world of animals, has to be seen not as an unnatural, evil form of behavior but rather as something natural. But this principle does not apply, indeed cannot apply, to human society. This is because man is the spiritual head of all things; and what's more, the law of the jungle is not in the best interest of man.

Chapter 14

The Belligerent Civilization

Wars encourage development and the creation of new civilizations. However, when viewed from a fundamental standpoint, war violates the principle of nature and forms a contradiction. It may create changes in some aspects of civilization. To achieve victory in war, all of the nation's energies are concentrated, and as a result there may be developments in civilization for the sake of war in weapon and manufacturing technology needed for killing. However, other aspects of civilization decline. True advances in civilization are achieved through the sincere efforts of the people and the nation's leaders, and through avant-garde elements and scholars of the various fields during times of peace. This is evident when we look at history, and it is a principle of Nature.

It is my opinion that a truly advanced civilization capable of ensuring human peace and happiness is only possible when excessive tendencies towards war and violence have been suppressed via the natural and rational control of man's instinctual desire for supremacy, and when human intelligence and sincere efforts are put forward cooperatively to find ways to engage in fair competition with freedom and good motives. For this to happen, the full efforts of both the people and the country's leaders are required.

Chapter 15

My Views on Human Life

I would like to discuss, in concrete and practical terms, the primary acquired phenomena listed below in terms of their fundamental, symbolic, and logical significance.

1. I must reiterate that the Do is the primal source and structure of Nature and the universe and, at the same time, is neutral.

2. Um and yang were produced through the Tao, which is a neutrality.

3. Um is stillness. Neutrality is central and regulating. Yang is movement.

4. Um elements mutually share the same nature and thus mutually transform yet remain contradictory principles that do not form a mutual synthesis.

5. Yang elements mutually share the same nature and thus mutually transform yet remain contradictory principles that do not form a mutual synthesis.

6. Um and yang, being of different natures, do not mutually transform but are a duality of a positive nature that form a mutual synthesis and mutually supplement one another in a positive way.

7. Neutrality, as mentioned here, refers to the regulatory role operating between um and yang for the sake of production.

8. In accordance with the natural process of transformation mentioned above, the Do harmonizes um (stillness) and yang (movement) to produce electrical energy. This serves as the productive force for the world's myriad images, forms, and entities.

9. In accordance with necessary principles, this world's myriad images, forms, and entities necessarily are different in terms of quantity or relative strength, but they possess electrical energy and, as a result, manifest magnetic energy. In the terminology of science and physics, this is known as gravity.

10. Through such a process, the Natural universe was produced.

11. This, in turn, necessarily implies the production of the law of balance.

12. Through this process, the myriad images, forms, and entities were produced. We human beings are therefore one particle within the composition of the universe. For this reason, man must live in accordance with the laws of balance, based on the fundamental principles of the Tao. Such a lifestyle becomes the basis for contentment—man's ultimate goal. If forced to give a name to this, we can call it "virtue."

13. The core of man is virtue; thus, in order to develop a virtuous character, to bring the ego to completion, it is important to live a rational life that follows the laws of balance. These imply the harmonization of time and place, um and yang, the environment, the empty and the full, movement and stillness, and the heart and mind.

Let us first ask, what is the method man is to follow if he is to realize his ultimate goal, true happiness. If we think of this as being difficult, it is difficult; but if we see it in simple terms, it is quite simple. This is because the solution, when all is said and done, depends mainly on us. In other words, it depends on the degree of our sincerity, interest, effort, and practical action. The starting point of human happiness is first, to calm the mind, and second, to be without desire. Third is training the body. The most ideal, rational, and suitable means of realizing these three essential prerequisites to happiness is the practice of Moo Do. And among the various types of Moo Do, I would recommend *Soo Bahk Do*. The reason is that it is widely recognized as being an ancient tradition, which is the most natural and rational and is one that has been passed down continuously from primitive times to the present. In addition, Soo Bahk Do incorporates the three types of training (mind training, inner training, and outer training) and can therefore be practiced without any problem, anytime and anywhere, by both the young and the old and both women and men without any special implements. Furthermore, it is easily adjusted to naturally suit different body types and levels of conditioning. It also incorporates the philosophical elements of Moo Do Philosophy. It teaches mind training, showing how to spiritually develop the mind/heart, as well as physical training (inner and outer forms of training) and includes natural, rational, and practical forms and martial arts techniques to defend and preserve our precious lives. I therefore regard Soo Bahk Do as a central pillar of human happiness to attain paradise in this very world.

Below, I would like to discuss some of the practical requirements for man to attain contentment.

- Everyone in the world wishes, before all else, to achieve paradise in the present life, happiness, and the opposite of this is hell in the present life, unhappiness. In other words, everyone wants to be happy, no one wants to be sad.

- If man is to be happy, he must maintain and pass on life, and in order to do this, the first prerequisite is health. For the maintenance of health, that most valuable of possessions, the most important thing is living a lifestyle based on the laws of balance in accordance with the fundamental principles of Nature. When man enjoys true health, he develops as a matter of course, but when he lacks health, he naturally goes into decline and is destroyed. This is a truth of this world.

- For the maintenance of health, the body and mind are of prime importance. In particular, we must develop these in a balanced manner.

Since true health depends on the mind and the body, I would like to discuss practical steps to maintain physical and mental health. First,

I would like to say that I neither confirm nor deny the doctrine that heaven and hell exist after death. My reasons are as follows:

1. I have always said that human beings must always be honest regardless of the time or the place and I will continue to stress this in the future. And it is only when we realize honesty in actual practice that we see its true value. This is not just my understanding of the issue—it is something that everyone in the world agrees upon. Honesty, after all, is the source of happiness.

2. I have never been to either heaven or hell and I haven't seen these places, nor have I talked to anyone who has done so. Heaven and hell are merely abstractions and impressions.

3. Regarding this issue, I have never heard a convincing, verifiable explanation that was rational, logical, practical, or scientific.

4. I have absolutely no knowledge regarding the existence or nonexistence of heaven, paradise, or hell.

5. How could I confirm or deny the existence of heaven or hell— something I know nothing about, while claiming that we must be honest?

6. I have directly observed, as indeed everyone in this world has, that in our present lives, those who are good are happy and those who are evil are unhappy. For this reason, I propose the doctrine that heaven and hell exist on earth during the present life.

7. This doctrine of heaven and hell existing on earth during our present life implies that human beings need to put forth authentic effort. But fundamentally, this is nothing more that the manifestation of cause and effect from the past, which occurs with the harmonization of um, neutrality, and yang in accordance with the basic laws of Nature.

My Theory

The previous section in this chapter deals with my doctrine that heaven and hell exist on earth and my views on good and evil.

It is my opinion that whether or not we talk of heaven and hell existing on earth or existing elsewhere, the main focus is actually the quest for human happiness. In other words, paradise is the symbol for good in human society, while hell symbolizes evil. It follows that human beings, no matter who they are, hate hell and love heaven. We might say that the fruit of goodness is happiness and the symbol of happiness is paradise. We can thus conclude that man must live a life characterized by goodness and kindness. With this in mind, I am an advocate of the doctrine that heaven and hell exist during the present life on earth. In order to consistently follow this doctrine in a rational manner, one must have a fundamental theory about how life is to be lived. I would like to talk about this in concrete terms below.

It is my opinion that the appearance of the concepts of heaven and hell in this world's religions, etc., is in order to urge man to do good. The doctrine that heaven and hell exist here and now has a similar purpose. These two doctrines, therefore both share the same focus, encouraging man to do good.

Everyone on this Earth, after being born, will disappear from this space with the passing of time. This is a principle of Nature and there is, therefore, no getting around it. No matter how much man has advanced in terms of knowledge or science, he cannot elucidate the mystery inherent in this problem. In other words, when man dies, it marks the end of everything, so everything after death remains eternally beyond his knowledge. For this reason, instead of saying this or that about paradise or hell subsequent to death, I believe that we should focus on encouraging man to do good in this world by pointing out the necessary and practical relationship of cause and effect as it operates in the visible world. Or in other words, heaven and hell after death is an issue after we die, and as such, is vague. Since it has no direct, intuitive connection with us in spatial or temporal terms, it is something that man can ignore. However, the doctrine of heaven and hell in this life is a practical and pressing issue that has a direct and ascertainable spatial and temporal connection to us in accordance with the fundament principles of Nature as these come into play in our everyday lives. For this reason, this issue is not something we can ignore or put aside. To the contrary, it is a perennial issue of great importance. It is therefore the most effective impetus for man to do good, and therefore plays a vital role in establishing human happiness.

While perfecting the self in a natural, balanced, righteous, and good way, man must live for the sake of others. "Natural" refers to a lifestyle following the principles of Nature and balance. It is to become habituated to a lifestyle characterized by a true love for nature and a desire to protect it, and is a way of thinking and action that encourages contact with nature. And it means maintaining a balanced life. The three basic elements supporting such a lifestyle are: *Right Mind*, *Right Posture*, and *Right Composure*.

Right Mind (*jeongshim*) refers to man's authentic conscience, sincerity, and honesty. Since this is an important pillar of our lives, we must work to develop it, and this work necessarily needs to be accompanied by reflection, judgment, and discrimination.

Right Posture (*jeongja*) refers to man's proper essence and, therefore, corresponds to his refined *ki* and the middle way, his autonomy, and action. This is a necessary condition for health in man's life. For this reason, man must always maintain an interest in this and follow it up with practice and cultivation.

Right Composure (*jeongjeong*) refers to human rest. Man's life, being limited, is neither mechanical nor eternal, and there must therefore be a balance of stillness and action within man's life. Just because movement is necessary does not mean we can maintain unlimited movement. And just because stillness is necessary does not mean that we can maintain unlimited stillness. Right Composure therefore refers to tranquility and sleep. As necessary conditions for health, these must be accompanied by mental calm, physical calm, and positional stability.

You will not be able to achieve your goal if your understanding of this issue remains at the theoretical level. This must be accompanied by rational action.

The reason that I advocate Moo Do, specifically, Soo Bahk Do (mind training, inner training, and outer training), is not to merely advertise the effects of the type of training that I have been involved in during my entire life, nor am I saying this for the sake of fame or to blindly push this onto people. To the contrary, I am simply stating things as they are. *Mun* (academic study)[23] is characterized primarily by logic and calm, whereas *moo* (martial arts) is primarily characterized by action and movement. Since academic study is focused on logic and stillness, if you pursue it in a one-sided manner, you will cease to have its value as *mun*. Such actions, after all, run counter to the relativity of things inherent in the principles of the Tao. Although academic study is mainly logical and calm, it ends up having no value whatsoever if it is not carried out in action. *Mu*, on the other hand, is active and moving. But if a person pursues this in a one-sided way, it ceases to have its true value. Just as with *mun*, this is because such an approach runs counter to the relativity of the Tao's principles. For this reason, I firmly believe that the best method for attaining true human happiness, the highest of man's goals, is Moo Do. This is because Moo Do's basic teaching involves the dual cultivation of both *mun* and *mu* in a balanced manner. Sincere training in the form of Moo Do known as Soo Bahk Do is a mysterious technique of the greatest importance. Over two decades ago in May 1970, I discussed the martial art of Soo Bahk Do in detail in the *Soo Bahk Do Dae Kahm*, and in May of 1992, I published a short booklet explaining Soo Bahk Do in its entirety to include the actual practice, the *six paths*, etc. This was a translation of Book Four (the *Kwon Bup* Chapter) of the Korean martial arts classic *Moo Yei Do Bo Tong Ji*. Since these works have dealt with the matter in an orderly and detailed manner, I have omitted a discussion of concrete training techniques in the present work. I would now like to explain in simple, ordinary, and natural terms the philosophical, moral, and practical work to be done in order to realize man's highest goal—human happiness.

Man is not born into this world through his own will or through the will of another. His birth is a momentary process involving the harmonization of um and yang forces in accordance with the Tao's principles of equilibrium within the calm of infinite space and the active flow of time. Even though phenomena are different in terms of space and time, the universe's myriad images, forms, and entities all share a commonality. Born into this world, man lives for a limited time before he must go. During this time, he needs to live wisely, nobly, and happily, receiving respect from others. What must he do to live this way?

1. Live a life that is natural and love nature.

2. Live a balanced life. He must live a life appropriate to his role within society.

3. Be mindful to control his environment.

4. Understand that human happiness is the focal point of human life; for this reason, happiness is sought by all.

5. Understand that the first condition of happiness is health.

6. Understand and practice the basic elements of health of Right Mind, Right Posture, and Right Composure (Three Essentials).

7. Develop the following with the above Three Essentials.

reflection	effort
judgment	morality
discrimination	ethics
courage	non-desire
sense of autonomy	spiritual cultivation
investigation	praxis (disciplined application of things in everyday life)

8. For the effective achievement of everything mentioned above, practice and maintain adequate nutrition, exercise, rest, and sleep.

In everyday life, there are those who think of only their own benefit and live only for themselves. They cause others harm and suffering and are filled with envy and hatred. They conspire against others and are dishonest, tell lies, and fail to keep their word. They disregard others and look down on them with haughtiness. They try to take advantage of others and boast of qualities they don't possess while criticizing the faults of others. They flatter people when they are present but curse them behind their backs. They are violent and threaten others and at times even commit murder. They are attached to power and seek to live lives based on the abuse of power. When strong, they pressure the weak. Instead of empowering the weak, they rob from them. They become drunk with fortune and fame. They act out of arrogance and authoritarianism. With eyes blinded by material possessions and money, they become slaves to money, becoming excessively greedy. They love shallow pleasures and casual sex. Not wanting to work and sweat, they want to get everything for free and even steal from others. They may enjoy such things when they are doing them, but don't they realize that these actions will definitely have a price in the future? Having committed these crimes of their own accord, they have created their own suffering, unhappiness, and hell.

The above actions violate nature, so you should take care not to do them no matter what. Such actions don't do anyone else any good, and they do not lead to your own good either. For this reason, human beings, no matter who they are, should avoid such actions.

To do so, they need to look in the mirror and ask themselves the following questions:

How sincerely have I worked and sweated to develop myself?

How much have I served others and sacrificed for them?

How much blood have I shed for higher principles?

How much have I sacrificed for higher principles? Have I gone so far as to give my own precious life?

It is clear that the extent to which a person has done the above determines that person's status as an authentic human being. Since I have written in detail about human life and human beings earlier, I will only comment briefly on these things here. It is my hope that the list of various forms of unreasonable and evil actions above will, to some extent, be helpful to the people living in the perverse and immoral society of today.

IX

TRENDS IN MODERN

PHILOSOPHY

Trends in Modern Philosophy

Modern philosophy is the successor of philosophies of the near-modern period, but it is changing in both the East and West. These changes are largely brought about by social transformations, astonishing advances in science and especially physics, and developments in mathematics, capitalism, and materialism, but the most decisive cause has been the quantum physics of the 20th century. This has brought about change in Eastern philosophy, but its effects have been particularly strong on the West. In near-modern philosophy, a mechanical view, based on Newtonian physics, held sway, but this theory has had to change as it encountered quantum physics. The trend has led to a critique of Kant's philosophy—the bastion of near modern philosophy.

In my view, mathematic logic and phenomenology are merely methodologies; they do not represent theories with actual content. These appeared based on science. They were created in order to make science rational. Along with these methodologies, there arose other philosophical movements that did incorporate content, including the philosophy of becoming[24] and the metaphysics of neo-realism. The philosophy of becoming saw the world as a unified, organic, living totality.

This is because the world is not mechanical but is instead living, historical, and spiritual. Realism, on the other hand, rejected subjectivity, which was independent of the perception of man searching for that reality. These two philosophical movements came under criticism by Kantian philosophy—the mainstream current of thought during the near-modern period. At the same time, they served as the starting point for modern philosophy. Experience has played a major role in the trends of modern philosophy. In response to the monistic and deterministic worldview established by science prior to 1900 C.E., modern philosophy has taken up the issue of human character and the value of the spirit (consciousness).

The French philosopher Henri Bergson and the American William James are two Western philosophers representing this trend. When it comes to experience, Bergson's philosophy is a direct observation of the limits of scientific objectivity and a subjective interior. In this respect, his philosophy transcends the level of scientific experience and instead regards life experience to be the issue at hand. It therefore concludes that the true reality is the internal flow of experience itself. If man wants to understand reality in its true sense, he needs to look inward and observe it intuitively. This is explained by the fact that instincts, when functioning correctly, are intuitive, and their essential character, as well as that of man's nature, is to not analyze the various separate phenomena of the world. Thus, there is a reality, not as something obtained through analysis but as understood through internal intuition. This is the human character and the continuum of ego moving through time. Life's distinguishing characteristic is its nonstop creative evolution. Life is cyclic and creates from itself that which is new. In this respect, the process of life's evolution is by no means mechanical or determined as understood according to teleological theories.

Moreover, the basic thing that our experience tells us is not that experience becomes possible after there is consciousness, but rather that consciousness forms after there is experience. The conventional dichotomy between subjective and objective awareness is therefore rejected.

This is because experience originally is not an internal dichotomy but, rather, is something originally existing. In other words, only pure experience exists. Ernst Mach, reflecting on positivism, advocated an essential monism. Colors, sounds, smells, spaces, and times were said to be feelings, which were essences that admitted of no further analysis. He was not describing the subjective world generally described in physics. Instead, he was referring to the reality prior to the distinction between subject and object and self and world. Depending on man's particular viewpoint, this reality can be seen in terms of the physical or the psychological. Moreover, he believed that perception did not prove facts; it noted them. In the West, there have been numerous other thinkers who have created philosophical systems besides these, but those discussed above form the main current of modern philosophy, and it is these that have created numerous changes in the preceding systems of philosophy.

X

THE PHILOSOPHY OF THE

INFINITELY LARGE AND

INFINITELY SMALL

The Philosophy of the Infinitely Large and Infinitely Small

It is now, and always will be, impossible to describe the infinitely large and infinitely small in theoretical or practical terms. Even so, we human beings can use our imaginative powers to get some idea of these. I would therefore like to describe the basic framework of these two things.

The phenomenon of the infinitely large is something that has appeared after transforming within the "stage of complete emptiness and darkness," which is also the stage from which the infinitely small transformed and became manifested. In the end, then, they are actually equivalent.

The only difference is in terms of size and scope as well as from a conceptual vantage point. The infinitely large is treated in Eastern philosophy, while the infinitely small is treated in Western philosophy. The people of the world seem to be chiefly interested in the infinitely great and the philosophy that deals with it, whereas there doesn't seem to be much interest in the infinitely small or its corresponding philosophy. The image of the entity of the infinitely small, which is the philosophy of the infinitely small, transforms into energy (Great Ki) and engages in production through the mysterious and rational harmonization of um, neutrality and yang natures and principles of equilibrium, which are the fundamental principle of the Do. And it is the Great Ki, through the rational harmonization of um, neutrality and yang, produces the world's myriad images, forms, and entities. As a result, the phenomenon of the current philosophy of the infinitely large, the source and structure of the universe, has been produced and manifested in accordance with the manifestation of the philosophy of the infinitely small, (vast time, space, and evolution of the entities/behaviors of the infinitely small). In this sense, the basis and structure of the philosophy of the infinitely large can be said to be the philosophy of the infinitely small.

The entities/behaviors directly visible to the human eye develop into the concepts of the philosophy of the infinitely large, while those entities/behaviors not visible to the human eye can be described as the concepts belonging to the philosophy of the infinitely small. We are aware of entities/behaviors of the infinitely small through consciousness. For example, we know of cells, atoms, electrons, spirits, etc. and can predict that there are other unimaginable miniscule entities. I would like to make a more detailed, logical, and concrete account of this at a future opportunity. I am firmly confident that both philosophy and science will take more interest in the infinitely small in the future. Until now, interest has chiefly been in gases and liquids and animals and plants, and there has been little interest in solid bodies (i.e., mineral). I believe that this must change in the future; indeed, I think it will change.

Notes to the Introduction

1. Korean and other Far Eastern cultures typically use the names of individuals with formal titles and terms of respect, particularly when referring to high ranking martial arts practitioners. Virtually all of the persons named in the acknowledgements are senior ranking (4th – 9th degree black/blue belt) master instructors (*Sa Bom*) or instructors (*Kyo Sa*).

2. Much of the information contained in this section was taken from *The History of Moo Duk Kwan* by Hwang Kee (1995). Additional information was drawn from personal notes by Hwang Kee and interviews with his son, Hyun Chul Hwang.

3. The origin of many of the foundational elements of Okinawan karate, such as traditional forms (also known as *hyung* or *kata*) that may be traced to Southern China. *Hyung*, commonly referred to as "forms" in English, are predetermined patterns of movement for the purpose of offense, defense, breathing, energy development, and internal and spiritual conditioning. For example, *Jei Nam* is the original Chinese name for the series of forms know as the "*pyong ahn hyung*," which are traditional Okinawan forms.

4. For the purpose of this text, the English spelling of Do is employed rather than Tao to maintain a consistent relationship between the descriptions of Hwang Kee's art Soo Bahk "Do" and the "Do" or "Tao" that is a centerpiece of Asian philosophical thought.

5. Ki is also commonly spelled as"qi," "gi," or "chi." For the purpose of this text they are exactly equivalent. The spelling "Ki" is used when the term is used by itself. The spelling "gi" is used when referring to a specific type of "gi" or "Ki" (e.g., *gigong, ungi*).

6. The terms "*gigong*" and "*gonggi*" may be cause for confusion. For the purpose of this text, "*gigong*" refers to the total accumulation of both innate and acquired ki that one has. It may be loosely translated as one's ki power. In this case, "*gong*" refers to what one has achieved or merits. "*Gonggi*" refers to a specific type of ki that is considered air or empty ki.

7. Hwang Kee included his own translation of the *Tao Te Ching* and the *Chou I* in the original version of the *Moo Do Chul Hahk*. As indicated, they were not included in this text in order to focus the reader's attention on Hwang Kee's Moo Do Philosophy. His translation of these texts may be available at a future date and are wholly consistent with translations that are currently available for reference.

8. The term "dan" (pronounced "don") is literally translated as "degree" or "level." Most martial arts have a ranking system that leads to various colored belts, the most commonly known being the "black belt." Hyun Chul Hwang was the youngest ranking "dan" member awarded the equivalent of a 1st degree black belt at the time. The color of ranking system in Soo Bahk Do differs from many martial arts ranking systems. The highest ranking belts are midnight blue rather than black. This is a traditional color of Korea adopted by Hwang Kee for the Moo Duk Kwan. In contrast to black, the color of blue suggests the color of the sky, which can acquire progressively darker hues representing a continuous process of learning and mastery. Other colors of the Soo Bahk Do ranking

system have been described with respect to the seasons to refer to the level and characteristics of a student's learning and practice. In addition, Hwang Kee was the first to develop and use a method of recording and tracking seniority by assigning each practitioner who received dan rank (midnight blue) a unique number. Hwang Kee's first blue belt was assigned the number 1 and each subsequent dan was assigned a number in the order in which they were awarded dan rank. The sequence of numbers assigned is consecutive regardless of a practitioner's country of origin. Thus, someone assigned a dan ranking of 509, the dan number of Hyun Chul Hwang, translator of the *Moo Do Chul Hahk*, indicates he is the 509th person awarded dan rank by Hwang Kee and has a much longer history and seniority with Hwang Kee and the Moo Duk Kwan than someone assigned a dan number of 20510, indicating that more than 20 thousand individuals have been assigned dan rank prior to this individual. The dan number, also referred to as *dan bon*, is very highly valued (often more than rank) and frequently cited to authenticate a practitioner's level of seniority and their direct relationship to Hwang Kee and the Moo Duk Kwan. While other organizations have begun to issue dan numbers, only the numbers issued by Hwang Kee and his successor, Hyun Chul Hwang, authenticate a Soo Bahk Do practitioner's seniority in the Moo Duk Kwan and their relationship to Hwang Kee as the founder of Moo Duk Kwan.

9. *Mo che* is literally translated as "mother-body" or "mother figure." For the purpose of this book, it may be interpreted as the original mother, essence, source, or origin that nurtures and sustains that which emerges from it. For example, the term "Mother Earth" is often used to refer to the planet as nurturer and sustainer of all plant and animal life. Though not exact, it is in this sense of the meaning of "mother" as both the source and sustainer that *mo che* may be interpreted. *Mo che* has been translated as "source and sustainer," "womb," "matrix," and "logos." The use of "source and sustainer" throughout the text does not completely convey the meaning of *mo che* and is somewhat clumsy. The term "matrix" has been defined as an arrangement of things; a substance containing something; or a situation in which something develops. While "matrix" may be closer in meaning in the present context than "womb," it carries many other meanings that may be cause for substantial misinterpretation in this context. The term "logos" is a Greek term that has a number of meanings that have emerged and been used in philosophical and religious contexts to refer to "argument," "reasoning" and later in reference to a universal intelligence or governing force that is revealed to humankind and may be likened to the Divine. These terms do not convey the meaning or sense of both source and sustainer in the way of a mother. Since *mo che* has no translatable equivalent in the English language and it would require a cumbersome explanation in the text the term, *mo che* is used with only two exceptions where the term "source" appears to be appropriate.

Notes to the Translation

10. *Seongjeong* (pronounced "sung-jung"). *Seong* is "Nature" in the sense of "human nature." *Jeong*, usually rendered "feelings," are the phenomenal manifestations of this "Nature" (anger, joy, shame, etc.) when the heart has been stirred by external conditions.

11. These terms don't have exact counterparts in English. The term *shin* is used for gods, devas, God, spirits, and a person's spirit, while *jeong* originally meant a refined essence. In terms of traditional thought, *jeong* is the person's *ki*, which is highly refined as consciousness. In Korean, the two terms are combined in the word *jeongshin*, a noun denoting the spiritual or psychological.

12. In this context, "force" refers to the power projected by the poise and posture of a person.

13. The most important of these are: general deep breathing technique (*ilban shim hoheup beop*), six *ki* technique (*yookki beop*), closed *ki* technique (*pyehgi beop*), fine breath technique (*semi hoheup beop*), focused *ki* technique—here the syllable *ju* means "to pour into" or "bring to bear" (*jugi beop*), trained *ki* technique (*yungi beop*), cinnabar field breathing technique (*danjun hoheup beop*), rotating breath technique (*hoejun hoheup beop*), triangle breathing technique (*samgak hoheup beop*), square breathing technique (*sagak hoheup beop*), among others.

14. *Chunantong* and *chunitong*, respectively. These powers enable one to see and hear things beyond normal visual and auditory range. In the Taoist school, these abilities are called *muwi* (Chinese *wu-wei*), *musa* (non-thought), tranquility, the unmoving, and *bulhaengjigi* (unfortunate self-knowledge). In Buddhism, these are called *shintongnyuk* (divine powers).

15. These are *geumsuryeon*, *mokshijae*, *susubi*, *hwa-ipjuk* and *toseunggeup*.

16. These include *yongjaerok* (dragon again record), *hoyuksamsaeng* (tiger counteract three lives), *punggwansamsaeng* (wind observes three lives), and *kyejae* (stage of purification).

17. *Yeoksamsaeng* and *gwansamsaeng*.

18. Three basic relationships within society: that between (1) sovereign and subject, (2) father and son, and (3) husband and wife.

19. Moral rules to govern the Five Human Relationships: closeness between father and child; loyalty between sovereign and minister; distinction between husband and wife; order of seniority between elders and younger people; and trust between friends.

20. Chinese, *Sun-tzu*, *Pingfa*, Korean *Sonja*, *Byeongbeop*.

21. The religious form of Confucianism is known as *yugyo* in Korean.

22. Jushi in Korean and Romanized Chu-hsi in the Wade-Giles system. The leading Chinese figure in the neo-Confucian movement.

23. Literally, "literature," but here the reference is to intellectual study and knowledge.

24. For example, the theory of creative evolution as put forth by Henri Bergson (1859-1941).

References

ANZAC Day Commemoration Committee (Qld) Incorporated (1998). Korean War, 1950-1953. Snippets from the war. http://www.anzacday.org.au/history/ korea/snippets.html.

Burdick, D. (1997). People and events of taekwondo's formative years. *Journal of Asian Martial Arts, 6*: 31-49.

Capener, S. D. (1995). Problems in the identity and philosophy of T'aegwŏndo and their historical causes. *Korea Journal, 35*: 80-94.

Chan, W. (1969). *A Source Book in Chinese Philosophy.* Princeton, NJ: Princeton University Press.

Chi, S. (2001). The study of social status groups in the Choson period. *The Review of Korean Studies, 4*: 243-263.

Cleary, T. (2008). *The training of the Samurai mind: A bushido sourcebook.* Boston: Shambala Publications.

Cumings, B. (2005). *Korea's place in the sun. A modern history.* NY: W. W. Norton and Co.

de Haan, P. (2002).50 years and counting. The impact of the Korean War on the people of the peninsula. http://www.calvin.edu/ news/releases/_2001_02/korea.htm.

Della Pia, J. D. (1994). Korea's mu yei do bo tong ji. *Journal of Asian Martial Arts, 3*: 62-71.

Della Pia, J. D. (1995). Native Korean sword techniques described in the Mu Yae Do Bo Tong Ji. *Journal of Asian Martial Arts, 4*: 86-97.

Doll, D. A. (2002). *Confucianism: The key to Korea's survival during the Japanese occupation from 1910-1945. Unpublished masters thesis,* California State University Dominguez Hill.

Dong-kwon, I. (1963). Traditional sports of Korea. *Korea Journal, 3*: 34-37.

Drury, B. and Clavin, T. (2009). *The last stand of Fox Company.* NY: Atlantic Monthly Press.

Dyke, J. M. (2006). Reconciliation between Korea and Japan. *Chinese Journal of International Law, 5*: 215–239

Feng, G. F. and English, J. (Trans.) (1974). *Chuang Tsu. Inner chapters.* NY: Vintage Books.

Feng, G. F. and English, J. (Trans.) (1974). *Lao Tsu. Tao te ching.* NY: Vintage Books.

Fehrenbach, T. R. (2008). *This kind of war: The classic Korean War history*. Dulles, VA: Potomac Books.

Goldstein, D. M. and Maihafer (2000). *The Korean War*. Dulles, VA: Brassey's.

Haggard, S., Kang, D., and Moon, C. I. (1997). Japanese colonialism and Korean Development: A critique. *World Development, 25*: 867-881.

Halberstam, D, (2007). The *coldest winter: America and the Korean War*. NY: Hyperion.

Hancock, J. (April 1994). The history of tang soo do. *Inside Tae Kwon Do, 3*: 17.

Hong, C. T. (n.d.) The history of Taekwon-Do. http://www.geocities.com/psta_gtf/realhist.html?100828.

Huang, C. (Trans.) (1997). *The Analects of Confucius. A literal translation with an introduction and notes*. NY: Oxford University Press.

Hwang, K. (1949). *Hwa Soo Do Kyo Bohn*. Seoul, Korea: Author.

———. (1958). *Tang Soo Do Kyo Bohn*. Seoul, Korea: Author

———. (1970). *Soo Bahk Do Dae Kham*. Seoul, Korea: Han U Ri.

———. (1978). *Tang soo Do (Soo Bahk Do)*. Seoul, Korea, Sung Moo Sa.

———. (1992). *Soo Bahk Do*. Seoul, Korea: Author.

———. (1992). *Tang Soo Do Moo Duk Kwan: Volume 2*. Springfield, NJ: Author.

———. (1993). *Moo do chul hahk*. Seoul, Korea: Author.

———. (1995). *The History Of Moo Duk Kwan*. Springfield, NJ: Author.

Kim, B. J. (2003). Paramilitary politics under the USAMGIK and the establishment of the Republic of Korea. *Korea Journal, 43*: 289-322

Kim, D. C. (2002). Beneath the tip of the iceberg: Problems in historical clarification of the Korean War. *Korea Journal, 42*: 60-86.

Kim, K, Y. K. (1977). The impact of Japanese colonial development on the Korean economy. *Korea Journal, 17*: 12-21

Kim, K. J. (1986). Taekwondo: Its brief history. *Korea Journal, 26*: 20-25.

Kim, L (2004) *World Cultural Heritage, Koguryo Tomb Murals*. Cultural Properties Administration, ICOMOS: Seoul, Korea

Kim, M. B. (24 June 1998). East wind West wind. Unfinished
    businesses of the *war. Korea Herald.*
    http://proquest.umi.com/pqdweb?index=11
    &did=30479587&SrchMode=3&sid=1&Fmt=3&VInst=PROD
    &VType=PQD&RQT=309&VName=PQD&TS=1202258019
    &clientId=17862&aid=5.
Kim, S. H. (2000). *Muye Dobo Tongji: The comprehensive illustrated
    manual of martial arts of ancient Korea.* Wethersfield, CT:
    Turtle Press.
Kim, W. H. (1986). *Muyedobo T'ongji*: Illustrated Survey of the
    Martial Arts. *Korea Journal, 26*: 42-54.
Kirk, D. (March 03, 2006). Korea's bid for truth and reconciliation.
    The Christian Science Monitor. http://www.csmonitor.com/
    2006/ 0303/p25s01-woap.html.
Kristoff, N. D. (1998 October 9). Japan apologizes forcefully for its
    occupation of Korea. *The New York Times.*
    http://query.nytimes.com/gst/ fullpage.html? res=
    9F01E4DA133BF93AA35753C1A96E958260.
Lee, P. H., de Bary, W. T., Ch'oe, Yongho, and Hughes, H. H. W.
    (1997). *Sources of Korean tradition: Volume I. From early
    times through the sixteenth century.* (1997). NY: Columbia
    University Press.
Lee, S. Y. (2007). *The Metropolitan Museum of Art. Timeline of Art
    History. Yangban: The Cultural Life of the Chosŏn Literati.*
    http://www.metmuseum.org/toah/hd/yang/hd_yang.htm.
Library of Congress (2007). *Country studies. South Korea.*
    http://countrystudies.us/south-korea/.
Lim, C. H. (2006). The National Security Law and anticommunist
    ideology in Korean society. *Korea Journal, 46*: 80-102.
MacIntyre, D. (2002). A legacy lost. *Time.* http://www.time.com/ time/
    arts/article/0,8599,197704,00.html.
Tistory (n.d.). *A Practical Guide to McCune-Reischauer
    Romanization.* http://mccune-reischauer.tistory.com/.
Millett, A. R. (2001). The Korean War: A 50-year critical
    historiography. *Journal of Strategic Studies, 24*: 188-224.
Min, P. G. (2003). Korean "Comfort Women": The intersection of
    colonial power, gender, and class. *Gender and Society, 17*:
    938-957.
Moon, K. H. S. (1999). South Korean movements against militarized

sexual labor. *Asian Survey*, *39*: 310-327.

Nam-Gil, H. and Mangan, J. A. (1998). The knights of Korea: Hwarangdo, militarism, and nationalism. *International Journal of the History of Sport*, *15*: 77-102.

Pak Wan-so (1972). *A season of thirst*. Publisher unknown.

Pieters, W. (1994). Notes on the historical development of Korean martial sports. An addendum to Young's history and development of tae kyon. *Journal of Asian Martial Arts*, *3*: 83-89.

Safire, W. (2008). Waterboarding. *The New York Times*. http://www.nytimes.com/2008/03/09/magazine/09wwlnSafire-t.html.

Sawyer, R. D. (1994). *Sun-tzu. The art of war*. NY: Barnes and Noble.

Schnabel, J. F. (1992). *United States Army in the Korean War. Policy and Direction: The First Year*. Center of Military History, United States Army Washington, D. C. http://www.history.army.mil/books/P&D.HTM.

Shaw, S. (2004). The history of Taekwondo. http://scottshaw.com/taekwondohistory/.

Spiro, A. (1990). *Contemplating the ancients: Aesthetic and social issues in early Chinese portraiture*. Berkley, CA: University of California Press. http://content.cdlib.org/xtf/view?docId= ft138nb 10m&chunk.id=0&doc.view=print.

Sterngold, J. (1991 July 11). South Korea seeks return of its artworks from Japan. *The New York Times*. http://query.nytimes.com/gst/fullpage.html?res=9D0CE7D6163DF932A25754C0A9679 58260&sec=&spon=&pagewanted=2.

Tauber, I. B. (1946). The population potential of postwar Korea. *The Far Eastern Quarterly*, *5*: 289-307.

The Cleveland Museum of Art (2008). Education and Research. Asian Odyssey. Paintings after Ancient Masters. *Lao Tzu Riding and Ox* painted by Chen Hongshou (1598 - 1652) (CMA 1979.27.1.2). http://www. clevelandart.org/educef/asianodyssey08/html/1979_27_1_2pu.html.

The Metropolitan Museum of Art, New York. (2008).*Special Exhibitions. The Games in Ancient Athens: A Special Presentation to Celebrate the 2004 Olympics Panathenaic prize amphora, ca. 525–500 B.C.E.* http://www.metmuseum.org/ special/Athens/3.L.htm.

Tikhonov, V. (1998). Hwarang organization: Its functions and ethics. *Korea Journal, 38*: 318-338.

Truman Museum and Library, (n. d.). *The Korean War.* Harry S. Truman Library and Museum, http://www.trumanlibrary.org/ whistlestop/ study_collections/ korea/large/index.htm

U. S. Army Center of Military History (2001). *Army Historical Series. American Military History. Chapter 25, The Korean War, 1950-1953.* http://www.history.army.mil/books/AMH/AMH-25.htm.

Weider History Group (2008). HistoryNet.Com. Captain James Jabara: Ace of the Korean War. http://www.historynet.com/captain-james-jabara-ace-of-the-korean-war.htm.

Westover, J. G. (1990). *Combat support in Korea.* Facsimile Reprint. CMH Publication 22-1. Center of Military History, United States Army. Washington, D.C. http://www.history.army.mil/books/korea/22_1_6.htm

Wilhelm, R. and Baynes, C. (Ed. and Trans.) (1967). *The I Ching or Book of Changes.* Princeton, NJ: Princeton University Press.

Yi, K. J. (2002). In search of a panacea: Japan-Korea rapprochement and America's "far eastern problems." *The Pacific Historical Review, 71*: 633-662.

Yi, T. and Pak, C. (eds.). (1790). *Muye tobo t'ongji.* (rev. ed.). Shinhan Sorim.

Young, R. W. (1993). The history and development of tae kyon. *Journal of Asian Martial Arts, 2*: 45-69.

Glossary

Korean Term	Han'gŭl	Chinese	Translation and Meaning
baegil kido	백일기도	百日祈禱	Hundred-day prayer retreat
bi	비	悲	Sadness
bo bup	보 법	步法	Method of steps
bokhap chwisang	복합취상	複合取象	Complex adoption of image
bonbang	본방	本防	Innate, original, justifiable and unconscious defense
bonneung	본능	本能	Instinct or original ability
bonsung	본성	本性	Innate or original nature
bujaeng	부쟁	不爭	Non-struggle or non-conflict
bujungbyungjuhang	부정변주항	不頂扁走抗	Translated to mean that one should do one's best to not be excessive or insufficient in all of one's thoughts and actions; one should work to maintain adaptability and appropriateness; *bu* means one should not do something; *jung* means to lean towards excesses; *byun* means to fall short; *ju* means to maintain proper distance and refers to judgment and control; *hang* signifies resistance and means that one should not go to great excesses
bulhaengjigi	불행지기	不幸知己	Unfortunate self-knowledge

Korean Term	Han'gŭl	Chinese	Translation and Meaning
chaju	차주	次主	Bundled rice straw representing a protective deity that measured about one meter wide and one and a half meters high
chajukkari	차주까리	次主까리	A type of alter frequently placed in the back of the house considered a very solemn area where shamans conducted prayers and worship
che	체	體	Body; may also be translated as "fundamental essence"
cheon	천	天	Chinese term for God or Heaven
cheonsung	천성	天性	Heavenly endowed nature
choong	중	中	Centrality; center or pivot; middle; corresponds or relates to the spine
choongyong	중용	中庸	Middle way; the mean
chunantong	천안통	天眼通	Power to see beyond visual range
chung	정	精	Spiritual essence'
chung	정	情	Originally meant a refined essence; usually rendered "feelings,"; the phenomenal manifestations of human nature (e.g., anger, joy, shame, etc.) When the heart has been stirred by external conditions; *chung* is a person's ki that is highly refined as consciousness
chung	정	靜	Fundamental quietness; tranquility

Korean Term	Han'gŭl	Chinese	Translation and Meaning
chungshintong-il bup	정신통일법	精神統一法	Consciousness unification method; to unify or concentrate the mind into a single whole
chunin	천인	天人	One who has attained Do
chunitong	천이통	天耳通	Power to hear beyond normal auditory
daegi	대기	大氣	The atmosphere, literally great ki
Daehak	대학	大學	Confucian work entitled "Great Learning"
daejung	대정	大情	"Great emotion"; state of emotion that involves the detachment from feelings of like and dislike
danjun	단전	丹田	Internal point of body located approximately three centimeters below the navel
danjun hoheup bup	단전호흡법	丹田呼吸法	Cinnabar (dan) field (jun) breathing method; a method of abdominal breathing
dansun chwisang	단순취상	單純取象	Simple adoption of image
deuk	득	得	Earn; obtaining
dham toi sip e ro	담퇴십이로	潭腿十二路	Name of a pattern of ancient Chinese movements; "sip e ro" refers to 12 combinations of movements; "dham toi" translates as "spring leg"
do	도	道	The way; source of nature

Korean Term	Han'gŭl	Chinese	Translation and Meaning
doduk	도덕	道德	Way of virtue; morality
duk	덕	德	Chinese term meaning "Virtue"
geumsuryeon	금수련	金修練	Iron conditioning
gigong bup	기공법	氣功法	Ki conditioning method
gong	공	恐	Fear
gonggi	공기	空氣	Air; literally empty ki
guk	극	極	Ultimate; extreme focal point
gunja	군자	君子	Superior man
gwa	과	戈	Knife
gwansamsaeng	관삼생	觀三生	Seeing previous three lives of others
gwansang	관상	觀象	To intuit the movements and changes of an object; the study of the changes; *gwan* means observation; *sang* refers to movement
gyung	경	驚	Surprise; frightened
gyung	경	勁	Vigor; strong
haenggongshimhae	행공심해	行功深解	A level of training where one's understanding and insight deepens as a by means of action, training and conditioning.

Korean Term	Han'gŭl	Chinese	Translation and Meaning
hananeuunim	하느님	Not available	Korean term for God
haneul	하늘	Not available	Korean term for heaven
hang	항	抗	To resist or oppose
heub-yeol	흡열	吸熱	Taking in heat
heui	희	喜	Joy
heupki	흡기	吸氣	Taking in ki
hocheon	호천	昊天	See *Hwangje*
hoejun hoheup bup	회전호흡법	廻轉呼吸法	Rotating breath technique
hoyuksamsaeng	호역삼생	虎逆三生	Tiger counteract three lives
hucheon	후천	後天	Developed after birth; "acquired nature"; can be changed or influenced; must be purposefully developed or learned based on deuk (virtue)"
hucheonjeok	후천적	後天的	Has the same semantic meaning as hucheon; term used as an adjective to describe hucheon characteristics of something
hucheonseong	후천성	後天性	Literally means "hucheon nature"
huri	허리	Not available	Pelvic girdle or waist of the body

Korean Term	Han'gŭl	Chinese	Translation and Meaning
hwa	화	和	Harmonization
Hwa Soo Do	화수도	花手道	Original name used by Hwang Kee of the traditional Korean martial art he taught
hwabyung	화병	火病	Fire disease; conditions resulting from poor ki circulation due to mental discontent
hwaipjuk	화입적	火入籍	Fire enter register
hwal	활	活	Live, Revival
hwangje	황제	皇帝	Emperor
hwanjungbup	환정법	還精法	Transforming essence technique
hyo	효	孝	Filial piety
hyunhwa	현화	玄化	Mysterious transformation
ilban shim hoheup bup	일반심호흡법	一般心呼吸法	General deep breathing technique
jae	제	齊	Transliterated cleansing, purifying or cultivating the mind
je	제	帝	Emperor (see *hwanje*)
jeongja	정세	正姿	Right Posture
jeongjeong	정정	正定	Right determination or composure

Korean Term	Han'gŭl	Chinese	Translation and Meaning
jeongshim	정심	正心	Right Mind
jeongshin	정신	精神	Denotes the spiritual or psychological
ji or jigak	지(知) or 지각	知覺	Knowledge
jikgwan	직관	直觀	Korean term for intuition; literally means direct (*jik*) seeing or observation (*gwan*); object of intuition
jikshim	직심	直心	Straight heart
jugi bup	주기법	注氣法	Focused ki method—here the syllable ju means "to pour into" or "bring to bear"
kaesung	개성	個性	Individuality
ki	기	氣	Energy (Note: may also be seen spelled as "qi," "gi," or "chi")
kiun	기운	氣運	Vigor
kwon bup	권법	拳法	Fist method
kye	계	戒	Transliterated as that which prevents suffering, misfortune or calamity; refers to the cultivation and practice of mind training that prevents illness and leads to a life of health, tranquility and happiness
kyejae	계제	戒齊	Purification; refers to the cultivation and practice of mind training that prevents illness and leads to a life of health, tranquility and

Korean Term	Han'gŭl	Chinese	Translation and Meaning
li	이	利	happiness; Benefit, profit, gain, or advantage
mangyang yongjung bup	망양용중법	忘兩用中法	A Taoist method or technique of forgetting the two and adopting the center
manmul	만물	萬物	Myriad things; includes plants, animals and human beings
mo che	모체	母體	Literally "mother body"; also represents originality or essence of foundation; source and sustainer;
mo hyung	모형	母型	Literally "mother figure"; also may interpreted as "resembling" or "to be alike"; can also be interpreted to represent a "mold" or "model"
mokshijae	목시재	木試才	Wood test talent
moo	무	武	Martial; prevent inner and outer conflict
moo do	무도	武道	Martial way; also referred to as *wu tao* in Chinese and *budo* in Japanese
Moo Do Chul Hahk	무도철학	武道哲學	Martial (Moo) Way (Do) Philosophy (Chul Hahk) *chul* is literally translated as sagacious or wisdom; *hahk* is translated as the study of something
Moo Duk Kwan	무덕관	武德館	Name of the organization of practitioners of Soo Bahk Do and Tang Soo Do (Martial Virtue Institute)

Korean Term	Han'gŭl	Chinese	Translation and Meaning
Moo Ye Do Bo Tong Ji	무예도보통지	武藝圖譜通志	Title of ancient manual of martial arts of Korea
Moo Yei Si Bo	무예시보	武藝時報	Title of newspaper published by Hwang Kee describing the history, culture, philosophy, and technique of Soo Bahk Do
mooye	무예	武藝	Martial art
mu (wu-wei in Chinese)	무	無	No or not; without limit; non-being
mua	무아	無我	Korean term for the stage of non-self
muagyung bup	무아경법	無我境法	Fasting and prayer, meditation and stage of non-self technique
mugeukkyung	무극경	無極境	Non-being ultimate
mun	문	文	The ancient and original meaning of *mun* is "pattern." This meaning is now differentiated by putting the radical for "thread" to the left of the character. The character eventually took on the meanings of "Culture" (the patterns of society), "civilization" and "literature" (patterns on paper). Traditionally, the scholarly or "cultured people" were known as *munin* (a *mun* person).
mungyum haenggong bup	묵념행공법	默念行功法	Silent thought technique
munhak	문학	文學	Literature as a field of study

Korean Term	Han'gŭl	Chinese	Translation and Meaning
munin	문인	文人	Scholarly person
musa	무사	無思	Non-thought; tranquility; the unmoving
musang	무상	無像	Invisible thing
muwi	무위	無爲	Non-action; not doing; refers to a type of selfless non-action
myeong	명	明	Luminosity
myungmyung bup	명명법	明明法	Technique of expanding luminosity
nae gung	내공	內攻	Inner training or power
no	노	怒	Anger
paeja	패자	覇者	Regional despots
pogi bup	포기법	佈氣法	Unfolding ki technique; a special mind training technique involving the treatment of diseases using ki by another person due to rash mental or physical behavior, or due to irregularities in environment or diet by a person
punggwansamsaeng	풍관삼생	風觀三生	Wind observes three lives
pyehgi bup	폐기법	閉氣法	Closed ki technique
ri	리	理	Principle; principles and laws by which things are manifested

Korean Term	Han'gŭl	Chinese	Translation and Meaning
ryun bup	련법	鍊法	Method of conditioning
sa	사	思	To seriously ponder or think about something; may also refer to phenomena—that which is manifested in the world
saenggi	생기	生氣	Birth ki; a basic element of life
sagak hoheup bup	사각호흡법	四角呼吸法	Square breathing technique
sam t'ae sung	삼태성	三台星	Three Great Stars
samgak hoheup bup	삼각호흡법	三角呼吸法	Triangle breathing technique
samjae	삼재	三才	Heaven, earth and man
samsaeng	삼생	三生	Refers to man's current life, the past and the future
sang	상	象	Movement
sangje	상제	上帝	Chinese term for God.
sanshillyeongdang	산신령당	山神靈堂	A type of alter referred to as the "mountain spirit altar" for the conduct of prayers, worship and rituals.
sari	사리	事理	Phenomena, facts, or reason.
seh bup	세법	勢法	Method of postures.
semi hoheup bup	세미호흡법	細微呼吸法	Fine breath technique.

Korean Term	Han'gŭl	Chinese	Translation and Meaning
seong	성	性	Nature in the sense of human nature.
seongjeong	성정	性情	Seong is "Nature" in the sense of "man's nature," etc. In other words, the natural proclivities of the human heart in its natural state. Jeong, usually rendered "feelings," are the phenomenal manifestations of this "Nature" (e.g., anger, joy, shame, etc.) when the heart has been stirred by external conditions.
Shakyamuni	석가모니	釋迦牟尼	Korean name for Buddha; also known as Prince Siddhartha.
shim	심	心	Mind; heart.
shim gung	심공	心攻	Mind training or power.
shin	신	神	Spirit; also term used for gods, devas, spirits and a person's spirit.
shinju	신주	神主	Divine sovereign.
shinsun	신선	神仙	A Taoist hermit with super natural power.
shintongnyuk	신통력	神通力	Divine powers.
sip sam seh	십삼세	十三勢	13 influences.
Soo Bahk Do	수박도	手搏道	Current name of the traditional Korean martial art developed by Hwang Kee.
sulli	순리	純理	Accordance with principle.

Korean Term	Han'gŭl	Chinese	Translation and Meaning
sulli bup	순리법	純理法	Accordance with Principle Method; following the fundamental principles of the Do in order to achieve mind training.
sun	선	仙	State of being natural; natural conditions; purity.
sun bi	선비		A Taoist adept or hermit, scholar.
sun do	선도	仙道	Path of cultivating the Do for the sake of *muwi* or non-action in the sense of spontaneous action without selfish motives and non-desire.
suncheojeok	선천적	先天的	Semantic meaning same as *suncheon*; term used as an adjective to describe *suncheon* characteristics of something .
suncheon	선천	先天	Literally translated as "before Heaven"; that which is innate or natural; developed before birth; characteristics or nature that one is born with; natural; may be translated as "innate nature."
sung-in	성인	聖人	A sage.
sungwangdang	성황당	城隍堂	A type of alter referred to as the "abundance king altar" for the conduct of prayers, worship and rituals.
sunin	선인	仙人	A practitioner of sun do; a Taoist adept or hermit.
sun-wu	손무	孫武	Also known as Sun Tzu, author of the *Art of War/Military Methods*.
susubi	수수비	水受牌	Literally, "water reception steel."
t'aegukkyung	태극경	太極竟	Realm of the Great Ultimate; the realm with images but no forms; the world of Nature.

Korean Term	Han'gŭl	Chinese	Translation and Meaning
tae keuk kwon	태극권	太極拳	Also known as tai chi chuan; ancient Chinese martial training method typically comprised of patterns of movements.
taeshikbup	태식법	胎息法	Fetal breathing technique.
taeyang	태양	太陽	Sun
taeyanggye	태양계	太陽系	Korean word for solar system; literally means Great Yang System.
Tang Soo Do	당수도	唐手道	Name used by Hwang Kee after the Korean War for the martial art he taught.
tao	도	道	See *Do*
tayjayun	대자연	大自然	Great nature
teoju daegam	터주대감	曰主大監	His Excellency of House guardian deity.
teojuragi	터주라기	Not available	Often used to refer to the same or similar entity as *teoju daegam*; no Chinese characters available.
tong	동	動	Action
toseunggeup	토승급	土昇級	Literally "earth ascending level" or "earth up grade."
u	우	憂	Being concerned or worried about something.
um	음	陰	Korean equivalent of the Chinese term for "yin" referring to female and passive characteristics of nature; opposite of *yang*.

Korean Term	Han'gŭl	Chinese	Translation and Meaning
umin jungchaek	우민정책	愚民政策	Literally translated "foolish people policy."
ungi	운기	運氣	Literally translate "transport ki"; refers to circulating or moving ki.
weh gung	외공	外攻	External training or power
wu-wei	무위	無爲	See muwi
yang	양	陽	Refers to male and active characteristics of nature; opposite of *um/yin.*
yangban	양반	兩班	The two upper classes of old Korea.
yeoksamsaeng	역삼생	逆三生	Seeing previous three lives.
yeong	령	靈	Spirit; spiritual force
yin	음	陰	See *um*
yong	용	用	Function; use; can also be used to refer to phenomena perceivable by man; may also refer to relationship between non-existence (see *musang*) and existence (see *yusang*).
yongjaerok	용제록	龍再綠	One of several stages or levels of spiritual purification that allows the ability to see the past, present and future, previous lives and the ability to see the intentions and mind of others. This stage is symbolized by the dragon.
yookki bup	육기법	六氣法	Six ki technique

Korean Term	Han'gŭl	Chinese	Translation and Meaning
yu	유	有	Being
yungi bup	연기법	練氣法	Training ki technique; also Opposition of Principle Method; opposition to Nature's principles.
yunjin	연진	燕津	Literally translated to mean swallowing one's saliva; determination.
yunsu bup	연수법	軟醉法	Refers to the light dregs technique used to correct certain conditions resulting from poor ki circulation due to mental discontent or chaotic change.
yuwi	유위	有爲	Action

Appendix

Brief Listing of the Achievements and Contributions of Hwang Kee to the Development and Advancement of the Traditional Korean Martial Art, Soo Bahk Do.

Date	Achievement/Contribution
1936	Began martial arts studies in Manchuria, China
1945 November 9	Founded Moo Duk Kwan style and established first Hwa Soo Do class in Ministry of Transportation
1947 March	Attempted to unify the five major existing styles in Korea: Moo Duk Kwan, Chung Do Kwan, Yeun Moo Kwan, Song Moo Kwan, YMCA/Kwon Bup Bu
1947	Presided as chairman at the first Hwa Soo Do demonstration in the Transportation High School gymnasium
1947 May 7	Established first regional branch Tang Soo Do school in Dae Jun City, Choong-Nam Province
1947 June 5	Established Hwa Soo Do (Tang Soo Do) school in the Department of Railways
1947 July 7	Established Hwa Soo Do (Tang Soo Do) school in the Labor Department
1949 May 30	Authored the first Hwa Soo Do textbook in Korea
1950 June 25	Korean War begins and suspends teaching for seventeen months
1951 January 4	Relocated to Dae Gu City, then to Pusan City
1951 November	Established temporary Moo Duk Kwan Headquarters in Cho Ryang-Dong, Pusan
1952 April	Began teaching at the Police Academy in Pusan
1952 October 1	Began instruction at the Ministry of Defense in Pusan

Date	Achievement/Contribution
1953 September	Returned to Seoul to re-establish Moo Duk Kwan Headquarters after Korean War ends
1953	Established Korean Tang Soo Do Association, presiding as Chairman
1953 November	Established Tang Soo Do studios in middle and high schools throughout Korea
1953 December	Applied to join the Korean Athletic Association
1954 April	Established Tang Soo Do studio in Mapo Correctional Facility
1954 July	Attempted to unify Korean Tang Soo Do Association and Korean Kong Soo Do Association (Chong Do Kwan, Ji Do Kwan, Chang Moo Kwan, Song Moo Kwan)
1955 May	Grand opening of headquarters (43-1 Dong Ja-Dong, Choong Gu, Seoul)
1955 July	Established the following provincial Moo Duk Kwan branches: 1) Seoul 2) Gyung Gi 3) Gang Won 4) Gyung Buk 5) Gyung Nam 6) Chun Nam 7) Choong Buk
1955 Aug.	Ministry of Education prohibits teaching Tang Soo Do in middle and high schools throughout Korea
1955 Aug.	Established Tang Soo Do studio in Seo Dae Moon Correctional Facility
1955 August	Established Tang Soo Do studio at Korean Air Force Headquarters
1955	Organized and chaired first International Goodwill Demonstration between Korea and China
1956 March	Begins teaching at the Korean Air Force Academy
1956 March	Dispatched instructors to the following bases: Soo Won, Sa Chun, Dae Gu and Dae Jun Air Force Academy

Date	Achievement/Contribution
1956 May	Begins instructing at the Korean Naval Academy
1956 June	Established Tang Soo Do studio at Korean Naval Headquarters
1956 June	Established Tang Soo Do studio at In Ha Engineering University
1956 October	Established Tang Soo Do at Korean Military Police Headquarters
1956 October	Established Tang Soo Do at Army Printing Corps
1956 November	Established Tang Soo Do at the R.O.K. 2nd Army
1957 March	Established Tang Soo Do studio at Korean Army Headquarters
1957 May	Established Tang Soo Do studio at Korean Marine Corps
1957 July	Established Tang Soo Do studio at Han Yang University in Seoul
1957 September	Established Tang Soo Do studio at the U.S. 8th Army in Young San
1958 July	Authored second Tang Soo Do textbook
1959 May	Established Tang Soo Do Studio in Seoul Agricultural University in Soo Won
1959 July	Established Tang Soo Do studio at Koryo University in Seoul
1959 October	Established Tang Soo Do studio at Air Force University
1960 June	Authored Tang Soo Do self-defense textbook
1960 June	Created name "Soo Bahk Do" from ancient name of Soo Bahk, Soo Bahk Ki or Soo Bahk Hee
1960 September	Published *Moo Yei Si Bo*

Date	Achievement/Contribution
1960 June 30	Using ancient Korean martial arts name, incorporated and registered with the Korean Ministry of Education under the name of *Dae Han Soo Bahk Do Hoe* (Korean Soo Bahk Do Association) becoming the first member association
1960 July	Ji Do Kwan becomes second member to join Korean Soo Bahk Do Association Moo Duk Kwan
1960 October	Instructors assigned to the following USA 8th Army branch studios: 8th Army Headquarters; Moon San; Dong Do; Chung; O-San; Inchon; Pusan
1961 May 14	Formed the Asian Tang Soo Do Association among Korea, Japan, Taiwan
1961 June	Established Chun Buk Province regional branch
1961 June	Established Tang Soo Do studio at Hong Ik University
1961 October	Established Moo Duk Kwan in Michigan, USA
1962 May	Established Tang Soo Do Association in USA
1962 May	Established Moo Duk Kwan in France
1962 June	Re-registered Korean Soo Bahk Do Association due to ruling of new government
1962 Sept.	Established Tang Soo Do Association in Canada
1963 July	Established Tang Soo Do Association in England
1964	Participated with Korean team in first Asian Tang Soo Do championship in Japan
1964 July	Established Tang Soo Do studio at Yeun Sae University
1964 November	Established West German Tang Soo Do Association
1964 December	Board of Directors of Soo Bahk Do changed and registered with government

Date	Achievement/Contribution
1964 December	Moo Duk Kwan announces revised charter and bylaws
1965	Sponsored and organized second Asian Tang Soo Do Championship
1965 January	Established Moo Duk Kwan regional branches in Washington D.C., New York, Michigan, California, Washington, Texas and Florida
1965 May	Korean Soo Bahk Do Association's legal status revoked; decision appealed to appellate level and relief granted
1965 August	Established Moo Duk Kwan branch in Philippines
1965 December	Appeal granted restoring legal status to Korean Soo Bahk Do Association
1966	Established Moo Duk Kwan branch in France
1966	Established Moo Duk Kwan branch in West Germany
1966 January	Korean Government appeals appellate decision to Supreme Court
1966 June	Korean Supreme Court rules in favor of Korean Soo Bahk Do Association
1966 November	Revised Moo Duk Kwan regulations
1966 December	Revised charter and by-laws of Korean Soo Bahk Do Association as required by the Korean government
1967	Established Moo Duk Kwan in Malaysia
1968	Established Moo Duk Kwan in Italy
1968	Sponsored and organized first World and fifth Asian Tang Soo Do Championship at Citizen Hall, Seoul
1968 August	Election of new Korean Soo Bahk Do Association Board of Directors and registration with government

Date	Achievement/Contribution
1969	Participated at second World and sixth Asian Tang Soo Do Championship (Philippines)
1973	Awarded "Da Ma Roo" from Philippines' President Marcos
1973 May	Established Moo Duk Kwan in Greece (Instructor: H.C. Hwang)
1974 March	Established Moo Duk Kwan in Belgium (Instructor: B.J. Lee)
1974 October	United States Soo Bahk Do Moo Duk Kwan directors convention and general meeting of all USA Dan members at Burlington, NJ
1975 June	United States Soo Bahk Do charter convention and special seminar by Grandmaster Hwang Kee (Hilton Hotel, NY)
1975 June	Participated in first Pan-Hellenic Martial Arts Championship in Athens, Greece
1976 October	Each foreign branch holds Soo Bahk Do meeting and convention
1977 May	Organized and conducted special seminar at each foreign Moo Duk Kwan branch
1978 July 22	1st United States National Tang Soo Do Moo Duk Kwan Championship at Concord Hotel, Monticello, NY
1978 October	3rd World Soo Bahk Do Moo Duk Kwan Championship at London, England
1980 July	Sponsored and participated in World Ko Dan Ja meeting in Newark, NJ
1980 December	Sponsored and organized Goodwill Soo Bahk Do Moo Duk Kwan Champion- ships between Korea and USA held at Jang Choong Gym, Seoul

Date	Achievement/Contribution
1981 September	Sponsored and participated in world Ko Dan Ja Meeting, regarding 1982 World Championships in Atlantic City, NJ
1982 May	Special Soo Bahk Do Moo Duk Kwan seminar and clinic held at U.S. Air Force Academy in Colorado
1982 November 4	International and Fourth United States National Tang Soo Do Moo Duk Kwan Championship at Atlantic City, NJ during which Hwang Kee presented the first public presentation of material translated from the *Moo Yei Do Bo Tong Ji* (Hwa Sung Hyung)
1982 December	England national Soo Bahk Do Moo Duk Kwan Championship
1983 August	Sponsored and organized special Chil Sung Hyung Seminar and Clinic
1983 December	Organized and attended first week-long Ko Dan Ja test
1984 October	6th United States National Tang Soo Do Moo Duk Kwan Championship at West Point Military Academy Gym, NY
1984 November	All England National Soo Bahk Do Moo Duk Kwan Championship
1984 November	Special Chil Sung Hyung Clinic for European region at London, England
1985 March	Attended special Chil Sung Hyung Clinic for South East Asia region at Sarawak, Malaysia
1987 July	Special International Summer Training Camp at Pathwork Center, NY
1987 December	Attended special Chil Sung Hyung Clinic for South America at Buenos Aires, Argentina
1988 March	Organizes special clinic for European region at Athens, Greece

Date	Achievement/Contribution
1988 May	Grand opening ceremony for new building for World Moo Duk Kwan Headquarters, Seoul, Korea
1988	Special clinic and Ko Dan Ja meeting for Southeast Asia region at Kuala Lumpur, Malaysia
1988 July	Annual International Summer Training Camp at Pathwork Center, NY
1988 November	Attended Tenth United States National Tang Soo Do Moo Duk Kwan Championship at West Point, NY
1988 December	Sponsored and organized world Ko Dan Ja special training in Seoul, Korea
1989 January	Attended Ko Dan Ja meeting and initiates discussion of "Mission 2000" agenda
1989 May 15	Sponsored and attended International Soo Bahk Do Goodwill Demonstration and clinics in Seoul, Korea
1990 January	Announces "Mission 2000," along range plan for the future of the Moo Duk Kwan
1990 March	Conducted International Seminar, London, England
1990 March	Conducted National Clinics in Belgium, Italy and Greece
1990 April	Organized special Ko Dan Ja meeting of Korean Soo Bahk Do Association Moo Duk Kwan in Seoul, Korea
1991 March	Conducted the first yuk ro clinics presenting material and movements translated from the *Moo Yei Do Bo Tong Ji.*
1991 June	Published *Soo Bahk Do* (Korean version) describing the yuk ro movements from the *Moo Yei Do Bo Tong Ji*
1991 December	International demonstration and clinic, March Del Plata, Argentina
1992 March	Published 424 pages of *Soo Bahk Do* (Korean Version)

Date	Achievement/Contribution
1992 March	Conducted yuk ro and chil sung hyung clinics, Headquarters, Seoul, Korea
1992 June	Attended the International Demonstration and Clinic at Athens, Greece
1992 November	Published Soo Bahk Do (Tang Soo Do) volume II (English version).
1993 April	Conducted the annual European clinic, Bruxelles, Belgium
1993 June	Published *Moo Duk Kwan* (Korean Version)
1993 August	Published *Moo Do Chul Hahk* (Korean version)
1993 September	Published *Instructional Guide for Soo Bahk Do Moo Duk Kwan*
1993 November	The 1st Youth Soo Bahk Do Moo Duk Kwan Goodwill Championship, Zurich, Switzerland
1994 February	Official announcement of the Moo Duk Kwan 50th Anniversary event in Seoul, Korea
1994 June	Annual European Clinic and meeting for preparing the European Soo Bahk Do Moo Duk Kwan Federation, Bruxelle, Belgium
1994 September 2	International youth good-will championship, Zurich, Switzerland
1994 September	Official birth of the European Soo Bahk Do Moo Duk Kwan Federation, Zurich, Switzerland
1994 October	Appointed Task Force member for future Mexican National Moo Duk Kwan Federation
1994 December	Published *Limited Edition for the Instructional Guide*
1995 April	1st European Soo Bahk Do Moo Duk Kwan Federation Clinic and meeting

Date	Achievement/Contribution
1995 September	50th anniversary Celebration of the Moo Duk Kwan, Seoul Culture and Educational Center, Seoul, Korea
2000	55th anniversary celebration of the Moo Duk Kwan, Seoul, Korea
2005	60th anniversary celebration of the Moo Duk Kwan, Seoul Korea

Table of Concordance

English Translation	*Moo Do Chul Hahk (Original)* English Titles	*Moo Do Chul Hahk (Original)* Han'gŭl Titles
Preface by Hwang Kee	Preface	머리말
Section I: The Importance of Philosophy	Section 1: Forward	서론(序論)
Chapter 1: Personal Reflections	Chapter 1: Reasons for Writing this Book	저자(著者)의 서정(敍情)
Chapter 2: Space and Time	Chapter 2: Theory of Space and Time	공간(空間)과 시간(時間)론
Chapter 3: The Source of Man's Transience	Chapter 3: Theory of Man's Transience	인간 무상론
Chapter 4: The Source of Philosophy	Chapter 4: The Source of Philosophy	철학(哲學)의 유래(由來)
Chapter 5: The Goal of Philosophy	Chapter 5: The Meaning of Philosophy	철학(哲學)의 의의(意義)
	Chapter 6: The Goal of Philosophy	철학(哲學)의 목적(目的)
	Chapter 7: The Importance of Philosophy	철학(哲學)의 중요성(重要性)
Chapter 6: The Changes of *Chou I*[1]	Chapter 8: Condensed Record of the *Chou I*	고대철학(古代哲學)인 주역(周易) 약기(略記)

English Translation	Moo Do Chul Hahk (Original) English Titles	Moo Do Chul Hahk (Original) Han'gŭl Titles
Chapter 7: World History, High Antiquity and Philosophy	Section 2, Chapter 9: World History, High Antiquity	세계사(世界史) 상고사(上古史)
Chapter 8: Eastern and Western Philosophy	Chapter 9: Eastern and Western Philosophy	동양철학(東洋哲學)과 서양철학(西洋哲學)
Section II: Realm of the Infinite Unlimited	Section 2: The Infinite Unlimited Realm	영원무한경(永遠無限境)
Chapter 1: Forward	Chapter 1: Forward	서문(序文)
Chapter 2: Realm of Complete Nothingness	Chapter 2: Realm of Complete Nothingness	완전허무경(完全虛無境)
Chapter 3: Realm of the Non-being Ultimate[2]	Chapter 3: Realm of the Non-being Ultimate	무극경(無極境)
Chapter 4: Realm of the Great Ultimate	Chapter 4: The State of the Great Ultimate	태극경(太極境)
Chapter 5: Universe of the Mysterious Realm	Chapter 5: University of the Mysterious Realm	신비계(神秘界) 우주(宇宙)
Chapter 6: Realm of Reality	Chapter 3 (Passages 7-8):Realm of the Non-being Ultimate	7절:인간(人間)의 개념음 8절: 도론(道論)
Chapter 7: Realm of the Future, Passage 1	Chapter 6: The Concept of God	신(神)에 대한 관념(觀念)

English Translation	*Moo Do Chul Hahk (Original)* English Titles	*Moo Do Chul Hahk (Original)* Han'gŭl Titles
Chapter 7: Realm of the Future, Passage 2	Chapter 7: The Concept of Heaven	천(天)에 대한 관념(觀念)
Section III, Chapter 3	Chapter 8: Regarding Innate Nature	선천성(先天性)에 대하여
Section I, Chapter 7	Chapter 9: World History, High Antiquity	세계사(世界史) 상고사(上古史)
Section III: The Logic of Virtue	Section 3: The Logic of Virtue	덕(德)에 대한 논리(論理)
Chapter 1: Introduction	Chapter 1: Introduction	서론(序論)
Chapter 2: Man's Uniqueness	Chapter 2: Man's Uniqueness	인간(人間)의 특이성(特異性)
Chapter 3: Regarding Innate Nature	Section 2, Chapter 8: Regarding Innate Nature	선천성(先天性)에 대하여
Chapter 4: Regarding Acquired Nature	Chapter 3: Regarding Acquired Nature	후천성(後天性)에 대하여
Chapter 5: The Logic of Good and Evil	Chapter 4: The Logic of Good and Evil	선(善)과 악(惡)의 논리
Chapter 6: The Theory of Being Ordinary	Chapter 5: The Theory of Being Ordinary	평범론(平凡論)
Chapter 7: Heaven and Hell	Chapter 6: Heaven and Hell	극락(極樂)과 지옥(地獄)
Section IV: The Philosophy of Balance	Section 4: The Philosophy of Balance	균형철학(均衡哲學)

English Translation	*Moo Do Chul Hahk (Original)* English Titles	*Moo Do Chul Hahk (Original)* Han'gŭl Titles
Section V: Moo Do Philosophy	Section 5: Moo Do Philosophy	무도철학(武道哲學)
Chapter 1: Introduction	Chapter 1: Introduction	서론(序論)
Chapter 2: Sip Sam Seh and Moo Do Philosophy	Chapter 2: Sip Sam Seh, Eight Trigrams and Five Elements	십삼세(十三勢)와 팔괘오행(八卦五行)
Section VI, Chapter 2	Chapter 3: Sundo	선도(仙道)
Chapter 3: Energy	Chapter 4: Energy	에너지(熱)에 대하여
Chapter 4: What is Ki?	Chapter 5: What is Ki?	기(氣)란 무엇인가?
Chapter 5: Moo Do Practice through Reflection on the Do	Chapter 2 (Passage 16): Sip Sam Seh, Eight Trigrams and Five Elements	무도동작(武道動作)의 근본은 도(道)의 원리인 반사작용(反射作用)
Section VI: Practice of Moo Do Mind Training	See Section 5, Chapters 2-3	2장: 십삼세가(十三世歌)와 팔괘오행(八卦五行) 3장: 선도(仙道)
Chapter 1: Mind Training	Section 5, Chapter 2, Passage 17, Man's Uniqueness	무도(武道)인 심공(心功) 실기(實技)
Chapter 2: Sun Do	Section 5, Chapter 3: Regarding Acquired Nature	선도(仙道)

English Translation	*Moo Do Chul Hahk (Original)* English Titles	*Moo Do Chul Hahk (Original)* Han'gŭl Titles
Section VII: Education for Character Development	Section 6: Education for Character Development	교양(敎養)
Chapter 1: Introduction	Chapter 1: Introduction	서론(序論)
Chapter 2: Virtue	Chapter 2: Virtue	도덕(道德)
Chapter 3: Man's Mind is God	Chapter 3: Man's Mind is God	사람의 마음은 신(神)이다
Chapter 4: The Do which Avoids both Extremes	Chapter 4: The Do which Avoids Both Extremes	양극초월자(兩極超越者)로서의 도(道)
Chapter 5: Do as the Function of *Mu*	Chapter 5: Do as the Function of *Mu*	무(無)의 용(用)으로서의 도(道)
Chapter 6: Virtue as the Generator of the Generated	Chapter 6: Virtue as the Generator of the Generated	생성(生成)의 생성자(生成者)로서의 덕(德)
Chapter 7: Theory of Intuition	Chapter 7: Theory of Intuition and Intuition's Significance	직관론(直觀論) 및 직관(直觀)의 의의(意義)
Chapter 8: The Image as the Object of Intuition	Chapter 8: The Image as the Object of Intuition	직관(直觀)의 대상(對象)으로서의 상(象)
Chapter 9: Limitations of Intuition	Chapter 9: Limitations of Intuition	직관(直觀)의 한계(限界)
Chapter 10: View of Man	Chapter 10: View of Man and Its Significance	인간관(人間觀) 이의 의의(意義)

English Translation	*Moo Do Chul Hahk (Original)* English Titles	*Moo Do Chul Hahk (Original)* Han'gŭl Titles
Chapter 11: Human Types	Chapter 11: Human Types	인간(人間)의 유형(類型)
Chapter 12: The Way to Become a Natural Person	Chapter 12: The Way to Become a Natural Person	자연인(自然人)이 되는 방법(方法)
Chapter 13: Explanation of Vitality	Chapter 13: Explanation of Vitality	활(活)에 대한 설명(說明)
Chapter 14: Guidance for Training in Soo Bahk Do	Chapter 14: Guidance for Training in Soo Bahk Do	수박도(手搏道)의 수련(修練)지침(指針)
Section VIII. Personal Reflections	Section 7: Addendum	부기(附記)
Chapter 1: Lao-tzu's Political Philosophy	Chapter 1: Lao-tzu's Political Philosophy	노자(老子)의 정치관(政治觀)
Chapter 2: My Political Philosophy	Chapter 2: My Political Philosophy	저자(著者)의 정치관(政治觀)
Chapter 3: Lao-tzu's Economic Views	Chapter 3: Lao-tzu's Economic Views	노자(老子)의 경제관(經濟觀)
Chapter 4 A Brief Account of My Economic Views	Chapter 4 A Brief Account of My Economic Views	저자(著者)의 경제관(經濟觀) 약기(略記)
Chapter 5 Military Doctrine	Chapter 5 Military Doctrine	군대론(軍隊論)
Chapter 6: Some Concluding Remarks	Chapter 6: Some Concluding Remarks	결론(結論)

English Translation	Moo Do Chul Hahk (Original) English Titles	Moo Do Chul Hahk (Original) Han'gŭl Titles
Chapter 7: The Ideal Society as Envisioned by the Taoist School	Chapter 7: The Ideal Society as Envisioned by the Taoist School	도가(道家)의 이상적사회(理想的社會)
Chapter 8: The Ideal Society of the Confucian School	Chapter 8: The Ideal Society of the Confucian School	유가(儒家)의 이상적사회(理想的社會)
Chapter 9: Doctrine of Return	Chapter 9: Doctrine of Return	환원론(還元論)
Chapter 10: Human Insensitivities	Chapter 10: Human Insensitivities	인간(人間)의 불감증(不感症)
Chapter 11: The Difference between Hope and Desire	Chapter 11: The Difference between Hope and Desire	희망(希望)과 욕심(慾心)의 차이점(差異点)
Chapter 12: Man, as the Spiritual Leader of the Myriad Things, Cannot Become a Slave	Chapter 12: Man, as the Spiritual Leader of the Myriad Things, Cannot Become a Slave	인간(人間)은 만물(萬物)의 영장(靈長)이기 때문에 노예(奴隷)가 될수없어
Chapter 13: Regarding the Statement "Life is War"	Chapter 13: Regarding the Statement "Life is War"	인생(人生)은 전쟁(戰爭)이라는데 대하여
Chapter 14: Belligerent Civilization	Chapter 14: Belligerent Civilization	전쟁문명(戰爭文明)에 대하여
Chapter 15: My Views on Human Life	Chapter 15: My Views on Human Life	저자(著者)의 인생관(人生觀)

English Translation	Moo Do Chul Hahk (Original) English Titles	Moo Do Chul Hahk (Original) Han'gŭl Titles
Section IX: Trends in Modern Philosophy	Section IX: Trends in Modern Philosophy	현대철학(現代哲學)의 동향(動向)
Section X: The Philosophy of the Infinitely Large and Infinitely Small	Section X: The Philosophy of the Infinitely Large and Infinitely Small	무한대철학(無限大哲學)과 무한소철학(無限小哲學)

[1] This chapter included a translation by Hwang Kee of the *Chou-I* that is not included here.

[2] This chapter included a translation by Hwang Kee of Lao Tzu's *Tao Teh Ching* that is not included here.

Index